DORIS LESSING

DORIS LESSING

A Biography

Carole Klein

CARROLL & GRAF PUBLISHERS, INC.
NEW YORK

First Carroll & Graf edition 2000

Carroll & Graf Publishers, Inc.
A Division of Avalon Publishing Group
19 West 21st Street
New York, NY 10010-6805

Library of Congress Cataloging-in-Publication Data is available.

ISBN: 0-7867-0806-9

Manufactured in the United States of America

Contents

Acknowledgements

I am delighted to have the opportunity to acknowledge the help of a number of people and sources in researching and writing this book.

Moore Crossey, former curator of the African Collection at Yale University was infinitely patient and helpful in locating material from that unique archive.

The Library of Special Arts in Johannesburg supplied me with articles that added to my knowledge of African history and literature.

The Elmer Bobst Library of New York University was an important resource for my research and its staff of librarians was unfailingly helpful.

The Zimbabwe Embassy in Washington, D.C. was always open to my questions.

The Rare Book and Manuscript Library of Columbia University permitted me to read the letters between Doris Lessing and her former agent, John Cushman, giving me insight into her career concerns.

I am eternally grateful to the late William Koshland of Alfred A. Knopf for making accessible the rich correspondence between Doris Lessing and Robert Gottlieb.

I am indebted to Tom Shaw for providing me with his impressive collection of Lessing material, and to Grover Askins, a very special bookdealer for his excellent stock of Lessing writings, as well as bringing me together with Tom Shaw.

Many people provided me with interviews that were invaluable. My deep appreciation is sent to Clancy Sigal, Neil Claremon, Peter Worsley, Paul Hogarth, Bernard Kops, Stewart Hall, John Mortimer, Jutta Laing, Bob Mullen, Stanley Mitchel, Lin Chun, Raphael Samuels, Robin Blackburn, Ralph Miliband, Marian Miliband, John Leonard, Florence Howe, Leslie Hazleton, Oskar Lewenstein, John Willet, Norm Fruchter, Ann Edwards, Susan Brownmiller, Elaine Dundy, Helena de Bertodano, Fiametta Rocco, Jane Kelly, Jane Cushman, and Margaret Walters.

In addition to this list of interviews are a great many others who would only speak to me on promise of anonymity. While I regret not being able to thank them formally, I honor their concerns and requests.

Thanks to Richard Marek for his reading the book in process. Deep thanks as well to Edward Weiss, for his invaluable and tireless research assistance. My gratitude and admiration to Angela Darling, who so carefully typed my manuscript and was always flexible about time changes and constraints.

My participation in the Biography Seminar at New York University, and the Women Writing Women's Lives group of the CUNY system were a source of both concrete help and creative renewal.

Finally, thanks to my agent and friend Lois Wallace for her sustained advice and efforts on my behalf. My appreciation as well, to my editor, Martin Rynja, at Duckworth for his attentive guidance.

List of Plates

(between pages 118 and 119)

To Ted,
for his encouragement
and support

Prologue

In 1969, Doris Lessing agreed to visit America to publicise her new book, *The Four-Gated City*. Lessing, an inveterate wanderer, usually tried to reward herself for these publicity tours. Often her compensation was to visit some new or interesting place. On this trip, it was Arizona she wanted to see, because she had heard it resembled Rhodesia's desert country: broad skies and open spaces. Lessing had lived in Southern Rhodesia (now Zimbabwe) from the age of five, in 1925, until she was twenty nine years old, when she moved to London to make a career as a writer. Like generations of artists from all over the world, she felt impelled to leave the narrow possibilities of her provincial homeland for the more sophisticated, sympathetic diversity of a cultural centre.

Yet leaving Africa for England only deepened the puzzle that has always surrounded Lessing's idea of 'home.' For her colonialist parents, the homeland was England, even though their daughter had visited it only briefly as a young child. Their family life revolved around English values and customs that had little meaning to a girl who roamed the African veld.

Doris Lessing was raised hearing whites talk about Rhodesia the way Americans once spoke of the West: as if the land they claimed had been empty before they got there, or, if not empty, whose native population had no rights to it. Yet even as a young girl she sensed that this was a false picture, one that made her, in effect, an alien in her own country. This point was driven home from the moment she learned that as a white Rhodesian child it was unthinkable for her to play with African children.

'Africa belongs to the Africans, and the sooner they take it back, the better,' Doris Lessing wrote in 1956, when she was fully aware of the horrors of colonial history. But, she added, expressing the persistent, plaintive hope of an expatriate, surely 'a country belongs to those who feel at home in it.'[1]

Helpless to alter her position as a young girl, she tried to find pleasure in her isolation. She wandered among the extraordinary varieties of animals, jagged rocks, rushing streams, aromatic bushes and trees. It was the type of landscape you could lose yourself in, made for introspection and flights at self-invention.

When she told her editor and friend, Robert Gottlieb, about her wish to go out west, he quickly made the arrangements. Lessing had met Neil Claremon, a young writer, on a previous visit to the States; he was then running a program in Arizona that brought writers into local schools and universities. Gottlieb had Claremon schedule her for readings and a lecture at the University of Arizona in Tucson. Neil and his wife, Judy, were passionate about Lessing's work. They were thrilled when she accepted an invitation to stay in their small home, rather than in university quarters or a hotel.

Their house stood all by itself in a large desert area. On the first morning of Lessing's stay, Neil Claremon awoke at 6:30, thinking he heard his cats stirring. Instead, it was Lessing walking out the door in her nightgown. Claremon quietly went to investigate and saw her climbing the land behind the house which sloped up to a big knobby hill.

'It was a gorgeous desert morning,' he recalls, 'and I knew she was thinking of African sunrises. When she got to the top of the hill, she pulled up her gown and started dancing. She has beautiful legs. Her hair was loose, free and loose. She was about to celebrate her fiftieth birthday, but she seemed almost girlish.'

Lessing asked Claremon to take her for drives in the mountains, and once at a peak, she'd climb out of the car to look at the scenery. 'She'd stand there for a long time, gazing out over the landscape, and then she'd say 'This could be Africa. If there were animals out on the plain, it could be Africa.'

* * *

Doris Lessing's early writing is Africa-based, revealing both her passion for the country and the painful sense of not belonging. In a preface to her *African Stories* (1964), she wrote: Africa 'is not a place to visit unless one chooses to be an exile ever afterwards from an inexplicable majestic silence lying just over the border of memory or of thought.'[2]

Lessing's exile from Africa is both physical and a metaphor for other displacements in her life. She has been exiled within her family. She is also a voluntary exile, an inner and outer expatriate. She seems to experience life at a remove, perhaps to soothe a painful sense of homelessness. Her disquiet and disaffection powerfully energise her work. When she coolly observes the world we know, she is able to render it for her readers in a new, clarifying way. Unfettered by boundaries, as a writer she has never stayed fixed within any genre, belief system, or locale – even ranging beyond our planet. Her restless imagination suggests the exile's wanderings, but finally, it is writing itself that is Doris Lessing's truest home.

1

Born into a Broken World

'We use our parents like recurring dreams,' writes Doris Lessing, 'to be entered into when needed; they are always there for love or for hate.'[1]

Like a detective on an elusive case, Doris Lessing has studied old photographs of her parents. Are there traces to be found of the people they became? Would she discover the ultimate source of her own years of waking nightmares?

There is a photo of Lessing's mother, Emily Maude McVeagh, in adolescence. She is a tall girl with a round, confident face. Her hair is pulled back and tied with a black bow. She wears a school uniform, blousy white shirt and long dark skirt, a proud young citizen of her beloved British Empire. Born in 1884, Emily was named after her mother Emily Flower, who died giving birth to a son when Emily was three years old.

Emily Maude's father, John William McVeagh, had worked himself up to the middle class, from office clerk to manager of a bank in suburban London. Class was immensely important to him, the yardstick by which he measured his opinions and decisions. He must have been smitten with his beautiful young wife. How else could he have overlooked the fact that during her short life she had never really abandoned her working-class habits and tastes? Had she lived past the age of thirty two, their marriage might well have foundered as McVeagh became increasingly preoccupied with his social position.

As it was, McVeagh never mentioned his wife to his children, and their home contained not a single picture of her. It was almost impossible for young Emily to conjure up a truthful image of her mother. There were only the vague memories of her earliest childhood and the obvious disapproval of the household staff who raised the three children after their mother's death. With no one to counteract the servants' version of her mother as an imprudent, common woman, Emily Maude adopted that view as well. In *Under My Skin* (the first volume of her autobiography), Doris Lessing recalls the disdain in her mother's voice whenever she mentioned Emily Flower. Her pursed mouth and little sniff seemed to imply that Emily Flower's death was fitting punishment for her lower-class ways.

McVeagh remarried when his three children were still young, but his elegant new wife had little interest in taking on a mother's role. McVeagh was not troubled by his wife's aloofness towards his children. He was equally remote as a father, stern and demanding, with never a gesture or expression of love. The only family life Emily experienced was when everyone attended what her father considered important public rituals of the empire: the funeral of Queen Victoria, Edward VII's coronation, or the visits of the Kaiser and other heads of state.

To her daughter, Emily expressed no love for her father, but did insist that she respected and admired him. His formal portrait hung on the mud wall of their African childhood home in Southern Rhodesia. Doris detested the man she saw inside the ornate frame. His corpulent form and chubby face, greased hair and old-fashioned, tightly tailored clothes were the very embodiment of what Doris disliked about England. In that image she saw the arrogance and repression of the British empire and the class system that went with it.

Despite her loveless background, Emily Maude was a lively girl with many friends. She often went to the theatre, musicals, and late suppers with her friends. She liked the rough and tumble of hockey and lacrosse, and less boisterous sports such as tennis and bicycle excursions. She did well in school, far better than her dull-witted brother. And, unusual for the time, her father considered sending her to university. One can imagine McVeagh's enthusiasm when he told his daughter of his enlightened plans, and his dismay when she rejected the rare and costly opportunity of a university education.

Emily stood her ground. Although she was a talented musician who dreamed of becoming a concert pianist, her practical nature together with a genuine desire to care for people, made her feel she should first be trained as a nurse. McVeagh was furious. Respectable middle-class girls did not become nurses. If Emily went through with these shocking plans, she would get no help from him.

That might have been the end of it, but John McVeagh underestimated his daughter's determination. Emily went off to train at London's Royal Free Hospital, where the work was hard and the wages low. Despite the obstacles in her path she passed her final exams with high marks, which no doubt bolstered her self-assurance.

By the time Emily Maude graduated to being Sister McVeagh, she had put the dream of being a concert pianist behind her, although later in life she would grow melancholy about abandoning music. She would lament who she once was and might have become. As a newly licensed nurse, however, she was happy with her work. She loved being needed. The gratitude of her patients when she came to their bedsides was like an expression of their love, which Doris Lessing believes was her mother's true motivation for entering nursing. Emily fed her hunger for love through the people who needed and valued her.

Despite the heavy demands of her workday, Emily filled her evenings with a busy social life and played the organ at various churches. When she could, she went on holidays with friends, and no matter how crowded her life, she found time to read prominent authors of the day such as George Bernard Shaw. Nursing was always arduous work, but its demands dramatically escalated with the onset of war in 1914. Trainloads of soldiers arrived at the Royal Free Hospital. Sister McVeagh ministered to these wounded bodies with such dedication that a number of the men wrote poems to her. She was proud of these tributes, and kept them in an album that she treasured long past her nursing days.

* * *

Doris Lessing's father, Alfred Cook Tayler, was born in 1886 in a small farming village near Colchester where his father was a bank clerk. The job was respectable but lowly and the family had to make do on very little money. Alfred's mother, Caroline, who appears in a baby picture of Alfred, is described by Doris Lessing as a 'fat, plain woman' with 'the face of a head cook.'² And indeed, Mrs Tayler worked wonders in the kitchen on her limited resources. Decades later, when Alfred suffered from diabetes and had to follow a Spartan diet, he rhapsodised over memories of suet, and treacle pudding and ham and sausages smoked at home.

Besides the all-important Bible there was apparently little interest in books and certainly no money for them. On Sundays, the family went to church three times, and all week Alfred anxiously anticipated that day which always recurred too quickly. Alfred had an older brother who was superior to him in school and their father beat his younger son when he didn't do as well. When they finished school both young men became bank clerks like their father, but Alfred remained a clerk while his older brother rose quickly to a managerial post. Lessing says her father found little pleasure in his clerk's job. But, he tried hard to improve his skills and he even laboriously changed his handwriting because one of his superiors disparaged it. Alfred may have felt that he would not mind his bank clerk's job so much if his personal life were richer.

Whatever the reason, one day Alfred decided to live on his own in Luton, about an hour away from the family home. It was a happy move. Away from his family and the narrow confines of his little village, he was free to indulge the side of him that loved to play, to be expansive, to be free of imposed, arbitrary constraints.

He swam and rowed, played football and cricket, sang at musicals and danced with the local girls, thinking nothing of walking ten or fifteen miles to attend dance parties that might be held two or three times every week. He would stay until the very last, walking back under

the stars. By the time he reached home he could often see the beginnings of a rising sun. Buoyed by the previous evening's pleasures, he
would wash and shave, make tea and porridge, and set off for work.

The girls in Luton all loved him. For a time he was engaged to one
girl, and then broke it off and became engaged to her sister. Their
mother was equally smitten with their charming, handsome suitor and,
until the second broken engagement, welcomed him into her house as
if he were her son. Doris Lessing recalls that when Alfred told this story
in front of his wife, (he repeated it many times, like all his reminis-
cences) he would invariably add, 'Just as well I didn't marry either of
them; they would never have stuck it out the way you have, old girl.'3
As Lessing reports statements like these her tone is biting. In all her
writing about her parents and their sadness and suffering at fate's
perversity, she rarely suggests that they cared for each other and tried
to protect each other from the hardship they shared.

One of Lessing's judgements that rings grimly true is that war was
a defining element of her life. The carefree young Alfred was irrevocably
changed by the experience of battle. Among the many early photographs of her father, the largest presents a darkly handsome young
man wearing a World War I officer's uniform. He holds his body erect,
his jacket is smartly buttoned and decorated with badges. He is ready
to do his duty for the British Empire, enlisting as a soldier in 1914
because he was horrified at the German abuses in Belgium. Filled with
idealism, he was eager to do his part, even though he 'knew' he would
be injured.

The source of his prescience was a fortune-teller. Doris Lessing
writes about this fanciful streak in her father's past: 'I concluded at the
age of about six my father was mad,' assuring the reader that it 'did not
upset me.'4 The fortune-teller told Alfred that although he would twice
be in great danger, he would not die because he had the protection of an
ancestor – his existence unknown to Alfred – who was a famous soldier.
She also said Alfred would sense beforehand his imminent injury.

At the front, Alfred did become seriously ill with what he thought was
a ruptured appendix. A few days before he was felled by the terrible
pain as anticipatory dread overtook him. The feeling of dark warning
was so intense before a second illness, about two years later, that he
wrote to his parents from the battlefield telling them he was about to
be killed. Once more, the fortune-teller's prophecy was fulfilled when
his legs were riddled by shrapnel. Alfred did not die. Indeed, he would
look back on it as the luckiest thing that ever happened to him because
ten days after he was taken to the hospital his entire company was
killed in the battle of Passchendaele.

On a surgical table at the Royal Free Hospital, Alfred Tayler's leg
was amputated at mid-thigh. He was also suffering from shell shock
and, despite his belief that he was lucky, he fell into a deep and

prolonged depression. The combination of traumas kept him in the hospital for nearly a year. Even when he was free of physical pain, his thoughts were sombre, and at night his dreams were terrifying. A physician assured Alfred that what he was experiencing was common to people who had gone through such severe stress and that Alfred was not, as he had begun to fear, going mad. Most people had a hidden store of troublesome feelings, the doctor said. When Alfred Tayler told Doris the story years later, he always cautioned her to remember that no one could know what battles people had to wage inside themselves.

Lying in his hospital bed, Tayler brooded over his war experience, which had been so different from his ideals. When he first entered the service, filled with patriotism and a sense of honour, the war had satisfied all his chivalrous instincts. The English soldier was the best in the entire world, he would maintain for the rest of his life. He had never experienced such friendship as he did on the field and in the trenches. This courtesy was extended to the enemy. Once, Alfred and a German soldier came face to face. As if by silent agreement, they lowered their guns, smiled at each other, and walked away. It was his Christmas of 1914, when some British and German troops gave each other presents, sang carols together, and played a rowdy game of soccer. Alfred used to wish, he said later, that he could get the opposing generals into those trenches for just twenty-four hours to see what the ordinary soldier faced every day. A firsthand look would surely persuade them to end the war. Gradually, he realised that such a visit would have made no difference at all. British authorities were horrified by stories of compassion. Soldiers were urged by every voice of society to defend his flag ruthlessly against the wicked Hun.

Crippled and his future uncertain, Alfred felt bitterly estranged from the country he had fought for. No one in government seemed to appreciate what price had been paid by the young soldiers in the trenches. Nor did most civilians want to know about the slaughter he had managed to escape. Alfred Tayler began to call the war he had joined so proudly 'the Great Unmentionable', and wrapped up in this sardonic appellation lay his conviction that he had to leave England once he was out of the hospital.

Alfred Tayler's war stories used to bore Doris Lessing when she was growing up, but in an experiment with mescaline in the early 1960s some of the sense memories that came to her were her father's experience of battle. This frightening event proved to her that the Great War had been an overriding influence on her life as well.

* * *

Alfred Tayler's nurse at the Royal Free Hospital was Emily McVeagh. She was kind to him and he was grateful and responsive to her. They spent many hours together and, although she didn't understand his mental anguish, she diligently tried to ease his physical suffering. When Tayler was finally ready to leave the hospital, he asked Emily to marry him.

The proposal threw Emily into confusion. She had been offered the matronship of St. George's Hospital in London, a highly unusual opportunity for a woman in her early thirties. The idea made her proud. But the truth was, she liked nursing better than administration. Even more important, she was still mourning the military doctor she'd fallen deeply in love with who had drowned when his ship was torpedoed. There were very few men left in London and, although her photographs contradict her, Emily thought of herself a plain woman. She was nearly thirty-five, well past the conventional age of marriage.

Understanding her dilemma, Alfred Tayler sympathised with Emily's loss and was patient with her. Long after they did marry, his wife kept the doctor's picture on her dressing table. Alfred's voice contained genuine sorrow when he told Doris and her brother, Harry, 'Your poor mother ... he was a good chap, that young doctor.'[5]

Perhaps the major reason Emily finally accepted Alfred's proposal was that she very much wanted to have children – although not right away. Alfred was still quite depressed and she felt oddly ill herself. This debilitating weakness may have stemmed from the cumulative effects of her years of war work or a mild form of the devastating Spanish 'flu that swept the world after the war. She felt that if they did marry, it would be best to wait until she and Alfred were stronger before thinking about starting a family.

As his release from the hospital drew nearer, Alfred was increasingly determined not to stay in England. Here he was, a cripple with a wooden leg, and out on the streets able ex-soldiers were selling matches in order to survive. There was no hope of dealing with his bitterness and anger unless he got away from its source.

Alfred asked the bank that had employed him before the war to transfer him to one of their branch banks in Persia, then dominated by France and Britain, with Britain controlling most financial matters. To Alfred's delight, he was offered the job of bank manager at the British-run Imperial Bank of Persia in the town of Kermanshah.

The news of this job had encouraged Emily to accept Alfred's marriage proposal. She was excited at the idea of sharing in the social status of his managerial position in an exotic country. She would go to parties, wearing lovely clothes, and serve elegant dinners and teas to 'nice' people. Yes, she would marry Captain Alfred Tayler.

The wedding, in January 1919, was small and informal. Both bride and groom were too emotionally burdened to pretend to the naive joy of a traditional ceremony. There was an additional constraint: Caroline Tayler was not at all happy with her son's choice. Sister McVeagh was used to ruling people's lives, and Mrs Tayler was certain her daughter-in-law would assume the same control inside her home as she had in the hospital.

Nonetheless, they must have made a handsome pair – the good looking Alfred and the dynamic Emily, both suffused with the excitement of a ceremony that would change their lives forever. With Alfred getting his wish to leave England, and Emily happily indulging her love of shopping by acquiring stylish frocks that she would be able to wear regularly, the couple were as happy as their bruised past allowed them to be.

Everything seemed perfectly in order for the life they were about to start together. Except for one small matter. On their wedding night or soon after, despite their plans to postpone parenthood, a child was conceived – Doris.

2

A False Start

Although the pregnancy was unwelcome, Emily Tayler was probably not totally unhappy with the news. After all, she would be thirty-five when the baby was born; as a nurse, she knew bearing a first child at an advanced age could be problematic. She briskly decided she would make the best of it and began to acquire a suitable layette to take with her to Persia.

In Rhodesia, African babies seemed perfectly content to be carried naked in a cloth slung over their mothers' bodies, so Lessing was astonished when she later read a copy of her mother's elaborate infant inventory. Everything Emily took to Kermanshah for her unexpected child numbered in the dozens, from diapers to hand-tucked smocks that required careful ironing, to vests that were both short and long, for wearing under other complicated clothing. As the flapper age dawned, the new mother and child departed for Persia in an outfit that suited bygone Edwardian gentility rather better.

As soon as she arrived in Persia, Emily Maude Tayler dropped her first name. She had never really liked 'Emily,' probably because of its association with her long-dead mother. And she was drawn to her middle name because of the long, moving poem by Tennyson titled 'Maud.' When she decided that her husband should also have a name change – even though it was Tennyson's first name, she found 'Alfred' too undistinguished for his new position – she dubbed him Michael, after the youngest child in *Peter Pan*. Though Alfred thought his wife's fixation with class was absurd, his name didn't seem an issue worth arguing about. He only wished the his own dark discontent could be so easily discarded.

* * *

It was Michael and Maude Tayler who arrived at the huge, etched-stone house in Kermanshah that the bank provided. It had vaulted windows and wide verandas that looked out on fragrant gardens with 'a heavy, tropical smell,' Lessing recalls, 'thick and resiny.'[1] The city itself was very old, seated upon a mass of brown earth encircled by mountains sprinkled year round with snow. Sense memories of Kermanshah – air filled with the sounds of running water from streams and fountains, and the fragrance of dust – would remain with Lessing throughout her life.

Maude presided over a large staff of servants: gardeners, cooks, people to clean and others to shop. After years of ministering to others, she had no physical work to do. Michael, too, must have felt his spirits lift when he saw Kermanshah. He loved his capacious house, not because it was impressive but because it allowed him such freedom. All his life he had lived in small spaces that permitted little privacy or escape. His new post as bank manager also freed him from the petty demands of superiors. Maude and Michael seemed to be starting a better life than Emily and Alfred had ever known.

That names were so important to Maude Tayler lends particular poignancy to the story of how her daughter's was chosen. In a photograph Lessing has included in *Under My Skin*, her father is lying in his bed in the Royal Free Hospital looking handsome but, his daughter implies, privately unhappy. Sister McVeagh sits at his side, eyes lowered under her white nurse's veil to some sewing on her lap. The photo is dated September 1917, and there is also an inscription written later by one of Doris's parents, 'Before she was thought of,' 'she,' of course, being the couple's first child.

In fact, 'she' was never thought of. The Taylers were expecting a boy. If Maude was going to have a child before she was ready to, she wanted it to be a son – so much so that she had prepared no name for a daughter. The boy was to be called Peter John. Apparently 'John' was after the brother Lessing believes her mother resented for receiving more privileges, despite being so much slower than her. John had had no trouble obtaining a commission in the Royal Navy, which Lessing believes – though this seems somewhat implausible – led to a deep seated bitterness in her sea-loving mother. It is interesting to note that both names occur in Maude's beloved Peter Pan, where John is Michael's older brother; Lessing, however, does not explore what complicated reasoning would lead Maude to give a son the name of someone she disliked. Equally puzzling is Doris Lessing's later decision to emulate her mother and name her first son John and her second son Peter.

Maude's pregnancy was difficult, and the birth, on October 22, 1919, in the tall stone house, even worse. Labour was lengthy. When at last the infant was ready to be born, the doctor had to use forceps to remove her, which left an ugly mark on the baby's face that lingered for days.

Maude was too exhausted, too angrily disappointed, to come up with a name for her unwanted daughter. Despite the doctor's urging, she refused to even try to think of something to call the girl. So it was finally the doctor – weary from the long night and needing a name for his records before he could go home – who looked down at the baby and tentatively offered, 'Doris?'

The doctor took Maude's silence, which was more likely a further expression of her indifference, as agreement. The infant girl might have forced her way into life, but her existence remained denied.

To complicate matters, exhaustion from her work during the war, perhaps coupled with her long labour, had apparently dried up Maude's milk, and Doris was bottle-fed from the moment of birth. In the early part of the century non-nursing babies were fed cow's milk even though it sometimes didn't agree with them. Maude diluted the milk according to standard English practice, not realising that cows in Persia produced a far thinner milk than English cows. And so Doris was ferociously hungry for nearly the entire first year of her life.

Her starvation made Doris scream with anguish, but Maude, like most women of her time, was a believer in scheduled feedings, and she was irritated at the demanding child who refused to adjust to her regime. As a result, Maude left most of Doris's care to a Syrian nurse-maid, who found the infant even more infuriating than her mother did, and made no attempt to hide her dislike.

As an adult, under the influence of morning glory seeds, Doris Lessing was able to envision the old stone nursery of her infancy. She lay in a crib, which to her unconscious experience was 'like a prison cell.'[2] Outside the cell, she could hear grown-up footsteps, but they never came her way. Frequently left alone, hungry from her diet of thin milk, Doris Tayler no doubt sensed as a baby, if only on a primitive level, that no one cared about her. Because of the strict, insensitive schedule of the household, she had to wait what seemed an eternity for relief from her emotional and physical pain. When she finally was picked up, it was usually by the impatient nursemaid, who scowled in annoyance, handled her brusquely, and hurried her care so that she could be put down again: alone, isolated, exiled.

Over the years of Doris's childhood, Maude liked to regale her friends with the story of her daughter's disappointing birth: how Maude had been so determined to have a son that she had no name ready for a girl, how the doctor had to provide one so that he could leave and get some rest. Then she would skip blithely to the lengthy misunderstanding about Persian milk, nonetheless labelling Doris a difficult baby, and now, an immensely irritating child. She presented it all as an amusing anecdote, never feeling any constraint merely because the story's subject was listening nearby.

Even as an elderly woman, Doris Lessing is incensed by the image of her mother smiling brightly while she recounted her terrible story, its hurtful theme utterly beyond Maude's understanding, as was the story's effect on her grim-faced little daughter listening from across the room.

In the 1960s mescaline trip during which Lessing experienced the anguish of her father's war service, she also gave herself a different birth, one that marked her entrance into the world. This one was not painful, though it was a complicated process, for she was both mother and baby, but at the same time neither. The baby was 'philosophic,' arguing with God from the womb, fighting against being born, especially to these parents.[3] She did not want to repeat her bitter real experience. There were voices behind the baby, one of them Maude's, easily recognisable because she was using some of her particular phrasing. Lessing wept profusely during the drug trip, and she is, she says, a woman who rarely cries. She remembers what she felt as the happy birth progressed, how a series of bitter, unhappy, sensations evaporated into a welcoming radiance.

* * *

Some of Lessing's other early, embittering memories revolve around her brother's birth and her mother's joy and excitement at finally having her son. Whatever cursory attention Maude had paid to Doris before his birth was withdrawn completely after Harry was born. She left her daughter's care exclusively to the nursemaid, while she took charge of the longed-for son herself.

At the same time, Doris was told Harry was 'her' baby, and she must love it. At two and a half, the girl already sensed she was being manipulated. This was not *her* baby. It was her mother's, and she would never know the love this baby would always receive as his birthright. She was achingly aware that this little boy would win their mothers' affection and attention in a way she never had and never would.

They are memories that cling tenaciously, undimmed by the passage of years. In Lessing's 1996 novel, *Love, Again*, the protagonist, Sarah Durham, is a sixty-five-year-old woman whose sexual life is calmly behind her. (At the time of publication, Lessing was seventy-six.) Then, during a single summer, Sarah falls passionately in love with not one, but two younger men.

Toward the end of the book, Sarah, suffering with frustration, witnesses a scene in a London park that helps her come to terms with her recent experience. A young mother is treating her small daughter with ruthless cruelty, while cooing adoringly at her infant son. The little girl's neediness and futile attempts to win a loving response from her mother are all too familiar to Sarah. As she stares compulsively at the painful tableau, she imagines the lifelong impact the young mother's coldness will have on the girl. In turn, she realises how the emotional starvation of her earliest days has influenced her own search for affection, even in her sixties. She silently tells the rejected little girl in the park, 'Hold on, hold on. Quite soon a door will slam shut inside you because what you are feeling is unendurable.'[4]

Before Doris Tayler was able to shut that door, barricading the raw pain, her fury could not be contained. Explosive bursts of rage marked her childhood, and deepened her mother's portrait of her as a wild, ill-tempered girl. Comparisons were invariably made to docile, loving Harry, who was called 'the baby' until he was seven years old and quietly, but firmly, protested against the infantilising label.

* * *

Doris's relationship with her father was different from that with her mother. Doris loved her father and believed that he loved her. But he didn't make a habit of openly expressing his affection. In fact, he had a detached quality that Maude found difficult to deal with.

Lessing does not mention her own response to his emotional distance. Yet a distinct physicality permeates her memories of her father, frequently related to his wooden leg. In writing about him, she employs graphically suggestive descriptions, without any additional reflection or comment. The effect is that of blatant, but unintentional, double entendre. It is as if Lessing is unaware of the implications of her description of the leg as 'a big hard slippery hidden thing.' She recalls a mixture of terror and excitement at being lifted up onto a horse to sit in front of her father, then pressing into his belly against the 'hard straps' of the leg's harness as the horse bounces her along.[5]

Smells, a powerful element in Lessing's writing, are a part of this disturbing memory of the horse ride they took together. She is acutely conscious of the blending of the smells of the horse and the smells of her father. The odours are burningly intense.

In general, Lessing's autobiographical writings suggest a highly developed sexual awareness unusual for a small child, an awareness often found in children who have experienced precocious sexual stimulation. Lessing remembers fleshy scenes, such as her parents swimming with friends when they lived in Persia: 'Loose bulging breasts. Whiskers of hair under arms' – all an 'unpleasant revelation' of what lies under their daytime clothes.[6]

When Harry was a little older, the family engaged in pillow fights nearly every evening. Doris's memories are of excitement and hysterical cries, until the dreaded but electrifying moment that always arrived, when her father seized his daughter and pushed her face down between his living and dead legs. She smells his crotch, and the odour makes her head ache as he starts to tickle her, wildly, while her head pounds and she starts to scream, and finally to cry. Supposedly, she is being taught to be a good sport. But Doris learned a different lesson. The treatment gave her nightmares. In combating them, she developed techniques for dealing with the dark side of dreams.[7] Because of what she has written about her parents, Lessing has occasionally been referred to as an abused child. She disdainfully denies the charge, labelling the current concern about sexual abuse as an irrational frenzy.

Martha Quest, the first volume of Lessing's *Children of Violence* series, novels she has acknowledged to be 'extremely autobiographical',[8] contains scenes that seem to the reader suggestive of incestuous feelings. In one of them, Mr Quest goes into his bedroom and finds his adolescent daughter, nearly nude, admiring herself in the mirror, the only wall mirror in the house. The moment is strained and much seems unspoken. In another instance, a deeper meaning to an encounter between the fictional father and daughter is more overt. Martha, wearing a revealing white evening dress, seeks out her father. She wants to show him the dress, which is an act of defiance against her mother, who still wants her to dress like a little girl. Turning to her father, Martha asks,

'Do I look nice, Daddy?

He gave a queer, irritable hunch to his shoulders as if he disliked a pressure, or distrusted himself. "Very nice," he said slowly. And then, suddenly, in an exasperated shout: "Too damned nice, go away!"'[9]

If Doris Lessing reveals no consciousness of untoward sensuality in her relationship with her own father, she is equally opaque about how she felt about his being an amputee. What did she think when she saw him holding on to the wall of the swimming tank while his wife and friends cavorted, unable to join in because of his missing leg? We do not know, for she does not tell us.

But there is another Persian memory that does suggest some of the feelings his helplessness evoked in her. Her mother was still pregnant with Harry, and the family was on its way to a new post for Michael in the larger city of Tehran, travelling in an open car over steep mountains. Doris was terrified looking down the rocky cliffs to deep valleys as the car circled higher and higher up the narrowing ridges, ever closer to the edge. The driver had difficulty executing one rock-filled turn, and he told the Taylers to get out of the vehicle while he attempted the manoeuvre.

Maude's pregnant body made it difficult for her to climb out of the car, but Doris knew that her father's artificial leg created equal problems. Finally standing outside, Doris hovered behind her father. First she was certain that the car would plummet over the cliff, and then she became convinced that a huge bird flying overhead would swoop her up in its beak. Doris clung to her father's legs for protection. One small hand was comforted by the feel of his warm flesh, the other found no solace in the hard, lifeless wood of the artificial limb.

Lessing seems to have powerfully denied this disquiet about her father's amputation. Her memories of Michael most often place the wooden leg in the context of his insouciant handling of experiences that were potentially humiliating for a proud man, such as the swimming pool memory; or in Africa, when he tried his hand at hunting for gold, being lowered in a bucket down a mine shaft like a dog or infant, or laboriously climbing up a tree to a tree house, where his daughter waits and watches his struggle.

* * *

Michael Tayler was not happy with his transfer to Tehran. For one, he was no longer bank manager, but had to report to, and take orders from, a superior officer. The house he and his family would now occupy was reminiscent of the pretentious English homes he remembered and deplored.

Maude, on the other hand, loved the new home for exactly the reasons her husband disliked it. Now her children would be in a proper English nursery, with velvet and lace curtains, and a brass-trimmed fireplace. Better still, her well-appointed parlour would be filled with guests who were truly prestigious. As the country's capital city, Tehran was host to – one could almost hear Maude's sigh of delight – 'embassy people.'

Maude was never to be as happy again as she was in Tehran. She dressed up in her pretty clothes and went to picnics, embassy receptions and dances, garden parties and dinner parties. When she entertained at home, she played the piano while the guests sang in jolly unison 'The Road to Mandalay' and the 'Indian Love Lyrics.' Only when Maude was by herself did she play the classical music she preferred as she felt her fun-loving visitors would likely find it boring.

Meanwhile, Michael grew increasingly irascible. As his wife revelled in the city's social life, he began to attack what he saw as the venal nature of Persian society with the same bitterness he had felt toward England after the war. This unhappiness with unscrupulous local business practices was no doubt based on a deeper dissatisfaction. Clearly he did not find what he was looking for in Persia. He had come thousands of miles to find himself trapped in the same type of mid-level banking job he had always disliked. On top of this, he was once again living in a society of fellow Brits that must have seemed a microcosm of the very country he had tried to escape. His new life in Persia seemed to be falling back on the same old routine, though in a storybook setting. Perhaps he longed to have a storybook life as well.

Beginning Again

After five years in Persia, Michael Tayler was given leave for a visit to England. Although he hardly felt more kindly disposed to his homeland than when he had first left it, his animosity toward Persia had reached such a point that he welcomed the break.

Because the leave started in summer, Maude decided the family shouldn't sail across the Red Sea as the weather was bound to be fiercely hot. Instead, they would travel through Russia, even though it was 1924, and the fledgling Soviet Union was still embroiled in the turmoil that followed upon years of revolution and civil war and Lenin's recent death.

Since few people were as determined, or perhaps as unaware of the implications of political turmoil, as Maude, the Taylers turned out to be the first foreign family since the Revolution to cross the Caspian Sea and travel overland to Moscow. For the rest of their lives, Maude and Michael would talk about what a disaster the trip was: the filth that Maude was sure would bring them typhus and Michael's illness with flu, which with everyone sharing the same small cabin might have infected the children as well.

When Doris would hear their complaint-filled story in later years, it seemed a meaningless recitation of colourless detail. The difficulties they described had little to do with the emotional chaos of her own recollections of the journey. Like other memories she recounts in her autobiographical writings, these are symbolic fragments filled with dreamlike messages and subjective meaning.

The small cabin the family shared on the first, most dangerous part of the trip, crossing the Caspian Sea on a broken-down oil tanker, is remembered by Doris Lessing as huge, an immense space covered with threatening shadows, made more menacing by her parents' obvious anxiety.

In one account she has written about the journey, Lessing says her mother stayed up all night, shining a light on her children's sleeping bodies to keep the lice away. In another, she ascribes the vigil to both parents. In any case, it went unnoticed that the light did not cover all of Doris's arm, so that when she awakened, it was puffy and distended with ugly red bites. Harry remained untouched.

The train they boarded in Baku to continue their journey to Moscow was essentially a troop train, crammed with soldiers. Lessing's remembrances again include smells: more lice, and the insect powder her mother scattered in futile attempts to kill scampering mice. The four-year-old girl slept with her face pressed against the cracks in the filthy window to escape these dank, oppressive odours.

Maude's first challenge came at the Russian border, where an immigration officer said they had the wrong visas. Ignoring his rifle, Maude briskly told him 'not to be so silly.'[1] This was Michael's favourite part of the story. He'd repeat Maude's scolding of the officer to friends, laughing till tears came to his eyes. Maude did not share his amusement. She was only doing what she had to do, had a right to do, and it had worked, hadn't it?

Something else Maude had not anticipated was that no food would be available on their train. Nothing in her middle-class background could have led her to imagine that a train would not have dining facilities. Instead, she had to leave the train at various stations to try to purchase food from the crowds of peasants who packed the platforms. All she usually managed to find were hard-boiled eggs and some bread. To Doris, however, more disturbing than the meagre rations was the sight of the ragged men, women, and children peering in at them at every stop, feet wrapped in rags and begging. It is a sight she has never forgotten.

One day, perhaps because she had even greater difficulty than usual in finding some food to buy, Maude didn't get back to the train in time and it took off without her. Doris was struck with terror and the mixed emotions of need. She now longed for the return of the mother she told herself she hated. She was being abandoned.

It is this memory that evokes a brief awareness of the effects of Michael's infirmity. She clung to him for comfort and tried to believe his assurances that her mother would rejoin them, but she was also aware of his silence as he watched his children share some leftover raisins and a single egg. Suddenly she realised that when the raisins and egg were gone, her father would not be able to jump off the train to find them more food like Maude. Lessing herself cannot recapture the feeling of being hungry, although her parents afterward told her she was. When she thinks of her mother vanishing, the little girl who appears in her mind is not asking for food.

It took less than two days for Maude to catch up with them. She was proud of herself for managing such a feat in a country full of turmoil, and whose language she did not speak. She'd pushed herself onto another train, and instructed the – to her mind – incompetent crew to telegraph the train her family was on and make sure they waited for her.

In Moscow, the family stayed at a hotel that became the setting for one of Lessing's strongest memories. She sees her four-year-old self in the hotel corridor, watching strange people disappear into rooms. The knob on the door of her family's room is out of her reach and she bangs on the door weeping, shouting, to be let inside. It seems hours until the door opens although Lessing knows it must have been only minutes. The feeling that still lingers is of being barred from the family centre, unable to open the door that may release her from terror and helplessness.

* * *

The power of memories like this are a continuing source of interest for Lessing. She is fascinated with what has been called autobiographical memory. She seems to revel in the use of her senses as tools for recapturing the past. Smells are especially evocative instruments. When she remembers Africa, her nose feels 'the smell that comes with the rains. That marvellous wet earth.'[2] A later visit to Singapore with its dry and tangy Eastern odours suddenly brought back memories of the sad little girl in the big stone nursery in Persia.

Lessing is intrigued by the validity of memory. As she asks in the first volume of her autobiography, *Under My Skin*, how can we know that what we recall is more important than what remains hidden? How can she reclaim a child's experience of time? Why is it that most of her memories are so sad, overpowering what must have been happier moments?

'People say I have a very good memory. I do have a good memory. But having said that, there are whole stretches of one's life, months that are blank. Why, then, this total recall for a weekend or a week, and then a blank?'[3]

Lessing says that what she recalls of her life has been different at different ages. The autobiography she wrote in her seventies is very different from what she would have written at fifty, or might write at eighty. Recollections change and in so doing allow us to rewrite our lives. Furthermore, Lessing has speculated, you can create a scene that contains nothing factual, and yet that scene is more true than accurate recordings of actual happenings. There is no question that subjective truth can be 'truer' than objective fact. Some reviewers who found a lack of emotional resonance in Lessing's memoirs pointed readers to *Martha Quest* or *The Golden Notebook* to get a real feeling of what she was like as a young woman.

Lessing knows how the impressions of childhood are powerfully felt and brilliantly coloured. Her account of the journey through Russia clearly shows the contrast between a child's sensitivity to the horrors of the outside world and an adult's ability to ignore them for the sake of survival. If Maude Tayler had experienced the same anguish as her young daughter, she would have been unable to surmount the considerable obstacles placed in her way during the trip.

For years, Doris Lessing thought about writing an autobiography told through dreams and dreamlike memories. The project evolved into the novel *The Memoirs of a Survivor* (1974), which she called 'my imaginative autobiography.'[4] In this novel the narrator becomes conscious of an adolescent girl living in a parallel world behind a wall in her apartment building. She comes to believe that the girl's life is actually that of her own youthful self. The wall divides reality and dream, the two components Lessing feels are necessary in creating a complete picture of someone's past. It was therefore extremely irritating to Lessing that critics and readers ignored her stated autobiographical intention, as if they were disconcerted by her using imaginative techniques to draw the story of a real life.

* * *

Lessing's memories of the family's six-month leave in England are uniformly grim and ugly. No pretty gardens or thatched cottages come to her mind. Only cold and dampness and recoiling at the fish carcasses on the fishmonger's wagon or the bloody sides of beef in the butcher shop window, not to mention the unpleasant faces of family members she had never seen before. These six months, in child time, were interminable.

Michael Tayler disliked being in England almost as much as his daughter, yet he dreaded going back to Tehran and what he considered its corrupt and frivolous way of life. He knew, of course, that Maude couldn't wait to return to Persia and there seemed no way out of his dilemma.

Then one day, the Taylers decided to visit the 1924 Empire Exhibition in Wembley. The Southern Rhodesia booth, decorated with corn cobs a foot and a half long, displayed huge posters that said people could become wealthy in five years by growing maize. Michael had grown up with farmers' children; there were even some farmers in his family, and he now knew that he didn't want to spend the rest of his life working for a bank. He had about a thousand pounds saved, plus his war pension, and veterans were being given a special purchase price for land in Africa. Impulsively, he bought the rights to 1500 acres, and began making plans to move to Southern Rhodesia.

Maude, who had just suffered the loss of Tehran's social swirl, would now be torn from London, the city she thought of as home. Still, she went along with her husband's eager plans to emigrate to Africa, in part because she too believed the promises of the exhibition. She looked upon the move as only temporary. After all, in five years they would be rich enough to move again.

Maude also thought she was going to some place like Kenya, which was considered quite fashionable at the time. Consequently, she took along all the accoutrements of the glamorous life: lovely clothes, her piano, calling cards, and a governess for her children.

The voyage took several weeks, and Michael was ill for almost the entire time. Maude, however, thoroughly enjoyed what would turn out to be her last taste of the social whirl she so adored. She played cards and deck games, went to concerts, and after dinner, for which she dressed up in her pretty clothes, danced with other passengers, and even with the ship's captain. Her hardy constitution impressed the captain and facilitated a genuine friendship. Sometimes during the rough passage only Maude would be on deck with him, all the other travellers fighting seasickness below.

The governess who accompanied them to Southern Rhodesia was a twenty-one-year-old girl named Biddy O'Halloran. She was as eager for a good time as her employer, and took her child-care duties lightly. The nightly routine aboard ship was for Doris and her brother to be put to bed in their cabin while Maude and Biddy, dressed in their best gowns, went to the lounge. They locked the cabin door so that the children couldn't get out. Harry invariably did as he was told and went to sleep immediately, but Doris was consumed with rage at her mother's unfairness. Maude told her she would not like the adult activities. Doris, however, knew she would like them very much. She was furious with her mother for telling her what to feel. Her mother was lying again, the way she'd lied about Harry being Doris's baby.

One night Doris thought of a way to get even. While Harry slept, she found her mother's nail scissors and cut holes in one of Maude's beloved evening dresses. Maude was horrified, but Doris was not punished. Instead, she was held on her mother's lap, while Maude talked to her of love and being good to people who love you.

Maude invariably used love as a form of pressure. But no matter how much Doris heard the word, she knew her mother felt no such emotion for her. Not that Maude would ever admit to such a horrifying thought. Mothers and daughters love each other. Any other possibility was blasphemy, and not allowed into her consciousness.

* * *

When the family arrived in Rhodesia, Maude, Harry, Doris, and Biddy stayed in a compound of huts called Lilfordia, twenty miles from the capital, Salisbury (now Harare), while Michael went to look for land nearby. This was a region from which black residents had been removed to the 'native reserves,' or told to find themselves land that the whites had not yet taken over. Derisively, Lessing says this was considered civilisation 'being brought to savages.'[5] Doris Lessing rarely openly criticises her father for racist attitudes. There is no doubt that he was less prejudiced than his wife, but he shared the prevailing ethos of colonialism.

When Michael felt he had found something suitable, he came back for Maude and she went off with him to see it. Doris and Harry were left in Biddy O'Halloran's care. Biddy was affectionate to Harry. Other children on the compound included Harry in their games, but left his sister out. Quick to leap on a weakened prey, a group of older children relentlessly bullied the five-year-old girl. Just a short time ago Doris had had to cope with her mother's disappearance in one strange land. Now, both parents had vanished in another.

The few days of their absence were once again, in childhood's measure, endless. Her anxiety manifested itself in lying, shouting, and stealing anything she could get her hands on, from trinkets to actual money. But she did not steal to acquire. She stole to express her fear and hurt, and to seek revenge for it. If her mother ever did come back, it would be a vindictive triumph to have her hear how wild her daughter had become.

Maude did indeed learn of Doris's bad behaviour, which she blamed on the disruptions in the child's routine. The family's life had been too filled with travel, and lacked the order all children require. Quickly, she accelerated the plans to bring them to the place that would become their new home.

One morning soon after her parents returned, Doris and Harry climbed with their mother and Biddy into a covered wagon drawn by sixteen oxen, while Michael rode alongside the wagon on horseback. Not all of their possessions were in the wagon, although it was packed to the brim. The larger and more valuable items, such as the piano, several Persian rugs, and pieces of sterling silver, would come by train. Also on the train were yards of English fabrics to make curtains and slipcovers.

A journey by covered wagon was certainly primitive, but to Doris, so recently frantic with rage and apprehension, the change was wonderfully comforting. The painful transition period was over.

Doris Lessing's love of Africa began on that journey, watching as 'a hurricane lamp swings' illuminating 'the dark bush on either side of the road.'[6]

4

Interlude

The country Doris Lessing grew up in has rivers lined with graceful trees, and is dotted with mounds of sharp rocks and towering stones. These hillocks, called *kopjes*, are a unique curiosity of this part of Africa, wondrous in their ability to withstand centuries of eroding weather. *Kopje* is of Dutch origin, but the word has been incorporated into the vocabulary of all English-speaking African residents.

Southern Rhodesia, as it was called in Lessing's childhood, situated in the southern hemisphere, north of the Tropic of Capricorn, lies entirely within the tropics. During the rainy season, the grassy land is lush and green, but even when the season ends, and the grass wilts, the expanse is still beautiful, for the drying grasses turn a shimmering golden colour. A fifty-mile-wide central plateau, the highveld, a high point of the geography of southern Africa, stretches through the country for four hundred miles.

This is the region where Lessing's family lived. The highest sector, the Eastern Highlands, has an altitude of some six thousand feet. To the north is the Zambezi river valley, where the highveld suddenly ends in a huge drop of fifteen hundred feet. The region of the middleveld stands two thousand to four thousand feet above sea level. Finally, the lowveld, less than two thousand feet above sea level, makes up a small piece of land in the Zambezi river valley and a wider band in the country's southeast corner.

Although the country has no seafront, two famed rivers bound its territory. The surging Zambezi which divided Southern Rhodesia (now Zimbabwe) from Northern Rhodesia (now Zambia) in the north, and in the South the comparatively calm Limpopo River formed the border with the Republic of South Africa

The Zambezi River builds up along the mountains in Angola and courses through Zambia, forming a number of tributaries on its way to the Zimbabwe border. Along the border, the river takes a spectacular drop over the Victoria Falls, which are more than a mile wide and 355 feet high. Rainbows, singly and sometimes in twos, colour the sky in moonlight and sunlight. There is always mist rising from the falls, accompanied by the majestic sound of plunging water, so that local people refer to the Victoria Falls as 'The Smoke That Thunders.'

If Doris Lessing was deeply moved by the extraordinary beauty of the veldland, with its magnificent array of natural phenomena, so was Cecil Rhodes before her. Once glimpsed, it had to be his. Rhodes came to southern Africa in 1870 when he was seventeen years old, in hope that the climate would cure his chronically weak lungs. He was immediately struck by the land's fantastic topography. Once, looking out at the horizon from the Matopo Hills, he declared that the perspective offered nothing less than 'a View of the World.'[1]

Rhodes, the founder of Rhodesia, was certain it was morally right for the British to rule Africa. A man of paradoxical values and behaviour, he spent his life in relentless pursuit of wealth, yet had simple tastes. He lived away from England for most of his adult life, while being consumed with admiration for his home country. He loved Africa as it was, but was determined to annex as much of it as he could for English rule. He drove hordes of blacks off the land, and used them ruthlessly for his own ends; despite this abuse and destruction, he was the only white person to be given the Zulu royal salute of 'Bayete' and a king's burial by the people he had conquered.

Rhodes envisioned a country where the British, the Afrikaners (South Africans of Dutch descent), and the indigenous tribes would live together peacefully as one nation. His overriding dream, however, was to create an all-British-controlled zone from the Cape of Good Hope to Cairo. To do this, he planned to take advantage of the mineral wealth rumoured to be present in much of the region.

The discovery of this mining potential had significance for a world undergoing considerable transformation. In 1870, when Rhodes arrived in Africa, Germany was engaged in war with France, America was reconstructing itself after the changes wrought by the Civil War, the Suez Canal was newly opened, and America and Europe were looking to tropical countries for raw materials to feed the mushrooming factories of the industrial revolution. International finance was growing, and ambitious men, in greater and greater numbers, looked to its practice as a way of getting rich quickly.

So when Rhodes heard that the land north of the Limpopo River, then called Matabeleland, contained great mineral wealth, he was determined to claim the land for his beloved Britain, with the idea of establishing an African federation, resembling the American federation of states.

To take African land away from its ruling chiefs might be seen by some as immoral, Rhodes acknowledged as he planned his incursions. But he defended the takeover as being beneficial to the black race. They would be taught British values and ideals and thus would become 'civilised.'

Rhodes knew that his coveted Matabeleland was not a peaceful place. Mashona tribes lived there in uneasy subjugation to the Matabeles, powerfully controlled by King Lobengula. The king wanted to turn away all the white men besieging him for mineral rights, but he did not want to make war with them. He hoped that by not openly clashing with the white interlopers, he could avoid being conquered, and could hold on to his country's latent wealth for his own people. Lobengula would use what military might he had to extend his influence north and east into Mashonaland.

Early in 1888, Rhodes sent a party to see King Lobengula, painstakingly coaching them on what to say. After several months of negotiations, J.S. Moffat, a missionary who was an agent of Rhodes's, finally succeeded in making a treaty with Lobengula, giving the king British protection in exchange for mining rights. According to lore, Moffat's argument in part was that it would be sim.pler to deal with one Englishman than a succession of greedy men from less honourable countries who wanted to mine all of the king's land.

Such an argument seems ironic in lieu of what happened over the succeeding months. For the various political machinations and intrigues that took place between Rhodes, his agents, competing interests, the British crown, other European powers, and King Lobengula shortly after the treaty are so complicated that they are still the subject of passionate debate amongst historians today.

The end result, however, was quite clear. In 1890, Rhodes formed the so-called Pioneer Column, a group of some two hundred colonists of several professions, primarily mining and farming, protected in their move into the black man's country by five hundred 'Chartered Police' – mercenaries.

They marched north through Matabeleland and into neighbouring Mashonaland, claiming both territories in the name of Rhodes's British South Africa Company (or, as it was commonly called, the Chartered Company.) It was on May 3, 1895, that the British South Africa Company officially named the land in honour of its driving force, Cecil Rhodes. 'Has anyone had a country called after their name?' he asked. 'Now I don't care what they do to me.'[2]

He wasn't feeling so carefree a year later when the Mashona and Matabele finally put aside their differences and joined together to rebel against their white conquerors. Ten percent of the white population was killed, but the tribesmen were no match for the British soldiers brought in to help the settlers in the battle.

In exchange for their surrender, the tribes were promised they could resettle some of the land they had held before the whites took it over. Most of these promises were kept, but the British South Africa Company still held title to the land. Africans who had refused to surrender were hunted down, and many of them were hanged.

* * *

In her introduction to *African Laughter* (1992), a report on four visits back to her homeland after an absence of more than thirty years, Doris Lessing writes, 'There is nothing in this bit of British history to be proud of, but the story of the Mashona Rebellion and how it was quelled was taught to white children as a glorious accomplishment.'[3]

Certainly many white settlers held this view. They were the people who were appalled when Rhodesia was named Zimbabwe in 1980. Maude Tayler, had she lived, would no doubt have felt the same.

In 1991, Doris Lessing told an interviewer that her mother 'just didn't like anything I did. She didn't like my short stories, she didn't like anything I wrote.' When the journalist asked whether this was because Maude disliked the idea of her daughter being a writer, Lessing answered: 'No, no. But I should have been writing something different – the biography of Cecil Rhodes, perhaps. Full of admiration for Cecil, she was.'[4]

Tom Toms and Chopin

The fifteen hundred acres of virgin bushland that Michael Tayler was able to purchase in 1924 with his limited funds plus an additional loan from the Land Bank were in the district of Banket, in the Lomagundi area of northeastern Southern Rhodesia. Although it was only seventy miles from the capital city of Salisbury, Banket was sparsely settled. Farms were very large, and miles apart from each other. As far as Doris was concerned, the unpopulated vastness of the veld was glorious after the recent narrow boundaries and crowded streets of London.

The Tayler acreage was unfenced, adding to the feeling of limitless expanse. Two rivers ran through the property, flowing to mountains seven miles away. On the other side of the mountains, after miles of more bushland, was Portuguese territory. Native Africans hoping to escape their white masters, or being sought for arrest for some minor offence, climbed these mountains in hopes of reaching the border.

Lomagundi had been part of Cecil Rhodes's gold country, and mining was still an active preoccupation for many of the colonists. But Michael Tayler had not yet spun that dream; he was impatient to become a farmer, to be outdoors all day, in comfortable khakis, instead of locked into a banking office and a suit.

While a parcel of the land was being cleared to build the family's home, the Taylers, along with other newly arrived settlers, boarded in lodgings on the site of a small gold mine that had formerly been part of Rhodes's *British South Africa Company*. Southern Rhodesia, no longer administered by the *British South Africa Company*, had become a self-governing crown colony in September 1923.

Staying in their small quarters, the Taylers received their first introduction to the bugs that are as much a part of southern Africa as the plains and wild animals. They were about to learn that life in Rhodesia was a constant battle against insects, especially ants. Despite all attempts to banish them, a stream of ants would circle the walls like veins, branching out in different directions. There were also spiders, beetles, and shiny black hornets that zipped around rooms as freely as they did out of doors.

One evening, as Doris and Harry lay sleeping under the mosquito netting that would shelter them on all their African nights, an older girl from a different family wandered into their room, and unthinkingly placed the lit candle she was carrying on a box a few inches from Doris's cot. Before she could leave, Maude also came in to check on her children. Seeing the flickering candle, she leaped across the room to seize it, waking her daughter. Had Doris put a foot or hand out, the netting, Maude believed, would surely have reached the candle and burst into flames, maybe spreading to her little brother and even destroying the flimsy hut.

Maude stared in cold disbelief at the errant, now weeping girl, and demanded to know how she could have done something so senseless. Lessing sees in Maude's reaction not just a mother's protective instincts, but her inability to understand that other people were not as clever or capable as herself. Lessing, who dismisses her fans when they ask 'stupid' questions, might be seen to share her mother's contempt for the less gifted.

The house that Michael Tayler had the dispossessed Africans build for him was made of materials from the bush, 'soil and grass and tree.'[1] Called a pole-and-dagga (mud) house, it was like the Africans' homes, only considerably larger. For the white settlers, such houses were to be temporary dwellings, meant to last only two years or so, after which, with money earned from farming or mining, they would build a proper home, of brick and plaster.

Michael went every day to watch his farm take shape under the supervision of the 'bossboy.' The two men sat on a dead tree log, discussing the work going on in front of them. Michael usually smoked his pipe during these sessions, while Old Smoke – and this was the reason for his nickname – inhaled the local brand of marijuana.

Maude Tayler generally joined her husband at their homesite in midafternoon, bringing the children with her so that they could see their new house taking shape. Doris sat on her father's good leg, listening to the workers' shouts and watching the intricate assembling of nature's own building materials.

First the land was cleared so that a trench could be dug in the shape of the house, which was long and narrow. Trees were cut down to a designated size, and bound together into a framework . Mud was applied to the tree trunks to become the walls of the house. Every African knew that dirt from anthills was the most desirable, because the ants had already mixed the earth by chewing on it. After soaking the soil, the workers squeezed it with their feet until it was the right texture. Doris and Harry were allowed to help them, and the feel of the dark, cool, sweet-smelling mud under their flexing toes must have been as sensuous as helping to build their own house was thrilling.

Lessing remembers that the workers refused to continue using one ant heap because they found in it skeletons of men who had once been tribal chieftains. Before they refused however, they had already pummelled the ant heap into mud for the house, and so, Lessing writes, 'the walls of our house had in them the flesh and the blood of the people of the country.'[2]

The tallest grass was used to make the thatched roof, thick and deep. Doors and windows were fitted, and finally the floor was finished. Cow dung, fresh blood from an ox, and water were mixed in with the ant heap soil, and the workers stomped on it to smooth it and eliminate unsightly bumps, then covered it in linoleum.

It was a happy time watching that house rise on the land. Michael had been advised by other farmers not to build his house high on the kopje as oxen would have to carry all their possessions and furnishings and provisions up that steep hill. Both husband and wife agreed, however, that the views from the hilltop were well worth any logistical difficulties.

Doris's bedroom was third down of the four rooms that made up the house. It was light and spacious, and had its own door to the outside. She used a stone to keep the door ajar so that she could see the hawks gliding down over the fields. The view included a mountain ten miles away that was called the chrome mountain because of its minerals.

The visual spectacle of Southern Rhodesia from her bedroom had a profound effect on Lessing. Some of the most evocative physical descriptions in her canon are of the vibrant colours and lush atmospheric effects she witnessed as a child: The red earth, yellow sun, and green corn fields whose stalks would dry when the seasons changed and shine like precious metals in the sun; the skies that could be filled with steam, smoke, or spinning multicoloured dust. Years later all of this would make London's muted tones difficult to bear when she adopted that city as her home.

The front room of the house on the skopje was ringed with windows, and Maude dauntlessly declared it was 'like the prow of a ship.'[3] In this room were all the accoutrements of the life she would never live again: Liberty curtains, the Oriental rugs, her piano, and some formidable decorated silver pieces. Much of the furniture, however, was made of petrol and paraffin boxes, stained black, that Maude did her best to enhance by dyeing and embroidering flour sacks as slipcovers.

At night Doris often fell asleep to the sound of her mother playing the piano. The usually plaintive classical pieces blended with the sound of beating tom-toms in the workers' reserve at the bottom of the hill. Doris was sure the workers were happily dancing, perhaps circling a fire in front of their shabby huts, as the drumbeat went on, and on, and on. Drifting off to sleep, she would listen to the drumming against the background of Maude's piano. In her mind, the two kinds of music connected to each other. 'I remember the shock when I realised that African drum music and Chopin were not part of the same phenomenon.'[4]

* * *

Lessing claims to have felt waves of pity for her mother, despite the relentless rage she carried toward her. Maude was invariably stoic in her acceptance of what must have been a terrible, aching disappointment at the impoverishment of their lives. The other settlers complained about their living conditions, about the unavailability of foods and other goods that in England they had taken for granted. But while Maude shared their yearnings, she tried to find relief in action.

She transformed herself into a human cornucopia growing more than enough fruit and vegetables to feed the family. In addition she made her own cheese and jams and jellies, all superior to the meagre supplies in the little store that was their only shopping source. Maude also raised chickens and rabbits. Everyone in the area respected her ingenuity and resourcefulness.

But there were other obstacles she could not overcome. On their side of the district, with its poorer, fickle land, farming was fraught with problems. She loved her mother country, but it was clear that its government had misrepresented the territory they had emigrated to. Crops were sparse and often attacked by locusts and other blights, veld fires, and deadly droughts.

Most terrifying of all, Maude knew within the first year of their move that her husband's love of farming did not translate into efficiency on the land. He was more likely to drift into a private fantasy than tackle a real-life problem. He was indecisive, ironic, accepting the vagaries of fate that Maude, ruled by common sense, knew one must relentlessly battle.

Biddy O'Halloran had quickly departed after they settled into the house. She wanted a more convivial life and one that didn't contain a critical, financially pressed employer and her unmanageable daughter. So Maude now had full-time child care to add to her enormous responsibilities, which had to be undertaken in an atmosphere that was in every way foreign to her urban tastes and experience. The elegant English lady of Teheran society might now find herself grabbing her husband's Army revolver to shoot a dangerous snake slithering through a patch of flowers.

Such demonstrations of her ability were hardly a source of pride to Maude. They were only a reminder of how wretched her life had become. And indeed, the bravery, the making-do, the shattered dreams took their toll. Before the first year was out, Maude suddenly became ill. She went to bed and did not get up for another year, diagnosing herself as having a heart condition. The local doctor was either incompetent or, like most other people – except for Doris – afraid to cross her, and he seconded Maude's medical opinion.

Looking back, Lessing wonders why Maude, as a nurse, did not see that she was in the throes of emotional collapse. She believes that in part the cause of her mother's illness was her great concern with social standing. The Taylers' neighbours were mainly of Scottish descent, thrifty and devout. The wives struggled to make ends meet while their husbands worked the difficult land, some of them drinking to soothe their hardship. On the other side of the district, the lands, and their primarily English and Irish owners, were far richer. Socialising rarely took place between these divided groups, though Maude and Michael mixed with both, the working-class Scots because they were neighbours and the wealthier English and Irish because Maude felt the need for 'nice' company. Michael had something in common with his neighbours regardless of their class.

Perhaps Lessing's feelings about her father's wound clouded her vision, for it was only as an adult that she realised that the men that gathered on social occasions shared the experience of surviving the First World War. Like Michael, several of the men had artificial limbs or wore eye patches. Conversation included descriptions of how it felt to have inside their bodies pieces of shrapnel that often moved from place to place. One man had a steel plate in his head, and another was supposed to have a steel shield for his bowels. Photographs of dead husbands or sons or brothers dominated the rooms where these families entertained the Taylers.

Although Maude didn't enjoy their constant talk about the war, at least the people were 'nice.' Back in her part of the district, this woman who had always surrounded herself with clever, socially acceptable friends refused to spend her days talking to ordinary farm wives about gardening and sewing and recipes. She was hungry for companionship, but she refused to be seen on a par with such boring, common people. And yet – and perhaps it did break her heart – on the surface, nothing set her life apart from theirs.

* * *

Undoubtedly there were deeper reasons for Maude's depression. She was caught in a trap that she was coming to realise she might never escape from. The terms of the lease meant they would not be able to leave the farm for five years. In dark moments, she believed she would be here, in this uncivilised country, in her primitive house, in this wilderness landscape, forever. That Doris loved everything about Africa Maude despised deepened the child's estrangement from her mother.

Several times a day, Maude called the children to her bedside, wanting them to console her. 'Poor sick mummy,' she moaned self-pity-ingly, to which Harry and Doris were expected to answer with murmurs of love, hugs, and kisses.[5] As always, Harry was obliging. Most of the time Doris went through the motions of embrace, but inwardly she recoiled. The struggle she experienced at her mother's bedside was terrible, and soon she began to resist coming when called. She didn't believe her mother was really ill, and she angrily told her father so when he urged her to visit the bedside.

Doris did go there, however, for Maude's lessons. Since their arrival in Africa, Maude had been educating her children, and in spite of her illness, she continued to do so. She taught them geography by using remnants of the mud and sand from building the house. She would make models in the shapes of different countries and continents and then put them in the sun to harden.

Similarly, Maude taught them mathematics using seeds and eggs and baby chicks. They played games to learn about the plants, and were expected to remember the names of a wide variety of animals and birds. They memorised the solar system by taking turns being the planets and moon and the sun.

Maude briefly signed them up for a correspondence course, but quickly decided, correctly, that her method of teaching was better, so she cancelled it and continued doing things her way, that is, the way things should be done.

Best of all, Maude told them elaborate stories of her own invention, and filled her bookcases with her beloved books, beautifully bound editions of Stevenson and Kipling that were never off-limits to her young children. She subscribed to two periodicals from England for her son and daughter, which were of a calibre, Lessing states, far beyond anything currently aimed at small children. The *Children's Newspaper* contained articles about inventions and archaeology and *Merry-Go-Round* had stories by writers as well known as Walter de la Mare.

Ironically, by encouraging Doris's love of literature, Maude was providing her daughter with the tools for escaping her.

Lessons – Some Better Left Unlearned

One morning Maude Tayler rose from her bed. She said her long hair was hurting her head. But after she cut her hair as short as possible, she did not return to the place of her year-long retreat. It was her children who climbed into the bed, covering themselves in her shorn hair and sobbing at their mother's changed appearance. Maude quickly became impatient with their emotional outburst, gathered up her hair from the bed, and threw it into the garbage pit. Her period of mourning for her dashed hopes was over. She had been dealt a bad hand, there was nothing else to do but play it.

Michael was relieved to have his wife back taking charge of their lives, especially now, when even he had to acknowledge that his lot as a farmer showed little promise. 'My father's dreams of getting rich in five years had become a brave family joke,' which the Great Depression only confirmed.[1]

Some years later her parents' struggle would prompt Lessing to make a solemn vow. There is a much commented upon scene in her memoir *Under My Skin*, where she observes her parents sitting together outside their deteriorating house. Their faces are worried, anxious, focused on separate inner struggles. She feels revulsion for their helplessness, and swears to always remember this appalling picture. She will never allow herself to be, like them, overpowered by desperation, dependency, and futility. She whispers to herself a phrase she will repeat over and over again for the rest of her life: '*I will not*, I will *not*.'[2]

Lessing also remembers that almost every evening her father sat outside, smoking his pipe, looking up at the stars in the vast African sky, as if in their glitter he might find some magic solution to his problems. Maude did not look to the stars for answers. Her sights were set on bettering the family's fortunes through actions, one of which was the education of her children.

Maude Tayler thoroughly enjoyed teaching her son and daughter and she sometimes fantasised about starting her own school for the young children of other settlers, but she knew it was an impractical notion.

Banket was not like farm districts in England. No real roads ran between the farms and it would be impossible to get the children back and forth every day. Anyway, without formal qualifications, even she probably could not talk the government officials into letting her be a teacher.

Still, she beamed when the educational examiners who came out from Salisbury to see how the rural children were doing told her that Harry and Doris were far ahead of their age in learning. However, the men also told Maude that she could not educate them at home indefinitely. Quite apart from formal instruction, her children also needed social contact, which they were not going to find on an isolated farm. This was a view that undoubtedly resonated all for Maude.

Harry and Doris were perfectly content to play by themselves, investigating the bush for wandering animals such as bands of baboons or wild pigs. This self-sufficiency did not sway their mother from her decision to start them on a conventional education, one that she hoped would culminate in their being accepted by a fine English public school. (And, please God, by that time Maude would be back in England herself.)

As a first step, she enrolled four-year-old Harry and seven-year-old Doris in Rumbavu Park, a boarding school on the outskirts of Salisbury. Harry was young to be away from home, but Maude never considered that a seven-year-old might be as well. As difficult as Doris could be, Maude was sure she loved 'the baby,' and would follow her parents' instructions to look after him.

And Doris *did* love the baby. But what prompted that love? In the park scene from her novel *Love, Again* where Sarah Durham watches a mother coldly rejecting her daughter while clearly adoring her infant son, the daughter makes ardent declarations of love for her brother. Sarah silently offers the girl a rational explanation for her behaviour. As a sister, the girl feels she must 'love that little creature ... so much because you think that if you love what she loves, she will love you.'[3]

* * *

In any event, it was quickly clear to Doris that Harry wouldn't need her protection. The school's older girls loved the idea of playing mommy to the adorable little boy. As it did at home, Harry Tayler's life at Rumbavu Park overflowed with affection.

But Mrs James, the matron of Rumbavu Park, did show Harry's sister affection as well, and Lessing still remembers the woman's warmth, how she brushed Doris's hair, and held her on her roomy lap as if she really loved having her there. Lessing recalls that when she showed Mrs James, a cultured woman, her writing attempts – little stories about 'flowers and birds' – the matron was extravagant in her praise, and proudly showed them to the other teachers.

Doris enjoyed Mrs James's attention. It was quite a different response from what she'd felt shortly before, when her mother sent a 'prose poem' by Doris to the *Rhodesia Herald*. The poem was printed in the newspaper, and Maude reacted with motherly pride, showing it to people, and relishing their praise of her daughter's precocious accomplishment. Doris felt ambivalent at best. She was happy to have her writing published, but she felt a sense of violation having her inner feelings made public. Wrestling with her confusing discomfort, she made another vow. Her next lyrical exercise would not be shared with others. Much to Doris's sorrow, Rumbavu Park closed at the end of her first term, because the owners, a family named Peach, had lost a great deal of money.

Shortly before the term ended, Doris suffered a blow that gave rise to a haunting, lasting question: 'why is it we expect what we do?'[4] The celebrated British actress Sybil Thorndike was touring Southern Rhodesia in a Shakespearean company. There were only a limited number of tickets for Rumbavu students. Mary Peach, the daughter of the school's owners, was to attend the performance, but she hadn't yet returned from a visit to England and Doris could take her place if Mary didn't arrive in time.

In childhood, time moves slowly and one can imagine Doris Taylor anxiously watching the clock, willing it to move to the hour when they could no longer wait for Mary's arrival only to have Mary suddenly there, standing in front of Doris, apologising for having to disappoint her. Doris managed to give her assurance that it was all right, it didn't matter, she understood. But behind the nonchalant facade she was bursting with rage.

Some seventy years after the incident took place, Lessing asks herself why her response that afternoon was so intense. She finds partial explanation in childhood's fundamental concern for fairness, but she recognises that this is not the whole story. What she remembers feeling in that forsaken moment was a sweeping sensation of total, absolute 'social injustice.'[5]

Lessing places her father at the centre of her excessive expectations and inevitable disillusionment. His sense of betrayal in the war had created an acute sensitivity to injustice in his daughter. Not to be allowed to go to the theatre while another child did was proof of the world's fundamental lack of concern for her. And the fact that Mary was a wealthy girl who had just returned from England, where she had had the opportunity to see numerous theatre luminaries would no doubt have made the situation all the more galling.

The event may simply have triggered a resentment that was long simmering in young Doris Taylor. To a child there is no greater inequity

1 love unfairly shared, and the world of Doris's childhood was filled
w. .h indifference of a quite specific sort: an absence of maternal love.
This neglect which had begun before her birth had increased a hundred-
fold ever since Harry was born. Lessing herself has acknowledged the
long-term effect of the different way she and her brother were treated
as children. After years without contact, Doris Lessing visited her
brother when they were both reaching old age. She recognised many
differences between them, but one in particular was sadly striking. 'He
was the much-loved boy, and consequently had an amazing emotional
response to everything. I would say I'm naturally a very affectionate
person, but I had a blight on me when I was young, and I had to lose
that.'[6]

Curiously, Doris Lessing has never acknowledged resenting her
brother for being the 'much-loved' boy. Yet every day of her childhood,
she could compare her maternal crumbs to her brother's feast. Innocent
accomplice or not, to a child's reasoning, Harry had taken from his
sister what was rightly hers.

* * *

After Rumbavu closed, Doris and Harry were sent to a day school in
Avondale, another suburb of Salisbury. To make extra money, an
ill-tempered local woman, Mrs Scott, boarded some of the school's
students, and Doris and Harry stayed with her. It was difficult for the
Taylers to find the money for board and tuition, but Maude managed to
cut more corners to achieve this all-important goal.

It was a miserable time, redeemed only by the reading Doris plunged
into at school. She was homesick and forlorn Lessing writes in *Under
My Skin*, but immediately adds, as though ashamed of that admission
of vulnerability, that conditions in schools today are far worse.

Lessing remembers Mrs Scott's daughter, Nancy, who bullied her
and tried to get her into trouble, but of the other child boarders she has
no recollection. More curious to her than this memory lapse is her faded
picture of Harry. 'Funny that I remember so little of my adored little
brother,' she muses in her memoir.[7] The detached, loving adjective
clings to Harry – the golden child. But it's difficult to tell how much of
this adoration Lessing shares, if any. Was she fond of Harry, despite the
fact that he was adored and she was not? Or did Doris deal with
resentment by pushing Harry out of her thoughts? As an adult she has
never expressed any real rapport with her brother, often telling friends
he had not the slightest sense of who she really was.

The Adventures of Tigger

After two terms at Mrs Scott's, Doris and Harry returned home in June 1927. Harry would be taught through correspondence courses for the time being and Maude had applied for a scholarship for Doris at a convent school in Salisbury. It had the reputation of being more refined than the local school. Maude needed no more reason than this to enrol her daughter. The only aspect of the convent that caused her concern was that the Roman Catholics would try to convert Doris from the family's Protestant faith. However, many other non-Catholic girls attended the school and she felt confident the benefits would outweigh the risks.

This was not a perception shared by Doris. She dreaded the day when she would have to separate once again from the farm. All too soon, a frightened, disconsolate little girl, dressed in her already hated uniform, went off, exiled once again to alien territory.

The convent was not an inviting sight. To the eight-year-old Doris, the central white building seemed massive, and students were denied access to much of it. It was left to their imagination what mysterious things the strange women in odd clothing were doing in the forbidden rooms.

Every night, in Doris's dormitory, a terrifying sermon was delivered to the twenty-four children lying in their narrow beds. The presiding nun, her face grim and cold, bade them good night with warnings of God watching them under the sheets, and seeing what was inside their heads. They might die this very night for their evilness and be eaten by worms forever. Pictures of a bleeding Christ, of mutilated bodies, of a woman being burned to death decorated the dormitory walls. The girls ranged in age from five to eleven and the younger ones were especially frightened, crying into their pillows after the nun went back to her own dormitory, where each sin-free bed was primly separated from the others by drawn white curtains.

When the sisters bathed, which was infrequently – 'The nuns smelled horrible' – they covered themselves with a white overgarment and pulled a wooden board with a hole in it over their heads so that they couldn't see their bodies when they lifted the white cloths to wash.[1] The girls were expected to wear the board as well in order to teach them not to be vain. They were permitted to bathe only once a week; only then could they put on fresh underclothing.

Doris knew her mother would be horrified at these appalling conditions. She wrote home to tell about it, but her letter was intercepted, and she was accused of being naughty and, worse, disloyal. Home for a midterm holiday, Doris was able to tell Maude the story. And by the time school began again, her mother had seen to it that the schedule for both bathing and wearing fresh underwear had doubled to twice a week.

There were also lice in the dormitory and no matter how much the girls protested, no real attempt was made to destroy them before they entrenched themselves in their hair. At last half a dozen of the Protestant girls wrote letters to their parents complaining about the problem, an act of disloyalty which resulted in the girls being brought to a heavy-set sister, who greeted them with an oversize ruler clenched in one large hand. She told them that she was going to punish them for their complaints by striking them six times on soaped palms. When Doris told her mother stories like this one, her voice was almost gay.

For Doris was settling into a new persona at the convent. In a spurt of good feeling, Michael and Maude Tayler decided the family should assume the characters of A.A. Milne's just-published *Winnie-the-Pooh* books. Michael was Eeyore, Harry was Roo, Maude was Kanga. Doris was Tigger, a lively character who giggled and joked and bounced her way through life. The rest of the Taylers slipped into these alter egos only intermittently, but Tigger – as a nickname and as an identity – would be part of Doris Tayler through the rest of her childhood, adolescence, and all the stages of her adult life in Africa.

Doris Lessing sees Tigger Tayler as a protective presence, shielding her from the outside world's demands and disapproval. But Tigger also shielded Doris Tayler from Doris Tayler. As Tigger clowned, Doris could avoid the fears and sadness that lay so deep inside that she felt more and more alienated from her own identity. While Tigger made jokes about life at the convent, Doris Tayler kept the extent of her misery secret: from her family, her schoolmates, and, in part at least, from herself.

* * *

If Doris Tayler defensively denied her depression and anxiety during those four years, she often acted it out. Rather than face her feelings, she would find some way to run away from them – on at least one occasion, quite literally. Home on a school holiday, when she was ten or eleven, swept once more with rage against her mother, which was now often expressed by Tigger's joking contempt rather than Doris's tearful tantrums, she was overcome with a need to escape. She mapped out her difficult route, a walk along a dirt road and abandoned mine track to the railway seven miles from the farm. There she would wait for a morning train to take her to some distant place where she would board a ship for an even farther place, so far that Maude would never be able to find her. It did not really matter where she ended up. The important thing was to get away.

Or was the most important thing to take Harry away? For she insisted that her brother come with her. He cried and protested, but Doris cajoled and exhorted him, whispering stories to distract him as they crept past their parents' window. Surely Doris knew that a small boy would be more of a burden than a companion as she fled, but perhaps on some level she felt that it might be worth the difficulty to deprive Maude of her beloved son.

The flight was aborted because the family dogs turned up suddenly on the road alongside their young masters and ran after them, jumping up and down, barking, wanting to play. Doris may have had second thoughts about her exodus through the dark bush, although she says it was not wanting the dogs to come with them that made her grab her brother's hand and turn back. Whatever the real reason, the following morning Tigger told Maude about her abortive adventure, making it extravagantly funny. She continued giggling even when her mother waved the story away as a silly lie. Behind the giggles, Doris was mortified at having been so naive.

Childhood was a prison of not knowing, of not understanding how to open the doors to your own life. As Doris's unhappiness continued, Tigger increasingly took over. If Doris liked to lie on her bed reading, Tigger craved activity and excitement. It was as if any action, no matter how risky or destructive, was preferable to facing her interior self.

Living in a house with a thatched roof, Michael Tayler was terrified of fire. One day, while Doris was at home on holiday, before he went off to the fields Michael warned his daughter over and over again not to play with matches. As soon as the admonition was offered, it was replaced by obsession, Lessing calmly recalls: she must burn something down.

Doris touched a lighted match to the little empty hut where the dogs sometimes took shelter. It seemed a relatively harmless prank, except for the fact that the kennel was quite near the building where they stored their food and, as that too went up in flames, the fire threatened to reach the house itself. Doris ran into the bush. She heard the dogs barking, and peeked out from her hiding place to see the workers running and shouting as they frantically poured water on the sheds.

Maude found her daughter when the fire was out, the house intact but the kennel and storage hut a mound of ashes. Didn't she know how little money the family had? – her parents asked, more in bewilderment than in anger. Now they would have to buy all new provisions, flour, sugar, groceries, when they could hardly afford stocking the storage hut the first time.

For once, Tigger was silent, and so was Doris. She was too frightened by the chain of events to protest. Recalling the incident in her autobiography, Lessing describes a desperate desire to grow up, to learn enough about life to foresee unintended consequences, rather than childhood remorse.

8

Lost

The beginning of the Great Depression in the 1930s was a particularly bad time for the Taylers to suffer the loss of all their stored food. Every day, economic conditions were declining. Some of the earlier settlers had become quite wealthy during the war, but even they were having difficulty during this period. In the depths of the depression, the price of maize dropped almost 60 per cent. White men were actually walking to farms begging for black men's work.

Michael was not that bad off, but he did have to borrow even more money from the Land Bank and the family went into further debt at the local store that was the source of most of their supplies. With increasing urgency, Maude tried to imagine ways they could settle their debts and leave the farm. They must find a way to put this terrible mistake behind them and return to England where they belonged.

Lessing blames her mother's relentless prodding for her father's grandiose 'solution' to their financial problems. Like other farmers, Michael did try to plant new crops, primarily tobacco, to compensate for the losses in maize. But increasingly he turned his attention to finding gold. He was not alone in this quest. When Doris and Harry played outside together – to Maude's sorrow, Harry was becoming ever more a bush boy, thin and quietly devoted to the animals – they routinely came across abandoned trenches that some gold prospector had laboriously dug, and rocks where pieces were chipped off as samples. The farm was quite near two working gold mines, and the children could hear the noise as they played. With every drop in the economy, new prospectors would bundle together some simple provisions, come to the territory, and camp out in the bush.

This activity had not gone unnoticed by Michael Tayler. A man who will look for deliverance from the stars could hardly be expected to ignore the prospect that it might lay beneath his feet. Indeed, most of the farmers did a bit of gold mining on the side. But Michael soon became obsessed with the idea. From the simple trenches dug by many of his neighbours, he progressed to actual mine shafts, diverting more and more of his time and energy and that of his farmworkers away from more practical duties.

No amount of failure seemed to deter him. Like a gambling addict who forever believes his next bet will come in, Michael waited tensely for word from authorities in Salisbury as to whether his samples were actually gold, which they never were.

Then the prospecting took a peculiar twist. Michael thought he could apply his skills for divining water to the problem. So he set about to perfect a method of divining gold. The idea triggered wild fantasies of commercial success in collaboration with powerful mining interests, and even a sort of training academy for gold divining.

For ten years Michael Tayler experimented with ways to solve the mystery of detecting gold. How did minerals attract or deflect each other? What was the relationship between the moon and these earth minerals? Such questions consumed him, and at dinnertime, he dominated family conversation with his excited talk about them. If Maude found the obsessive ranting depressing – her husband's dream of getting rich from gold was an even harsher joke than getting rich in five years from farming maize – Michael's children were fed up with it. They were equally tired of his other favourite theme, memories of his war experience. When brother and sister, both eager to get out to the bush, looked despairingly at each other and started to fidget, Michael became visibly angry and waved them away, sarcastically accusing them of being bored by 'the Great Unmentionable.'

Lessing acknowledges that she modelled the character of the stubbornly superstitious Alec Barnes in her long African story, 'Eldorado', after her father. Barnes increasingly neglects his farm as he becomes obsessed with gold prospecting and, more particularly, gold divining. When their son discovers the elusive mineral practically by accident, Alec's wife finds herself saddened by what she knows will be a terrible blow for Alec, even though she has railed so bitterly against his destructive fixation. 'After all these years of work with his divining rods and his theories; after all that patient study of the marsh light, gold, it seemed too cruel that his son should casually walk over the ridge he had himself prospected' and strike gold. Alec himself is quiet when he discovers his son's triumph, but soon recovers his insistent faith in his own powers. Lessing strikes a note of pathos as the father says proudly to the son, 'Well, that proves it. I told you, didn't I? I always told you so.'[1]

As Michael's dream foundered, he became more physically infirm – he developed a severe case of diabetes – and was more agitated. One of the manifestations of his bodily disintegration was his changed attitude toward the natives. Though Michael had consistently deplored his wife's condescension toward their workers, he now complained that it would take only two farm helpers from Europe to do the job of twenty ignorant 'savages.' Events such as these, made the injustice of prejudice seep further into Doris Tayler's consciousness and conscience.

One of Zimbabwe's most illustrious writers, Lawrence Vambe, is a contemporary of Doris Lessing. In 1972 he wrote a book called *An Ill-Fated People: Zimbabwe before and after Rhodes*. Lessing wrote the foreword, in which she says, 'It was painful reading this book. I hope it will be painful for other white people to read. I hope particularly that it will be read by the white-skinned British, who are responsible for the double-dealing, the negligence, the cruelty, the atrocities described here.'[2]

* * *

Lessing is the first to acknowledge that her own awareness of the true horrors of Rhodesian racism was delayed. It was one thing to know something was not right and another to truly understand its ramifications. She attributes her finally understanding her culture's racism to her generally critical attitude about life. 'I can't remember any time in my life where I wasn't sitting looking at the grown-up scene ... and thinking, this must be some great charade they've all agreed to play,' she told an interviewer in 1980.[3]

One of the complaints she overheard from the white farmers was that many African workers preferred mining to farming. Although mining conditions, for diamonds or gold, had improved from Cecil Rhodes's time, it was still brutal work. Nonetheless, it paid better than working the land, especially land that was so difficult to tame. The Lomagundi district had developed a bad reputation among Africans who had travelled hundreds of miles from the north to work for the early white settlers. Now many men went directly to the mining area without stopping off in Lomagundi for farm jobs.

Unproductive as Michael Tayler's farm was, in some seasons it might employ up to sixty workers, who were paid just a few shillings a month. 'They lived in these terrible huts, were badly fed and badly paid and they had to work because they had to pay the poll tax.'[4]

Confused and frustrated by what she saw, Doris stored up memories she would one day try to understand, if always within the limitations of her white consciousness. Even as a child, Lessing could empathise with the Africans' reluctance to work for white farmers. Their living conditions were patently abysmal. They were given only a day to build a makeshift hut and they were given meagre foodstuffs in comparison to the white farmers. There was actually an ethnocentric assumption that the Africans' nutritional needs were less than the Europeans' more complicated metabolic system required.

Cecil Rhodes's vision of the superior race did not include severe physical abuse of one's workers and Michael, for one, never resorted to it. Abuse, however, was routinely practised in Southern Rhodesia. Slaps and kicks, withholding of wages to insure against defection, and endless fines for the smallest infraction were habitual ways of keeping workers in line. Farmhands who had swallowed enough mistreatment from a white *baas* (Afrikaans for 'master') would alert his tribe members through the 'bush telegraph' – the slashing of trees around the edge of the farmer's land so that no worker would come there seeking employment. Lessing's story 'Leopard George' describes this custom.

Most whites derided this 'primitive' form of communication, but Lessing believes her former African neighbours often possessed even more exotic ways of connecting with each other: 'Bushmen in Africa used to know when strangers were coming three days before they arrived.' She enthusiastically recalled being shown a 'tree that had been used by the village as a telephone – and it really *had*.'[5] Disdainful of modern society's easy dismissal of phenomena it doesn't understand, Lessing has lamented that Western civilisation rejects these kinds of psychic and extrasensory faculties.

To further cement their economic and social control, the whites of Rhodesia proposed a segregation policy in 1930. The plan was to establish the optimal amount of racial segregation between black workers and white employers, and to have each race restricted to a specific geographic area. Of course, from the country's beginnings under Cecil Rhodes, there had always been a geographic separation between white and black. But it wasn't enforced by law until the Land Apportionment Act, celebrated as the white man's Magna Carta, was issued in 1930.

Despite the fact that whites constituted only about 5 per cent of the population, they dominated the country. The right to vote was related to property ownership and, consequently, nearly all the Africans were locked out of any chance to use voting as a way of changing their lives for the better. As they were also blocked from most union jobs, commercial transactions or access to public places like restaurants or hotels, the many restrictions against black Africans were characterised by a single term: the colour bar. In 1939, when Doris Lessing was twenty years old and becoming politically active in Salisbury trying to eliminate the colour bar, seventy blacks had a vote, contrasted with twenty-eight thousand whites.

The most exaggerated fear of the white Rhodesian was the 'Black Peril': sexual attacks by black men on white women. Lessing remembers that young white girls were always being warned not to go out in the bush lest they be raped. But she did walk around in the bush freely, without fear of attack. She raged against her mother's heightened worry as she approached adolescence, and defiantly flung herself out of the house. When she returned home she left the outside door to her bedroom unlocked. 'Anyone could have raped me fifteen times a night,' she said in a 1984 interview.[6]

The Africans did look in the windows when there were white parties in the district. It was another of the bizarre but taken-for-granted factors in the two worlds of Southern Rhodesia. Lessing recalled a story about a white person asking some black students at Salisbury University why in the 1980s they freely had sex, lay around in the grass caressing each other, and drank too much. The answer was that they'd been observing this behaviour among whites all their lives, and decided this must be 'civilised behavior!'[7]

Doris Tayler was progressively more appalled by what she observed of life in Rhodesia in the 1920s and '30s. But however instinctive her revulsion toward what she heard and saw, white supremacy seemed an absolute. She had no other frame of reference except literature, which was in any case another world. The ideals she had read about in books seemed too remote to apply to life in Southern Rhodesia.

Rebecca West is reputed to have said of Doris Lessing that she was the only person getting the mood of her times correctly. The mood, she explained, was a desperate search for a pattern. As Doris Tayler looked around at her beautiful African landscape, she was beginning to comprehend that a person's mental map can seem totally authentic and yet not be real to someone else. The same space could be occupied by two completely different but equally valid patterns. To the isolated, bewildered young girl, both seemed equally desolate.

9

Doris Tayler's School Days

Back at the convent, Doris kept coming down with illnesses. Perhaps it was better to be preoccupied with physical problems than to face her emotional pain. Being ill brought her into the sickroom, where she was nursed by one of the school's few compassionate sisters. Having found this gentle, affectionate woman, Doris Tayler did everything she could think of to stay in her presence.

Maude regularly visited Doris in the infirmary, more, it seemed, to tell the nuns what to do than to comfort her daughter. When Doris came home on holiday, Maude took her to see doctors although she often argued with their diagnoses and instructed them on her daughter's proper care. Maude's attentiveness seemed largely self-serving, making her feel important and keeping her child dependent. '[I]llness ... delivered me to her, helpless,' Lessing explains.[1]

One aspect of Doris's sickliness that Maude definitely did not enjoy – and that Doris gloated over – was that it stymied Maude's campaign to have her daughter excel at school. It was Maude's determined goal that Doris do well enough at the convent to win a scholarship to a prestigious boarding school in England. But as much as Doris wanted to be free of her mother's interference, nothing she remembered about England made her want to go there again.

Maude wrote to Doris every day, reminding her that she must score extremely high on the qualifying exam that was the key to her winning a scholarship. She got Doris a tutor, whom she barraged almost as much as she did Doris with letters and phone calls to make sure that her daughter succeeded. But Tigger joked rather than buckled down with the tutor, merrily answering her mother's almost unbearably anxious letters and blithely ignoring her fears and pleas.

* * *

Ultimately, Doris won her reprieve. A brief interest in Catholicism and an epidemic of lice and ringworm finally freed her from the harsh and lonely convent. She was brought home. Although Doris was thrilled to be back on the farm, her mother's demands were unabating. For years, her mother had sought surcease from the aridness and disappointments of her own life by trying to cannibalise her daughter's accomplishments. And her zealous need to cultivate her daughter's abilities had long been one of their continuing, bitter battles. Now this familiar pattern was being renewed with vigour as Maude focused her energies on Doris's artistic activities. No creative enterprise could be indulged in by Doris without a reaction from Maude. Each small effort whether it be a sketch or a music lesson was envisioned by Maude as the first step to a brilliant artistic career back in England.

Doris was contemptuous of these grandiose projections. To punish Maude, Doris dropped her other artistic experiments, but writing was something she could not give up. More than ever, she perceived Maude as a dangerous invader, a brutal thief of her emerging identity. Doris's solution was to hide her literary explorations as if her life depended on it. Her resentful, constantly enraged daughter, acted as if Maude's simple gaze would poison every fledgling page. Her boasts of Doris's future as a great writer would destroy any possibility of that glorious fantasy ever coming true.

One particular comment from her mother made Doris explode with fury. Wearing a bright smile, Maude assured acquaintances that she and her daughter were exactly alike. This assumption was so far from reality that it would have been laughable, if Doris hadn't also seen it as a dreadful, suffocating threat. It was as if her mother had placed a curse on her, a spell of possession that Doris might never be able to exorcise.

The more Maude pushed to take part in Doris's life, the more Doris retreated behind a wall of sullen silence or taunting belligerence. 'Why do you hate me so much?' Maude would finally ask, while Doris coolly protested to Michael, 'Why does she hate me? She has always hated me.'[2]

* * *

After several months at home, Doris, now thirteen, reluctantly entered Girls' High School in Salisbury as a boarding student. Overall, it was a better experience than the convent, but she was still miserable and isolated. Tigger again came to her rescue. She made the other girls, and even the teachers, laugh. Well, at least some of them. Other teachers found Tigger's irreverence insulting, and scolded her severely.

This time when Doris came home on holiday from Salisbury, she did not find the comfort the bush had always provided. There was no escaping the wretched atmosphere inside the farmhouse. Michael Tayler was barely recognisable as the person he had once been. It must have been impossible to muster sympathy for the querulous, emaciated, often raving, suddenly old man that he had become. His diabetes had worsened and Maude had put aside his doctor's prescribed Spartan diet and devised a plan of balanced foods that she was convinced would at least not make the condition worse. It seemed to work, although Michael remained frail and increasingly hypochondriacal, a characteristic that, despite her own series of physical complaints, filled his daughter with contempt. Returning to school seemed almost welcome, although once there, she hated it as much as ever.

When an epidemic of pinkeye struck, and Doris developed a particularly bad case. She could barely see through swollen eyelids shut tight with pus, and the thick bandages created frightening light shows as her puffy eyes pressed against the cloth. Maude came to see Doris when the condition was already greatly improved. Nonetheless, she took her to a physician, who confirmed that there was nothing wrong with Doris's eyes. The girl's vision was and would be fine.

Now it was Doris who insisted the doctor was wrong. She could not see well at all, she contradicted. Then, in a surge of rebellion, she told her mother that she would not stay at school with such a handicap. In what she knew was the ultimate assault on her mother's aspirations, Doris went home to the farm, turning her back on formal education forever. Maude was heartbroken. Doris was triumphant and resolute. At fourteen, she was severing the ties to a dependent childhood. With the intense conviction of a teenager she decided that if she were ever to find freedom from her mother, it had to be now.

10

Interlude

Just as teenage athletes look up to sports heroes, adolescent writers revere literary idols. Often there is an intense identification with an accomplished author whose work explores the same emotions as the aspiring writer, an identification that intensifies when details of a literary figure's life match those of the young aspirant.

Doris Lessing has described the South African novelist, Olive Schreiner as a sort of literary older sister. But when you consider the parallels between their lives, it is hard to believe that she was not a great deal more. Certainly, Lessing has acknowledged the profound impact of coming across *The Story of an African Farm*, fifty years after its publication. It was an extraordinary experience for the then fourteen-year-old Doris. It was not only the first 'real' book she'd read that was set in Africa, it was truth as she had never known it before, not in all the books she had devoured in her autodidact's education.

Like Olive Schreiner herself, Lessing had pored over the classics, and also contemporary works from English and Russian and French and American writers. But this South African writer's story, set in the very same emotional and physical terrain that made up Doris's own life, meant she did not have to make adjustments for a different cultural or geographical perspective. She was amazed as she devoured Schreiner's novel to find her own deepest feelings described, her questions about life validated, the painful joining of her passion for Africa with the isolation of a colonial intruder expressed in exact detail.

Schreiner's book not only contained descriptions of the world Doris saw every day, it told what it felt like to grow up inside it. Schreiner lost her loneliness in the boundless beauty of nature. As one of her biographers writes,

> She extolled not only the beauty of the South African karroo but its gifts of visionary insight into the symmetry of all being and the possibility of a human universe of love, peace, and equality ... No matter how hungry, nomadic, and desolate Schreiner's life and the lives of her fictional characters, they could roam miles of the karroo in exalted reflection and find comfort in the radiant blue sky, the invincible rocks, the sparse but hardy vegetation, and the animal life. At

times, she felt that the individual plants she gazed upon spoke to her and returned her love for them.[1]

In nature's silence, Schreiner could think deeply, nurturing her own perceptions. She saw nature as filled with connections that were available to everyone who cared to look. A tree, a fossil footprint, an animal's skeleton, the human body possessed affinities with one another. From earliest childhood she had seen the connection between herself and nature and never lost her belief in the unity of all things. Schreiner gave great credence to her dreams and often wrote in allegory. She made no apologies for this literary choice. If some found her writing ambiguous, she told them that true art was multilayered in meaning. Literary fashion would never guide her work.

*   *   *

Doris shared another of Olive Schreiner's feelings: resentment about the unfairness of growing up female. In much of her writing, and throughout her life, Schreiner angrily asserted that no matter what talents a girl possessed, no matter how she hungered for achievement, her sex imprisoned her. 'Throw the puppy into the water: if it swims, well; if it sinks, well; but do not tie a rope round its throat and weight it with a brick, and then assert its incapacity to keep afloat.'[2]

Doris had never heard such revolutionary thoughts from any of the girls at school or the daughters of her mother's few friends. These families were taught to embrace the Edwardian manners and values that had shaped their parents' lives. Boys hoped to grow up to be businessmen, perhaps with branches back in England, or the owners of large tobacco farms or diamond mines. The girls would marry these men, live in large houses, wear beautiful hand-sewn clothes, go to and give tea and cocktail and dinner parties, where all the work would be done by large staffs of servants whom they would treat with varying levels of contempt and indifference.

To see such a future as terrifyingly empty, to want to write, to have autonomy, fame, and power, increasingly fed Doris Tayler's sense of her own oddness and personal estrangement. Imagine, then, the welcome shock of reading the speech the young female protagonist makes to a male friend in *The Story of an African Farm*.

It is not what is done to us, but what is made of us ... that wrongs us ... the world tells us what we are to be, and shapes us by the ends it sets before us ... To you it says ... as your arm is strong and your knowledge great, and the power to labour is with you, so you shall gain all that human heart desires. To us it says – Strength shall not help you, nor knowledge, nor labour. You shall gain what men gain, but by other means. And so the world makes men and women.'[3]

'[T]he book became part of me,' Doris Lessing wrote in a foreword to a 1976 edition of *The Story of an African Farm*. From then on, she had only 'to hear the title, or 'Olive Schreiner,' and my deepest self was touched.'[4]

Lessing recoils from women who tell her how important reading *The Golden Notebook* or the Martha Quest novels was to them, how they feel so close to Lessing even though they have never met her, because she revealed and affirmed what lay buried in their hearts, but she does not scorn the same response in her fourteen-year-old self as she describes her intense identification with Schreiner's novel, and with the young woman who had written it, who 'felt so close, like a sister.'[5]

One important similarity to Olive Schreiner that Doris learned of as she read more about Schreiner's life was their relationships with their parents. Doris may have smiled in affectionate recognition at Schreiner's description of her father as gentle and kind but too soft and dreamy to cope successfully with the harsh South African life he had taken on as a missionary. But surely her heart leaped when Schreiner described her own mother as a class-consumed woman, ambitious and intellectual, who held her daughter at a cold distance, at least in her early years. When comparing her parents in a letter to Havelock Ellis, Schreiner said that her father was 'infinitely tenderer to us as children and had a much greater heart than my mother.'[6] Doris Tayler made her real break with her family at fourteen and surely her courage was stimulated by the writer she had just discovered, who had not only shared her dreams of escape and achievement, but, most important, had lived out the dreams, blazing a path for her to follow.

* * *

The account of how Olive Schreiner got *The Story of an African Farm* published must have had a powerful effect on Doris Tayler. Perhaps as powerful an effect as the book itself. It was Schreiner's first novel. One that she had carried in manuscript form from South Africa to London where she went to work as a governess. After numerous rejections the book was finally accepted by the T. Fisher Unwin, publishing house. In 1883, the twenty-eight-year-old South African governess had her novel published under the pseudonym Ralph Iron. *The Story of an African Farm* became an instant sensation for the same reason it had been rejected by so many publishers: it depicted an Africa that English readers were totally unfamiliar with.

As Iron/Schreiner says in the book's preface, 'It has been suggested by a kind critic that he would have better liked the little book if it had been a history of wild adventure; of cattle driven into inaccessible kranzes by bushmen; "of encounters with ravening lions, and hair-breadth escapes.'" But the untried author says defiantly, 'this could not be. Such works are best written in Piccadilly or in the Strand.'[7]

As soon as Ralph Iron's true identity was discovered, the obscure colonial governess became a celebrated and hotly pursued member of London's intellectual elite. Prime Minister Gladstone, the Irish novelist George Moore, and Oscar Wilde were impatient to meet her. The politician Sir Charles Dilke compared her book with *Pilgrim's Progress*. Schreiner began lifelong friendships with Eleanor Marx, daughter of Karl, and the young Havelock Ellis, who became famous for his books on sexuality.

Schreiner's almost daily correspondence with Ellis, much of which was destroyed at her instructions (only 607 letters remain out of several thousand) continues the themes of 'the woman question' and 'the sex question' that appear in her published writing: How can a woman find some balance between love, sexual desire, and the need for personal freedom? Olive Schreiner experienced intense sexual desire from a very early age. In several of her letters to Ellis, she declared that she was trying to stifle her carnal longings, that she was often unable to work because of sexual frustration.

Although they were immensely intimate, Ellis and Schreiner appar-ently never became lovers. Doris Lessing has suggested that Schreiner simply did not find Ellis sexually arousing. In his memoir, *My Life*, Ellis seems to affirm this, by suggesting the difference in their erotic needs:

> She possessed a powerfully and physically passionate temperament which craved an answering impulse ... For a brief period at this early stage of our relationship there passed before her the possibility of a relationship with me such as her own temperament demanded. But she swiftly realised that I was not fitted to play the part ... which her elementary primitive nature craved.[8]

During her stay in England (1881 - 89) Schreiner kept in touch with her homeland. She knew of Cecil Rhodes's activities in gold mining, and she was eager to see what changes the discovery of gold and Rhodes's Gold Fields of South Africa were making in her country. She was also intrigued by what she had heard of the man, so much so that as she sailed toward the Cape Colony, she felt a strong attraction to him, the sense that 'this man belongs to me.'[9]

She was certainly attracted to Rhodes when they first saw each other, admiring his energy and political passion. Although it is fairly certain that Rhodes was homosexual, he enjoyed Schreiner's admira-tion, and also being in the company of her celebrity. For a while, they spent considerable time together, with Schreiner even acting as hostess for Rhodes on some social occasions. But the more she realised what imperialist goals lay under his benevolent rhetoric, the more bitter and disillusioned she became. She determined to tell the world who she believed Cecil Rhodes really was, and quickly became his sharpest and most visible opponent.

One of her most stinging attacks was a blend of fiction and nonfiction titled 'The Salvation of a Ministry.' It railed against Rhodes's support for the 'strop bill,' which allowed police to administer lashes instead of fines and jail sentences for a native's minor criminal offences. Schreiner called the act the 'Every Man Wallop His Own Nigger Bill.'

For years, Olive Schreiner had been developing quite a different work, her own lengthy study of the woman question, called *Woman and Labour*, which she discussed in her letters to Havelock Ellis. It was to be her own mammoth 'sex-book,' an attempt to trace from prehistory the conditions of women's lives. She wanted to understand the historical path that had led to 'the secret torment' of her life.

An abbreviated version of *Woman and Labour* was published in 1911, and was immediately taken as a text for the growing British feminist movement. In it Schreiner declares that it is a woman's right to work and be financially independent, and warns that these rights cannot be blocked forever. In government and business and medicine and science, in any field formerly closed to women, doors would finally be forced open.

Doris Lessing says that Schreiner was the kind of woman who, in an ancient culture, probably would have been appointed a 'prophetess of a tribe.'[10] Clearly, Olive Schreiner had extraordinary sensitivity and sociological acumen. Her years in England had only strengthened her childhood observation that the 'parasitic' role of middle-class and upper-class women relied on a large, unnoticed body of working-class women who would not always be content to remain in the shadows. As outspoken about the world around her as Doris Lessing would be, Schreiner theorised with great foresight that the world would one day be dominated by America and Russia. She was enraged by the anti-Semitism that poisoned a large segment of white South African life. She was also far ahead of her time in condemning the cruel and pointless killing of African wildlife, and in demanding conservation laws and animal reserves.

Martha Quest, the first volume of Doris Lessing's Children of Violence series opens with an adolescent Martha ostentatiously reading an Ellis sex treatise to annoy her mother. And the novel's epigraph is a statement from one of Schreiner's letters to Havelock Ellis – 'I am so tired of it, and also tired of the future before it comes.'[11] The statement introduces readers to the young Martha Quest's struggle to escape a conventional, preordained life. Lessing's refusal to succumb to such future fatigue owes much to Schreiner's courage and prescient advice, articulated in Schreiner's *From Man to Man*.

You, you, yourself must save yourself. From those weak limbs strike off the fetters; with your strong hands bend down and heal the wounds your hands have made; remove the sand about the heavily sunken feet.

When they are healed and free and strong, they, they and not another, will bear you to the mountains where you would be.[12]

Beauty

Au Pair ...

For more than a year, war raged in the Tayler household. Doris's blossoming sexuality prompted a new set of battles. Maude wanted her daughter to dress like a little girl, or, if she must wear more grown-up clothes, in tasteful ensembles befitting her social class. Lessing now finds her mother's penchant for formality in dress quite poignant. 'I think of her going to the station, which consisted of three little buildings and a butcher's shop, wearing a hat, white gloves, stockings, and a proper dress.'[1]

But, like most teenagers, Doris's taste in clothes did not resemble her mother's. She taught herself how to use the family sewing machine and killed guinea fowl to sell to the butcher – once she simply broke a hen's neck instead of using her gun – so that she could buy fabric to create short, revealing dresses that showed off her shapely body and beautiful legs. Lessing exults in the memory of first claiming her youthful body. Out on the bush, holding a rifle, she pulled up her dress to look at her legs and preened with self-esteem.

Her face was lovely as well. The almond-shaped brown-green eyes and high cheekbones accentuated her sun-burnished skin. Her shiny dark hair, waved with home permanents, added to the resemblance between herself and the American movie star Gene Tierney that would later be remarked upon.

No matter what her arguments with her mother were about, Doris could no longer rely on Michael as an ally against her. As his body shrivelled from diabetes, he turned into a sorrowful old man obsessed with his own illness and unfulfilled fantasies. He certainly no longer had the capacity to ignore the constant friction between his wife and daughter. He wanted peace. If Doris was so unhappy at home, he finally said, if she hated her parents so much, why didn't she just go away for good?

Despite her mother's weeping protests, she took him at his word. Cheerful, fun-loving Tigger became an au pair for a young couple who lived just outside Salisbury. They had a four-year-old son and were expecting a new baby. Lessing recalls she was soon doing much more than child care, virtually running the household. But this introduction to life as a *hausfrau* did not satisfy her. She found herself drifting off into the romantic fantasies that have undoubtedly befallen many a bored au pair. Her other escape from drudgery was less typical. In between her domestic chores, Doris was beginning to send short pieces of writing off to magazines and a few were published.

* * *

After three months in her first job, Doris left to work for another family who lived in town, a location she much preferred. It was an empire-loving, conservative household, a couple and the wife's unmarried brother. Surprisingly, the husband supported the idea of improving the natives' lives. He believed the current system was hurting whites, because by keeping blacks uneducated and living so poorly, they could not develop into efficient workers.

Though the rationale was pragmatic and self-serving, it was the first time Doris Tayler had ever heard anyone from a conventional background speak critically about how black people were treated. Having often criticised her mother's colonial prejudices, Doris was not yet sophisticated enough in her understanding to make strong arguments against racism and she had often had to abandon her attacks. Doris's new employer gave her books to read that would prepare her for winning debates with her mother. But for once, this was not her real goal. What mattered more was that her eyes were being opened to what had been around her all those years, and that she was learning the legitimacy – and excitement – of radical thinking.

The couple's four-month-old baby was turned over to Doris's nearly total care. The mother liked her baby well enough, Lessing writes, and was even proud of him. 'She was simply not maternal.'[2] There is no hint of identification with the baby or anger at the mother is given in this detached observation.

Doris enjoyed the fact that the men of the house clearly found her attractive. She had no doubt that the husband would have liked to 'seduce' her, and was certain that only his conventional values kept him from making a pass at her. To compensate, she tried to lure the unmarried brother, but he too was unwilling to do what she wanted. He would lie down beside her, but only to kiss her lightly, and cuddle her with affection rather than passion. Ironically, Lessing who would later endure more than her share of philandering men, found herself frustrated by a household of males with strong Puritan values.

As a child, Doris had longed for such cuddling from both her mother and father. Once, sick in bed with the dysentery that had struck the family, she had begged Maude to stay with her a little while longer. Her request for cuddling was mimicked by her weary mother and became a family joke. She was twelve years old at that point. But now aged fifteen, cuddling was not enough. The mild responses resulting from

Tigger's efforts to get her unwilling paramour to consummate their affair were a source of irritation. Gentle expressions of affection were bland, pointless, boring.

Doris Lessing has postulated that young girls should be paired off with older lovers, who understand from the beginning that the relationship will not last.[3] The girl's heart might be broken in the process, but so what? Inevitably, it will be broken anyway, Lessing declares in a tone which is free of accusation. It is largely in the arena of sexuality and men and women's relationships that Lessing shrinks from sharing the label with other women writers of feminist orientation. Florence Howe, the feminist writer and publisher, remembers a visit she paid to Doris Lessing in 1966. Howe was a passionate admirer of *The Golden Notebook*. When she told Lessing that she disliked all the novel's male characters, Lessing was surprised, and asked why. Howe answered that the men all eventually left the women they were involved with. Doris Lessing was amused by this.

'Well, men do leave, after all,' she said. 'But that doesn't make them less marvelous.'[4] Nearly thirty years later, Lessing, who has jettisoned so many previous views, has retained a remarkably consistent approach to women's issues. Vocal in her criticism of the obstacles women suffer and the passive behaviour demanded of them by society, she has shown an equally determined antagonism to much of the sexual politics of mainstream feminism. As a woman who has made it clear that she values sexual satisfaction over fidelity, or long term commitment, it is not surprising that she would refuse to condemn men in the *Golden Notebook* (or men in general) for having a similar ethos. Lessing has never publicly supported the view that the detached and aggressively promiscuous side of male sexuality is a form of sexism.

In *Under My Skin*, Lessing illustrates her hostility to current attitudes about sexual harassment with a story about a good-looking physician who begins breathing heavily after inserting a finger inside her during an examination. A simple health question is enough to throw the doctor off track and end the encounter almost as soon as it's begun. It's a trivial incident as far as she's concerned and she mocks the idea that it would be appropriate to report such an incident and destroy a man's career.

Issues of appearance and self-worth raised by feminists don't register with Lessing, either. In her writing she displays early confidence in her appearance, as well as a joy in that appearance. The insecurities that so often accompany puberty did not visit her. She seems perplexed by the degree of discomfort many women feel in trying to relate their bodies to the idealised images projected by society. And this has led to a dismissive attitude towards feminist writing on the subject.

In a 1994 interview, Lessing explained her views. She brought up Simone de Beauvoir, whose career spanned about the same time as her own and said that de Beauvoir disliked her body as well as being a woman. That was not a view which Lessing shared, either then or later. In Salisbury, in the 1930s, Doris Tayler was as sanguine about the true relationships between men and women as she was confident about her appearance. To her, 'love' was coated with false sentiment, often invoked only to justify having sex.

* * *

The search for a sex partner wasn't Doris Tayler's only problem in her new household. Writing also had its frustrations. Most of it, chiefly poetry, went unpublished. But one article that she submitted to a Salisbury newspaper, written in Tigger's ebullient, irreverent, heedless voice was accepted and printed.

A Zimbabwean man named Philip Paul remembers that newspaper story. In early 1935 or '36, 'after I had returned to this country from an education overseas, I joined a party of young friends to go to a dance at the Grand Hotel in Salisbury. My partner was Tigger Tayler, whose company I thoroughly enjoyed.' But what Tigger Tayler's friends didn't realise as they carried on at the dance was that all the while she seemed to be taking part in the fun, Doris Tayler was recording every detail of their behaviour.

Shortly afterward, Paul recalls, the newspaper published Tigger's commentary. It made fun of several incidents at the dance and the people involved in them. Although no surnames were used, the writer did not bother to change Christian names, so that any parents knowing that their son or daughter had attended the dance could easily recognise the culprits. 'I enjoyed it,' recalled Mr Paul, 'but the family of one of the girls with us was very angry and wrote a vigorous protest, either to 'Tigger' or to the editor of the paper.'

Lessing's sharply observant eye has always served her writing well – though sometimes her style seems disturbingly detached. Paradoxically, her writing combines a deep insight into humanity with very little of the empathy that usually accompanies such insight. She has a unique unsentimental voice that can be traced to the uneasy feeling she had as a girl that she must constantly be alert to what was going on around her – the difficult effort to understand what was really behind a grown-up's statement or behaviour. With age, that understanding may no longer require strenuous effort. But her writing retains the perspective of the observant outsider even as she explores the most intimate of territory.

* * *

At seventeen, Doris Tayler left Salisbury to return to the farm in order to write a novel. She could not afford to stay in Salisbury without working, and the demands of her job would make writing impossible. Once home, she wrote two novels, both, at least to her mind, embarrassing failures. She destroyed them, and turned again to the short story form for more practice. Though she was writing, she still didn't consider herself a 'writer.' Maude tried to talk to her about other occupations, such as nursing, while Doris briefly entertained the thought of veterinary medicine. But despite her unhappiness over her novels, her desire to write was intense. Writing and discarding two consecutive novels might be devastating to most writers, aspiring or not. But the process left Doris unfazed.

Life in the Tayler house grew ever grimmer. Michael Tayler continued to fail physically, and became increasingly embittered by the news on the wireless to which he listened obsessively. Hitler was rising in Germany. It was clear there would soon be another war. Since Maude had never learned to drive, Doris often had to chauffeur her parents to Salisbury for Michael's medical treatment.

Doris was teaching herself typing and shorthand, in order to get a different sort of job than au pair. It was absurd to leave her parents' house only to be subjected to the rules of someone else's home. She wanted to be free of all authority, to live on her own, to come and go as she pleased. And the price she was willing to pay for such autonomy – and it would be heavier than she could imagine then – was leaving the bush. After her *African Laughter: Four Visits to Zimbabwe* was published in 1992, Doris Lessing told Fiammetta Rocco, a South Africa-born journalist, that she would have no fear of re-entering the bush as an elderly woman. It wouldn't frighten her to be temporarily lost to the outside world. But at seventeen, although she loved it so dearly, the last thing Doris wanted was to be lost in the bush.

Every day, Doris's desperate longing for escape grew stronger. She heard from a man who was passing through the region that there were jobs at the telephone exchange in Salisbury. For Maude, this was the ultimate atrocity. It had been bad enough to have her daughter be a nursemaid, but now Doris had entered a world that was even more crass and demeaning. This gifted child, whose talents had previously provoked her mother to incessant talk of a brilliant career in the arts, was about to humiliate the family by becoming a common telephone operator.

Of course Doris ignored her mother's pleas, and her rage, and immediately went to Salisbury to apply for the job. As soon as she was hired, she found herself a room in the home of a widow. This time there was no turning back. Doris Taylor had left her parent's home forever.

Smoke Got in Her Eyes

Since Doris refused to tell Maude anything about her life in Salisbury, Maude went there to see for herself, inquiring of the landlady how Tigger was spending her days and, worse, her nights. The results of the investigation fulfilled her darkest nightmares. Doris, her mother said in bitter, scathing letters to her daughter, would surely end up in a brothel.

Eighteen-year-old Tigger Tayler worked at the telephone company for a year, where, when the short working day ended, it was time for tireless socialising. The young people, men far outnumbering the women, gathered every evening for sundowner parties that began at six and might last nearly all night. Lessing professes to be amazed at the alcoholic excesses of those evenings, but her reminiscence is affectionate. The sweet and spicy scents of an African night were mixed with the bitter aftertaste of the gin she never stopped sipping, and the star-filled sky was seen through the haze of cigarette smoke.

Like her father, Doris was a wonderful dancer. Pressed tight to her partner, she glided in his arms to songs like 'Smoke Gets in Your Eyes' and 'Dancing Cheek to Cheek,' music she found bewitching. In November 1993, Lessing was interviewed on 'Desert Island Discs' in connection with the publication of the first volume of her memoirs. The program's format involved her choosing eight favourite pieces of music. One of her selections was 'I've Got You Under My Skin,' from which she had derived the title of the soon-to-be-published book. After the Bing Crosby recording, Lessing recalled, 'I danced, it seems to me now, every night for about three or four years. It's very powerful music, you know, this kind of thing. Very sentimental. Always yearning and longing and wanting.'[1]

Even when she put on weight, which she has done on and off all her life, Doris exulted in her body, and admired herself as much as the men did who danced with her, or watched her pass by. Sexual self-confidence is alluring, especially when it comes in a pretty package and Doris would have had no trouble finding one of the young professionals or civil servants to partner her in a dance or (if she so desired) something more. War seemed imminent and added to the desire to pack in experience, all of it heady and heedless, and – 'most important – fun.

* * *

The telephone job quickly became routine, and Doris looked for other work. But her energy remained primarily invested in her social life, although she continued with her reading, adding Virginia Woolf to the shelf occupied by Olive Schreiner. Reflecting on her early reading habits, Lessing is amazed at how many books she acquired and devoured while working and pursuing her social life. She ordered books from England, and when they arrived they were like the most luxurious gifts.

She was, she now realises, too young for some of them, such as Carlyle and Ruskin, but at the time she did not notice. She devoured the Russians. Tolstoy, Dostoyevsky, Chekhov, Turgenev filled her mind with new ideas about writing and the human condition, in sharp contrast to the atmosphere around her. Salisbury, like the rest of Southern Rhodesia was racist and narrow. Conversation was confined to the colour bar, athletic games, or careless, often mean-spirited gossip. Literature was an escape from all this, an anchor to hold on to.

One day a friend invited Doris to a meeting of the Left Book Club, a small group of Communists in Salisbury, for she had heard that Doris was becoming more and more sympathetic to the natives' plight. Doris was intrigued by the idea of meeting people who were brave enough to dissent from the prevailing politics and came along. But as she watched their faces, and listened to them speak, she became more and more impatient. The men slandered members of the group who hadn't bothered to show up and the women all wore clothes that were shapelessly unattractive, and they seemed to spend most of their time complaining about their husbands who had turned them into house wives.

Doris was contemptuous of the women's grievances. No one made them get married. No one made them have children. She speculated that their disgruntled air arose from having such a young, good-looking, free young woman watching them with obvious disapproval.

Although the heated talk of racial injustice resonated in Doris's mind, at this point in her life Tigger Tayler did not choose to associate with a group she found so drab. Political involvement was not then her first priority. Nonetheless, she followed the group's parting instructions to give up her subscription to the establishment magazine, the *Observer*, and subscribe instead to the *New Statesman*, considered a dangerous, disgusting, left-wing propaganda sheet by the rest of the white population.

* * *

It was one of Frank Wisdom's attractions that he also read the *New*

Statesman, and shared Doris's radical ideas about the racial question. Frank Wisdom (the model for Martha Quest's first husband, Douglas Knowell, in the Children of Violence series) was a civil servant, ten years older than Doris. Later in his life, he would become Master of the High Court, a civil service job in the upper echelons of Southern Rhodesia's Ministry of Justice. But when Doris met him, he was working his way up through fairly routine positions.

Aside from his political thinking, Frank was indistinguishable from the other men in Tigger Tayler's life. He danced, and drank too much, and played sports, and loved to flirt with women and behave laddishly with his buddies. And the girl who had looked at her parents and vowed 'I *will not*. I will *not*' decided she wanted to marry him. In April 1939, she did.

In *Under My Skin*, Lessing is cavalier about her decision to marry. It wasn't really a decision at all, she implies, for she was programmed by the approaching war, and by the heady dance music with its ardent lyrics. Everyone was getting married, and she was swept along in the tide.

Lessing does not consider that a different sort of programming may have been at work, one personal and internal rather than created by external events. The defences Doris Tayler constructed to protect herself from the pain of rejection had produced a person who seemed totally uninterested in love and attachment. But as defences often do, her refusal to show any emotional need may have created the very situation she was trying to avoid. By not letting anyone come close enough to hurt her, she was guaranteeing that her sense of isolation would continue. Doris may have looked to marriage as a means of connection and acceptance.

Lessing says she did not love Frank Wisdom, but, caught up in the tumult of the times, she didn't find it difficult to convince herself that she did. She also believes he did not love her. Indeed, he was engaged to a girl in Britain, but Tigger had no qualms about taking him away from his fiancé. Lessing presents her ability to dispossess that other girl with something bordering on pride. Women down through time have felt such behaviour is their right, she says; rather than making her feel morally ignoble, or unsisterly, it infused her with self-esteem.

In her wedding pictures, nineteen-year-old Doris Tayler is a smiling, happy, delighted new bride. Behind that mask is a girl numb to the unwanted festivities. She despised the charmless ceremony. It had nothing to do with what she wished for in life. But why should it? After all, Lessing says, 'It was 'Tigger' who was getting married.'[2]

Maude and Michael were predictably astonished that their rebellious, independent daughter had got married so young – and to a man who was respectably employed. Michael assumed Doris was pregnant, which she was, though she was not yet aware of the fact. She would remain unaware for some four and a half months, so removed was ᵗ ᵤₑ from the realities of her life.

After the wedding, Frank and Doris took off on a honeymoon in the company of another couple. They were driving to Beira, on the coast of Portuguese East Africa (now Mozambique), to see the Salisbury Sports Club rugger team play. They drove along dark, twisting roads, some of them little more than a rough path in the bush. They passed elephants and drank toasts to them. When they got to Beira, the town was like one big party, filled with rowdy athletes and their fans, and plenty of liquor.

When Mr and Mrs Wisdom came back to Salisbury, it was to a small flat owned by an older couple who were friends of Frank's. The woman gave kindly instructions on how to perform a married matron's duties. Under her tutelage, Tigger cooked and cleaned; she polished Frank's boots, and their new furniture, with manic energy.

At night they continued their sundowning, drinking and dancing at the Sports Club. Some of the people at the club noticed that Doris appeared to be pregnant. She thought the idea was laughable, until she realised it might be true.

Doris took it for granted that she would have an abortion, and Frank concurred. With only a vague connection to someone who might know someone to perform the operation, she took a train to Johannesburg, in search of the potential contact. The train was crowded, she had very little money and even less idea what was going to happen when she got to her destination. It took considerable doing to locate the young man she was looking for, and then the person whose name he gave her angrily turned her away. Somehow she did find a doctor who was willing, affable, and as luck would have it, intoxicated. She was warned by one of his female friends not to allow him to perform the operation because he had already run into trouble for operating while under the influence. Finally, Tigger located a decent physician who, although he did perform abortions, informed her how far along in the pregnancy she was, and why he would not do one at this stage.

Doris Lessing says she became pregnant because nature wants young women to have babies. She also believes that nature's demands caused her to deny her pregnancy until it was too late to have an abortion. Doris Tayler might not have wanted a child, but nature forced her into cooperating. With surprising frequency, Lessing looks back on her life and attributes her actions to Fate, to mother nature, to the Zeitgeist, or a hidden force or an era's commanding flow. Such passive yielding to higher powers is hard to understand in someone so fiercely determined to do things her way, and so self-absorbed. It is an attitude, however, that perhaps also allows one to evade responsibility for many of one's actions: if you are not in control of events, you can't be faulted for their outcomes either.

* * *

Doris Wisdom spent an uneventful pregnancy, lying in cool tubs, eating for herself and the child. Other young mothers-to-be felt ill, and they worried about the health of their unborn children. Doris was convinced that she would have a perfect pregnancy, an effortless birth, and an equally perfect child.

She claims to have been happy about her condition and a substantial factor in her contentment was that Frank, who was desperate to be in the service, was likely to be called up soon. A training school for the Royal Air Force had opened in Salisbury, and other Englishmen were arriving in the city to take part in war-related work. As Doris thought about being alone with the baby when Frank was off to war, she could fantasise about an affair with one of this new crop of men. She was also certain that with Frank gone, she would have time to write a novel and better stories than any she'd written in the past.

In fact, Tigger's labour was very painful, and she was virtually ignored by the overworked nursing staff. But at last, her son John's birth released her from the agony. Frank, still a civilian, was a proud father. During Doris's weakling confinement after the birth he would frequently show up at the maternity nursing home with a loud group of friends to help him celebrate.

A Proper Marriage, the second volume of the Children of Violence series, won Lessing some of her most devoted fans because the novel not only demythologised pregnancy and birth, it revealed the ambivalence of motherhood. Feelings that had never been connected, at least so openly, to this experience startled readers even as it made them feel less ashamed that they too had felt resentment mixed with love, a sense of entrapment with protective impulses. Lessing explored this experience skilfully in her fiction. 'Cycles of guilt and defiance ruled her living, and she knew it,' Lessing wrote of Martha Quest's relationship with her infant daughter.

> [S]he had not the beginnings of an understanding of what it all meant .... She was saying to herself, as she wiped off milk and grey pulp, Oh, Lord, how I do hate this business, I do loathe it so. She was saying she hated her daughter; and she knew it. Soon, the hot anger died; guilt unfailingly succeeded.[3]

In the maternity home, Lessing remembers she longed to hold her baby for more than the few minutes custom allowed, to feed him when he was hungry instead of only every four hours as the nurses insisted. But the rules that had kept Doris crying in her bed as an infant still applied and the nursery floor rang with the terrible clamour of hungry, shrieking babies. Ironically, when Maude came to visit she told her daughter that a four-hour wait to be fed was much too long for a newborn baby. This immediately brought Doris into agreement with the restrictions in order to prevent her mother from involving her in an unwinnable fight with the staff.

Once home, Doris continued to follow the prevailing rules about infant care, even though John's obvious hunger filled her with frustration. In her memoir she does, however, not connect what her son might be feeling to her own early feeding experience.

Lessing sees John as a baby and then a child who would now be called hyperactive, and while she remembers her exhaustion and helplessness at his anger and demands, she is pleased that the term did not exist at the time. Thus labelled, he would have been both stigmatised and filled with deadening chemicals to control his behaviour. Because John demanded more milk than she was producing, and the whole process was more trouble than it seemed worth, she put him on a bottle. Maude accused her daughter of selfishness and self-absorption.

As Maude's visits continued, Doris discovered that what absolutely tormented her mother, far more than arguing, was to agree tonelessly with everything she said, while clearly having no interest in any of her opinions. At each visit Doris would employ this strategy until Maude departed. But when the door closed, she was alone with her son, as Martha Quest was with her daughter in the novel *A Proper Marriage*.

Doris Lessing has been candid about the connection between the account of giving birth in *A Proper Marriage* and her own experience with John. It seems likely that Martha's post-partum experience is also derived from that period of Lessing's life. For Lessing's words about Martha serve as an apt summary for her own experiences as related in her memoirs: 'Her whole life was a hurrying onwards, to get it past ... hurry, hurry, hurry; and yet there was nothing at the end of it to hurry towards.'[4]

13

'The Excrutiating Divide'

To Maude's delight, Harry had got into the British Navy and was in Dartmouth, England, where he was studying to be an officer. Frank was equally excited to be joining the Army, training along with many of his friends from the Sports Club at a base in nearby Umtali. Like the other wives, Doris followed Frank, with John in tow. Rigid dieting had brought back her figure, and her hair had regained its lovely dark shine. But the cheap hotel she stayed at in Umtali was hardly the background she wanted for her newly returned self. The baby got sick and he cried even when he was better. Doris would push him in his pram up and down the town's unfamiliar streets. Sometimes she dreamed of some heroic soldier who would make desperate love to her, knowing that they would soon have to part.

Instead it was Frank who came to her, and for good. He was thirty years old and he had bad feet and, consequently, the Army did not want him. The Wisdoms went back to Salisbury, where Frank felt humiliated by being among the town's military rejects. They still went to the Sports Club, but it had become a different place. Insensitive girls teased Frank about being old and Doris found that with the group of men much reduced, most of them defective in some way, and herself a mother, the sexual attention she thrived on was almost totally absent. Housing was scarce, and they kept moving to spaces that were only slightly larger than the one they just left, all cheaply furnished with low quality manufactured furniture. When Frank went to work, Doris walked the baby and then joined other young mothers for morning tea.

She hated the women.

She hated Frank.

She hated her life.

* * *

Doris Lessing has never been one to idealise marriage. In 1972, Joyce Carol Oates visited Lessing, and they discussed the plotline of the novel Lessing had just finished writing, *The Summer Before the Dark*, about a 'woman who loses her husband and goes to pieces.' Oates remembers

Lessing's fascination with the idea that a woman could be so utterly 'defined by her marriage.'[1]

In 1980, when asked by a Spanish journalist about living alone for so many years, Lessing said she didn't think it was productive to try to form a couple. The inequities are too great. Men tend to want to dominate and women lose any position of autonomy and strength. When a younger friend from America was about to be married in the mid-1980s, she contacted Lessing, saying she was troubled about her partner: 'I wrote that I believed we had three centres in our souls: physical, emotional and intellectual. And that I had hoped when I fell in love to do it on all three levels. I found that this had not happened, and I was disconcerted by this, and wondered whether maybe I should wait until I found somebody with whom I could connect on all three levels.' Lessing wrote back, 'There's no point in waiting.'

Doris Tayler Wisdom was not happy to have found Frank. How terrible that she, who had recoiled at her parents' dependent connection, now found herself attached to a man, day and night, month by month, year by year, every moment constrictive and intrusive. Somehow Doris found time to compose poetry while she was pushing a baby carriage. But rather than offering some respite from the situation, her creative pursuits brought the conflicts with Frank to a head. For Doris's new work was contemptuous of Rhodesian society to a degree that Frank found unacceptable.

Frank had liberal ideas, to be sure, but Doris, he felt, was going too far. It certainly wasn't good for his career to have his wife making fun of everything most other people believed in. Besides, it was taking up too much of her time; time she should be spending with him. With every complaint from Frank, Doris felt more trapped. She fantasised about finding a sort of Uber-bohemian from the rollicking artists quarter of Cape Town.

If Doris was threatened by her emotional turmoil, Tigger knew how to push back the insistent feelings. When John was nine months old, she decided to get pregnant again. Doris's daughter, Jean, was quickly conceived and easily birthed, in 1941. The Wisdoms' landlord chose this time to announce he could make more money renting to Army and RAF men. The new father decided he was fed up with being at the mercy of landlords. This time, when they moved, they bought a house to accommodate their expanded family. Tigger acted as if she were thrilled with the idea, but Doris secretly felt more and more trapped.

Soon the Wisdoms were living in a home on one of Salisbury's better streets. The furniture that came with the house was everything Maude would have wanted for a daughter, except that this daughter mocked her mother's delight. Neither was Maude allowed to take pleasure from Doris's three servants: a 'cookboy,' a 'houseboy,' and a little ten-year-old, called a 'piccanin,' who polished shoes, did errands, and occasionally looked after the baby.

The servants lived in brick rooms on a lane that held repositories for the lavatory contents, carried there by cart twice a day. Their quarters were always vulnerable to visits from the police to see if unauthorised people were living there, such as wives, or girlfriends, or even children visiting their fathers from the country where they lived with their mothers or grandmothers or aunts. Although Doris Wisdom generally obliged her servants' requests for a letter saying she allowed them their visitors, she never called on them to see how they lived. She had no personal relationships with the servants so there was no reason to make a social call and also she wanted to respect their privacy.

John was an increasingly angry child. He flew into tantrums when Doris nursed the baby, and even when she took Jean off the breast, his jealous fury could not be contained. Jean was quiet and agreeable, but even with all the household help, Doris was often still terribly weary. She was overcome with malaise that sapped her energy and made her always feel on the verge of collapse. After she experienced a few episodes of fainting, she decided to take John to the sea for a month's vacation, leaving the infant Jean with a friend. Babies need cuddling and comforting, Lessing explains, but it doesn't have to be their mother who provides it. Because of that fact, she states: 'I did not feel guilty about this then and do not feel guilty now,'[2] But she also once said, 'Jean will be bitter until the day she dies because I am not the possessive mother. My daughter should have had my mother for a mother.'[3]

Harry, on leave from the Navy, visited his sister at her seaside resort for a couple of days. They sat on the hotel's veranda and admired each other's appearance. They hadn't really seen each other for years, and knew hardly anything about the other's life. Doris flirted with him a bit, in part, she says, to impress the other young women in the hotel who pushed their babies back and forth in front of the handsome couple.

After the publication of *A Man and Two Women* (1963), Lessing was asked to choose a couple of her favourite stories from the collection. One that she singled out was 'Each Other,' about a brother and sister, Fred and Freda, 'who are in love with each other. Not autobiographical at all, actually,' she said, anticipating what she seems to consider one of life's most irritating questions. But then she added, 'Perhaps I wish it were.'[4]

Doris Lessing is the master of the opening line; with a few words, she can capture readers in an almost literal sense. In 'Each Other' she employs a seemingly bland beginning that arches over the storyline with perverse ordinariness. The story starts, 'I suppose your brother's coming again?'[5] The brother will return the next morning, and the day after that and the day after that. The sister's name is Freda, the brother's, Fred.

The similarity of their names reflects their link to each other, as does their physical likeness. They both are tall and slim, with black hair and dark eyes. When her husband is away at work, Freda and Fred make love. Through their lovemaking, they deepen their bond, passionately attempting to fuse their identities. There are no parents mentioned in the story, but it's clear that Freda's husband and Fred's girlfriend are meant as substitutes. The siblings take spiteful pleasure in deceiving these conventional others.

There is a further twist to the story. Although the lovemaking is ecstatic, brother and sister stop just short of orgasm in each other's arms. They find excitement in seeing how closely they can approach sexual climax before having to pull apart. Freda says they can make love their own way because they can always turn to Charlie and Alice for 'coming.' Thus, the husband and girlfriend are being doubly used and deceived, a situation that Freda finds especially intriguing.

There is no reason to believe that 'Each Other' is autobiographical in terms of actual incest. But reading it against the background of Doris Lessing's family life elicits some thoughts about her relationship with Harry. Brother and sister in 'Each Other' are practically indistinguishable except for their gender, and sister wants to fuse with brother, be one with him, so that even that difference will be obliterated. To what end for Doris Lessing? If she were part of Harry, would she experience being the treasured child?

'Each Other' is also a story of control over feelings. Freda, holding back from orgasm, takes pleasure in renunciation rather than giving way. Doris Lessing's denial of any anger toward Harry may be, at least in part, a defence against her own fury. She was already so consumed by rage toward her mother that to acknowledge the same feeling toward her brother would perhaps risk her own emotional destruction.

Another man, casually met, tried to make love to Tigger, but she refused his advances because she was friendly with his wife. Still, the mere possibility of a lover increased her certainty that her marriage to Frank had to end. She knew she treated him badly when they were together, and that he didn't know what to make of her behaviour.

Once home again, she told him only that she needed time to pursue her own interests. Much to the shock of friends and her mother, she had a Shona girl move into the house and become Jean's nanny. Maude complained bitterly about this unconventional living arrangement. For a few blessed weeks during her vacation Doris had been free of her mother's relentless interference. How could she continue to bear it? And yet still she stayed married. If Frank accused her of flirting too much with other men, or worse, she considered the accusation not insulting but irrelevant. Her whole life seemed to be immersed in extraneous events.

Jean and John, both now toddlers, contracted whooping cough, and Doris caught it from them. The children were taken to Maude so that she could care for them while Doris recovered. When they were all well again, Doris drove out to the farm to bring Jean and John home. Her visits to her family had been intermittent at best, and she was shocked at her father's emaciation. They had little to say to each other, and just stood together on the grass, watching the attractive children play. Michael, distressingly drawn and thin, muttered, 'Yes, that's what you were like too, such lovely little things you were and look what you turn into. It's not worth it.'[6]

There is a similar period of separation in *A Proper Marriage*. Martha Quest sends her sick daughter to her mother's for some nursing care. She puts the child completely out of her mind during her absence 'as if Caroline did not exist, had never existed.'[7]

* * *

Doris Wisdom had reached a crossroads. She did not want to break up her home, but she could not continue the fiction of being a contented wife and mother. Tigger's pretences would not help her now. Doris's marriage had to end for her life to begin. And then, the inevitable follow-up thought, the inadmissible thought, the bold, thrillingly emancipating thought. To truly achieve that escape, she would have to leave the children as well. As she had run away from school at fourteen, from home at fifteen, at twenty-four she would run away from her husband and her two children.

In 1973, Lessing scholar Dee Seligman visited Rhodesia and talked to Harry Tayler, who recalled the excruciating period of his sister's desertion. Of all the hurtful things she had done to the family, he said, leaving her children 'broke our parents' hearts.'[8]

When Martha Quest leaves her three-year-old daughter in *A Proper Marriage*, she is amazingly calm and resolute. Martha is just doing what she has to do, and life for both mother and child will go on, better, it is implied, than before. 'You'll be perfectly free, Caroline,' Martha announces to her daughter. 'I'm setting you free.'[9]

The same rational voice is heard in what Lessing writes in her memoir about leaving her own children. She asserts that she was hardly leaving them on their own. They would be surrounded by caring and affectionate people who would look after them extremely well. Journalists' attempts to discuss Lessing's desertion of her children have been met with considerable disdain. 'Do I think I should have left the children? Yes. If I hadn't, either I would have had a very bad breakdown, or I would have become an alcoholic.'[10]

She sees no point in agonising about regret. To her mind, down that path lies bitterness and self-pity, two qualities she has little use for in her later years. To address the question that for many readers of her memoirs hovers over her actions – how, when Doris Lessing had suffered so deeply from her own mother's rejection, could she take rejection so much further by abandoning her children – she returns to the impositions of fate. She felt she carried a 'secret doom' that would have harmed her children as much as it had harmed her own childhood. 'It's all patterns repeating. Lots of patterns repeat.'[11]

But perhaps the repetition she feared was not some abstract 'doom' but bad mothering. Lessing was confronting a frightening mix of distaste for her stifling marriage and ambivalence towards her children. Perhaps there was a fear that life as a Rhodesian housewife would turn her into the remote, bitter mother she had always resented – that staying with Frank would transform Doris Wisdom into Maude Tayler.

Those who know Doris Lessing intimately, or as intimately as she allows anyone to know her, believe that she is not as chillingly detached as she presents herself. Her personal correspondence supports this view. In 1983, when her son John had another in a series of automobile accidents, injuring himself quite badly, she wrote to her editor Robert Gottlieb that she speculated on what might have been if she had made different choices.

'I have always felt,' says one friend, 'that Doris lives along the line of trying to forgive herself for past actions, and wanting to move on with her life. Behind her impassive facade, she is stuck forever on that excruciating divide.'

Finding a New Family

During the dreadful weeks when Doris longed to flee but could not yet summon the strength to do so, she found immense comfort in the activities of an underground radical group. One afternoon, she ran into her old friend Dorothy Schwartz, who had taken her to the Left Book Club meeting four years earlier. Standing under jacaranda trees, now laden with pale purple blossoms, the two women tried to catch up with each other's lives. Still needing to camouflage her inner chaos and confusion, Doris called on Tigger, with her sprightly delivery, to recount the story of a stuffy husband, silly friends, and the oppressive nature of white society.

After hearing her out, Dorothy Schwartz again encouraged her restless friend to become more politically involved. She assured Tigger that the left study group she was asking her to join now was truly revolutionary, not at all like the ineffectual bunch she had taken her to before. Besides, Dorothy said, many of the people had heard about Tigger's sympathetic views, and would like to meet her.

The idea that a band of intellectual radicals were interested in her was enormously gratifying. Nothing in her daily experience was making her feel even remotely interesting or significant. The life she was living was a sham, and had no bearing on her real self, whatever that was. Lessing has said she believes that she had always felt like a writer, but at this point in her life, even though she sold the odd piece or poem, she saw the word as an abstraction. With the exception of Olive Schreiner, who lived in a different era and had not, after all, been swept by fate into motherhood, no other woman from her background that Doris knew of became a writer in any pragmatic, operative way.

As soon as Doris was introduced to the group – mostly a mix of RAF men from the English working classes and refugees from Europe, many of them Jews – she felt a surge of hope that the bleakness of her life might begin to lift. Cut off emotionally from Frank and the children, her alienation from her parents increasing with each deadly visit home, Doris was nourished, as Martha Quest would later be, by the sense of community among these fascinating, confident men and women. It promised a sense of belonging that she had not yet experienced.

As she polished and sewed and pushed her babies in their pram, she longed for the moment when she could throw off the tight-fitting costume of wife and mother. In the afternoons, she would take off for the Meikles Hotel Lounge, where her friends gathered to drink beer, or a tearoom in an unfashionable part of town, where they sipped coffee or tea and buttered their scones like any proper British citizen while they eagerly devised anti-imperialist political strategies. As she swung through the door, they made room for her to join them, calling out in welcome to Comrade Tigger.

The loosely organised mix of liberals, radicals, socialists, and labour reformers proclaimed themselves Communists even before they were officially recognised by the Communist Party. Although the Rhodesian branch was not taken seriously by Communist officialdom even when it was given formal status, it was taken very seriously by its members, and no one was more ardent about its goals than Tigger Wisdom. She was eager for any task her comrades asked of her, no matter how visible the work made her to Frank's conservative civil service colleagues.

Sometimes, perhaps to placate Frank, she would take one of the children along on her bicycle when she ran political errands, such as picking up bundles of pamphlets for distribution. She would settle Jean or John into the canvas seat that she had attached to the handlebars. Generally, John enjoyed the trip, bouncing up and down while his mother sailed along as quickly as her bare legs – whose shapeliness she continued to revel in – peddled them to their destination. Jean was never a happy passenger. The speed and bumps frightened her. Doris took note of the little girl's fear, and assured her there was nothing to be afraid of, but she did not allow it to stay her journey. To acknowledge Jean's needs might have meant opening the door to her own most deeply buried feelings, which she was not ready to face. The woman who had once pleaded 'Mummy, come and cuddle me, come and cuddle me' was slow to respond to her own daughter's need for her.

Soon Doris was spending every night, and several hours a day, with her comrades. When she was not with them, she was reading books on Communist theory and history. As she had once devoured Proust and Woolf, now she stayed up all night reading Lenin and Marx and Stalin. For the young woman who had left school at fourteen, the Communist Party was a university, and many of the members her teachers and mentors. The more time she spent with them and their bold ideas, the more urgent the need to escape her other life became.

In later years, Lessing would say that her attraction to Rhodesian Communism was emotional rather than intellectual. As an autodidact, Doris was free to defend her opinions. No professor or classmate argued with her reasoning or conclusions. This allowed her to reject ideas that did not please her, and to embrace unquestioningly new ideas that touched some personal need, with no professor to challenge her. Neither love nor sex nor children nor even her writing was more important than

adopting and enhancing the Party's glorious plans. That Doris passionately agreed with the group's convictions enabled her to reconcile the
conflicting pulls that had caused so many years of torment: the need to
preserve her individuality, and the longing for connection. As a Communist she remained outside the social and political conformity of
Rhodesian society that she had found impossible to accept. But now
there were others standing beside her. Similarly, her double fears, of
dependency and isolation, had lost their threatening power. Here she
would not be isolated, here dependency was comradeship, built on
strength, not weakness.

Until now, Doris had tried to find herself primarily in opposition,
declaring what she was not. Not like her mother, not like Frank, not
like other white colonialists, not like other young wives. For the first
time, she felt she was moving toward real self-definition. What she
believed was not only approved of by people she respected, but affirmed
by the books and ideas on which they modelled their principles. She felt
she might at last elude the forces that had catapulted her into a life she
despised. She could slow down and think before acting. Like Martha
Quest in *A Ripple from the Storm*, she stopped trying to prove anything
while she steeped herself in the Communist rhetoric of her new friends.

* * *

There was also a satisfying sense of superiority that came from being a
member of the only circle that understood what needed to be done to
save humanity. Later, Lessing mocked the naive, self-congratulatory
delusion of that younger self, telling a South African interviewer that
she and her friends were convinced they could change the world. That
their insight would overcome the intransigence of the vast numbers of
thickheaded people who had been ignorant for so long.[1]

Frank Wisdom increasingly seemed to belong to that latter category,
and certainly so did Maude and Michael. Frank's sister-in-law, Dora,
however, was now living in the Wisdom home, and Doris genuinely
liked her. While Dora would never have thought of divorce, she and her
husband almost always lived apart. The mother of two sons, she adored
Jean, and gave her the physical attention Doris did not. A neighbour
who helped look after Jean was equally tender with the little girl. How
much better for Jean to be raised by two such caring women, Doris
reasoned, than by a mother whose love was dormant.

Doris's comrades supported her desire to leave her family for a
politically active life, but soon became impatient with her ambivalence.
It was wasteful and unproductive to be so indecisive about such a
bourgeois problem. There were more important issues to deal with, and
she had better get on with them.

The people Lessing presents as understanding her best were her children. Like a robber carefully explaining the reason for an intended burglary, she told them why she had to leave so as to make the world a better place for them. It was probably easier for her to believe that John in particular followed her argument. If she felt little traditional maternal love for her daughter at this time,' what I had always had with John was a kind of friendship. We had always "got on."'[2]

* * *

Lessing suggests that the reason her feelings for her children had never fully developed was not a response to her own lack of mothering, but rather was a natural defence mechanism that was triggered by her innate understanding that she had to go. There is no hint of awareness that the problems she was trying to head off by leaving her son and daughter might have painful repercussions in the future, for them and for herself. In *Under My Skin* Lessing has acknowledged that memory is selective; that in each of our stories what is forgotten may be as important as what is recalled. But she does not explore the phenomenon of protective amnesia. What fascinates her is the pattern of her actions, not the reasons underlying them.

The impact of the Martha Quest books, *The Golden Notebook*, and other early work relates in large part to Lessing's ability to explore in that fiction what she seemed unwilling or unable to do as she lived her life. Martha Quest and Anna Wulf come to a deeper understanding of themselves through the course of their stories.

Martha Quest tries to block off feeling, but suspects that the goal is ultimately impossible to achieve. She allows herself to see the connections between past and present, opening herself to the often painful images of involuntary memory. She worries that there is a breach between her present and her past, so that her thoughts are jumbled and unfocused. Her feelings for her daughter include moments of uncontrolled sorrow – 'The thought of Caroline caused her acute pain. A cold shell she had been careful to build around her heart was gone. She longed for her daughter.'[3] Doris Lessing's own cool detachment and defended reality is transcended in writing like this, replaced by insights and perceptions that seem to be felt.

Lessing's weapon against painful memories is most often the rationality she at other times rejects. In the early 1980s, Jean came to visit her mother in London, bringing along her two daughters, who were virtual strangers to their grandmother. (In 1998, one of Lessing's granddaughters lived with her while attending university.) Lessing's personal assistant remembers the days leading up to that visit as being extraordinarily tense. 'Doris was very frightened – that's the word I would use.' After Jean left, Lessing reported on that visit to Robert Gottlieb. She was pleased that Jean seemed a very nice woman whom she would be interested in getting to know better. Yet, she adds, the stay was fraught with tension. Regret seems to creep into Lessing's description of the almost unbearable pain that surrounded the reunion with her daughter. Then another, more familiar tone takes over. After all, she writes Gottlieb, Jean's hurt is part of the past, not her current life. There's little point in dwelling on those feelings now.

15

Comrade Veidt

In *Under My Skin*, Doris Lessing suggests some of the friction that precipitated her departure from Frank Wisdom, but she doesn't describe his actions in any detail. Whatever degree of acrimony existed, Frank drove Doris and her belongings in his car to yet another boarding house.

There has never been any suggestion that Lessing's real life conflicts approached the level that her fictional stand-in Martha Quest was subjected to in the novel *A Proper Marriage* – where the enraged Husband, Douglas, threatens to rape Martha and murder both her and their daughter Caroline before reconciling himself to the fact that she is leaving. But, undoubtedly, the conflicts in Lessing's own break-up helped fuel her imagination when she created that scene.

Doris quickly found a job as a typist in a law firm. Her salary was twelve pounds a month and after paying her rent, she had little left over for meals or clothes, but nothing could have been less important to her then. There was a moral grandeur to not caring about money or possessions or even proper meals. All of her new friends shared the same disregard for material things. It was one more link in their utopian vision. Though free of the familiar constraints that had hindered her sexual experimentation in the past, Doris Wisdom's main obsession was for now intellectual.

The time was right for this shift of priorities. Her relationships with men had been less than emotionally uplifting. Doris's great lover who would fully awaken her to life remained a steadily fading fantasy. Though her comrades' ideology included a vision of sexuality beyond the reactionary confines of bourgeois institutions like marriage, their fervour was political. While it seems unlikely that Doris would ever completely abandon her quest for an ideal sex partner, she had discovered that sex could lead to a stifling respectability. She was ready to accept her new friends' opinions that concentrating on the pleasures of the body could prevent her growth as a socially responsible person, something she desperately wanted to be.

As *A Ripple from the Storm*, the third volume of the Children of Violence series, begins, Martha Quest fervently embarks on her political education. She is a willing and eager pupil. A theme of the novel is the relationship between the individual and the community or collective. For the first time in Doris's life, she too was willingly submitting to a canon that placed group solidarity above her own goals and feelings. The sense of 'we-ness' must have been a balm for someone who had spent so much of her short life as an outsider. It was in any case a remarkable turnaround for someone so fiercely protective of her individuality.

An observer of her life at that time attempts to explain the shift. 'Doris was, and to my mind still is, an ideologue,' he says. 'People become ideologues because they've lost hope. Sexual liberation was part of her emancipatory project, but it wasn't working, and she was feeling even more estranged. Communism was exciting because it was another way to try and figure everything out.' Lessing seemed to echo some of this reasoning in a 1980 interview where she explained the attraction of the idealistic visions of Communism. She likened the appeal of Communism to the allure of religion, seeing the psychological pulls as comparable. Both institutions offer a haven from the isolation of self.[1] When she was in her active Communist phase, she and her group were positive that within a decade after World War II, the world would be free of all imperfections in its new Communist philosophy, a belief she says could have them classified as insane now.

* * *

Yet, however foolish the group looks to Lessing in hindsight, the odd assortment of socialist reformers gave great meaning to her life at the time. At the centre of the collective that sat in judgement of Rhodesia's white supremacist society was a core group that included Frank Cooper, a cockney RAF corporal whose hatred of the British class system was fierce and absolute. Doris admired his passionate convictions then. Later, she described Cooper as a fanatical madman.

Doris's friend Dorothy Schwartz was also in this inner circle, along with a handsome young man named Nathan Zelter. Doris respected Nathan's intelligence and social daring. Until his lover, also named Dorothy, became pregnant, they lived together without being married, an arrangement that was still the stuff of darkest scandal in Salisbury.

Zelter was a Jewish refugee from Romania and made his living working for a relative's import-export business. But money interested him even less than it did Doris. He was the most passionate of Communists and, according to Lessing, who seems to deride his naïveté, at the end of his life he still believed he could create the perfect world in the newly sovereign Zimbabwe. Zelter had endless projects, all undertaken with the same energy. One of these was a magazine, where some of Doris's short stories were published. She often consulted him on her writing, despite the fact that he might infuriatingly find it ideologically unsound. For instance, if she created an African character who hovered too close to some white stereotype of blacks, he would strongly disapprove.

Lessing acknowledges that Nathan Zelter was a warm and generous man, but she also calls him absurd in his unbending, unrealistic beliefs. When she returned to Africa in 1956, she stayed with the Zelters for a while, and was amused to see that despite his still firm Communist ideology, he had become quite wealthy. His hospitality didn't compensate for his still addressing her as Tigger, a name Lessing had by then banished from her life.

The bouncy, jokey, cheerful self Doris had used to mask her sense of isolation had always been a source of her own secret contempt. Once free of the society that only Tigger could thrive in, Doris abandoned her, though not forever. On her mescaline trip in the 1960s, Lessing discovered a part of her personality that seemed an adult variation of Tigger. The 'Hostess,' as Lessing called her, was willing to act in accordance with other people's wishes. As might be expected, Doris did not exactly embrace this newly discovered identity.

In fact, Lessing indignantly blames the couple who gave her the drug and stayed with her after she took it for bringing out the Hostess. She should have been left on her own. She would also have been more comfortable about her constant weeping, which had clearly disturbed the couple. Nonetheless, Lessing has said that she has found the Hostess useful in keeping her self secret.

* * *

There was another émigré in the inner circle of the Rhodesian Communists. His name was Gottfried Lessing. Gottfried Anton Nicolai Lessing is described by Doris Lessing as looking like Conrad Veidt, the suave, German movie star of the 1920s and '30s who later became a Hollywood character actor. He was born in St. Petersburg, Russia, in 1917 to a family of considerable wealth.

In *Under My Skin*, Lessing says that Gottfried's great-great grandfather, a Jew, was a self-made millionaire, having established various industries, from nails for horses to tankers and railways. Gottfried's father carried on the business tradition, but at heart he was a scholar. Lessing says, with clear disapproval, that Gottfried's mother did not share her husband's tastes. The daughter of a Russianised German family, she loved parties, entertaining lavishly while he spent most of his time studying history in the library.

According to Doris Lessing, Gottfried escaped to Berlin during the Russian Revolution as a baby in the arms of his nursemaid, along with his mother, grandmother, and older sister. Gottfried's sister, Irene Lessing Gysi, has a somewhat different account of her brother's early

life. She says her parents were separated for four years by the First
World War. The two children went with their mother to a little Russian
town called Pensa, while their father fought on the German side against
their mother's brothers. Speaking of her mother with affection, Gysi
recalls that when her father came to fetch his family after the four-year
absence (which would mean Gottfried was hardly a baby when he
arrived in Berlin), he seemed a stranger to his son and daughter. The
sense of alienation Irene and Gotti – as he was always known to the
family – had experienced with their newly returned father increased in
Berlin, where the two also felt 'like strangers to the other German
children.' Although the Lessings did not live ostentatiously, their home
was beautiful. The family regularly spoke three languages, German,
Russian, and French. The parents primarily spoke French with each
other, as Gotti and Irene's paternal grandmother was Belgian and
French was the language of her household.

Gotti finished university in Berlin, where he studied law. In 1939,
he went to London to work as a lawyer in an insurance agency owned
by a father of one of Irene's friends. In *Under My Skin*, Doris
Lessing offers a confusing account of the reason Gottfried emigrated to London. She writes that although his mother considered
Hitler an unimportant vulgarian who was not worthy of her attention, Hitler's rise to power had made him acutely conscious of his
Jewish lineage. The Lessing family was completely assimilated and
he was only one quarter Jewish, but Gottfried did not want to risk
being called up to fight in Hitler's armies. According to Lessing, the
Nuremberg Laws, which excluded Jews from citizenship in Nazi
Germany had been amended thus making Gottfried eligible to be
conscripted.

It's unclear exactly what amendment she's referring to however. And
in a 1989 interview with Sedge Thompson, (which has the industrialist
ancestor as Gottfried's grandfather), Doris says that Gottfried's sister
Irene was half-Jewish. This would of course make Gottfried, himself,
half-Jewish and (all the more) unlikely to be conscripted in Nazi Germany. Although it would certainly have provided him with ample
reason to leave the shrill antisemitism of his homeland.

Gottfried arrived in London with very little money, but a few connections. He was invited to dine at the lavish tables of his father's business
associates on a weekly basis. And though the meals would have helped
make ends meet, they must have been a sad reminder of his fallen
fortunes. Doris Lessing offers a rather dismissive explanation of
Gottfried's conversion to communism. He was completely uninterested
in politics when he came to England, she insists, but he became involved with a lovely young Communist, and he took on her beliefs which
were very pure. Consequently, he was completely committed to every
nuance of Communist ideology. She does not explore whether

Gottfried's experience with Nazism might have been a motivating factor in his swing to the left.

Gottfried landed in Southern Rhodesia, among all the Communist 'innocents,' because as World War II approached, German refugees were unwelcome in England, and had to choose between emigrating to Canada or Southern Rhodesia. Gottfried chose Rhodesia, where he went to work for the same law firm, Howe-Ely, that employed Doris Wisdom. He was vastly underpaid for his efforts and obviously superior mind, Doris Lessing writes.

The combination of his passionate commitment, total self-confidence, and personal history as first a wealthy young man in Berlin's decadent 1920s and '30s created an aura around Gottfried Lessing that awed the African Communists. Doris was not immune. In her memoir, Lessing presents an equivocal picture of Gottfried. At times she paints him as considerate and unselfish. But more often he is depicted as a cold, sarcastic, authoritarian man who lived by emotionless logic. When comrades were arguing unproductively about some issue, he would insist on analysing each point that arose, and then he would proceed to strip their rhetoric down to its essentials, brooking no interruptions.

Doris Lessing also seems to be of two minds about Gottfried's sister, Irene Gysi. She has written disparagingly about Irene's elegant, social girlhood in Berlin, but she has also described her ex-sister-in-law as remarkably courageous, even though Gysi was the sort of committed Communist Lessing came to hold in contempt. Irene Gysi was in France at the outbreak of war, and was arrested because of her Jewish background. Astonishingly, she was rescued by her Jewish lover and they nonetheless both decided to go back to Nazi Germany because they felt it was their Communist duty. Irene kept him hidden during the war, an act that would have got her killed if she had been found out. To feed him and several other charges, she would walk miles into the countryside to forage every week.

Irene Gysi visited Doris Lessing in London on several occasions and recalls with pleasure that her former sister-in-law wrote a warm inscription in her copy of *The Golden Notebook*. She wonders, then, why Lessing seemed to pull back from further contact later, and more important to Gysi, why she painted such a negative picture of Gottfried in her memoir and in interviews.

Gysi is only one of many people troubled by Doris Lessing's unflattering portrait of Gottfried Lessing. One intimate describes him as 'a very kindhearted person, a good man. The harshness that comes across in some of Doris's writing, I don't understand at all. He was very tolerant of people who believed differently than he did.'

Others find Doris's picture of Gottfried incompatible with their image of him, as well. A person who knew Lessing in Germany recalled him as 'very gentle, very understanding.'

Irene Gysi is clearly wistful about her relationship with Doris Lessing. Still fond of Lessing, her feelings do not seem to be reciprocated. The brave friend whose defiance of Nazi authority Doris Lessing once celebrated now rates only an annual Christmas card.

If at First You Don't Succeed

Shortly after Doris left Frank and the children, she became ill. The combination of eating poorly and sleeping little, and stress from the self-imposed changes in her life, simply became too much and, as her mother had done so many years before, she took to her bed. Her radical friends faithfully stopped by her boardinghouse when they finished work, and it was at this point that Doris made quite an impression on Gottfried Lessing. Gottfried later told Doris that he had first thought of having an affair with her when he saw her lying in her sickbed. The results of such imaginings, she writes, were, for her, disappointing. Gottfried, she reports, 'was deeply puritanical and inhibited'[1] and thus bad in bed. Uncharacteristically, Doris continued the relationship despite the sexual disharmony.

As an enemy alien and already under suspicion for his Communist activities, Gottfried was ill-advised to have an affair with a married woman. He had to be circumspect in his behaviour or risk an internment camp or even deportation. But a British Southern Rhodesian wife would keep Gottfried from being punished by the Southern Rhodesian government, and it would also strengthen his chances of becoming a British citizen.

Doris Lessing pleads political obligation in explaining why she agreed to marry Gottfried Lessing. According to her, it was quite common at the time for a couple in her circle to make this sort of marriage of political convenience. In *A Ripple from the Storm*, when Martha Quest tells Anton Hesse who Lessing says is not physically modelled on Gottfried Lessing, but was 'very similar psychologically'[2] that she will marry him, she is startled and upset at sensing he genuinely cares for her. But she does not allow herself to explore his feelings. Her own needs for growth and transformation are pre-eminent. 'Already she was feeling, under the pressure of the snapping jaws of impatience, the need to move forward, as if the marriage with Anton and what she might become as a result of it were already done and accomplished.'[3]

Doris Tayler Wisdom and Gottfried Lessing were married in 1943 at a magistrates office during a break between two Communist committee meetings. The wedding day and the events leading up to it, says Doris

Lessing, are described with uncomfortable accuracy in *A Ripple from the Storm.*

In the novel Martha oversleeps on the morning of her marriage to Anton Hesse because she was up till nearly dawn with her comrades the night before. What had consumed them all was creating a 150-page treatise that laid out in great detail how the country would be run should the Communists gain control. There were ambiguous overtones to the exhausting session, finally voiced by a young woman named Maisie. Like the child in the fairy tale 'The Emperor's New Clothes,' Maisie ingenuously asks Anton what the point of the long evening had been: None of them are candidates in any elections, so they will have no chance to execute any of their plans.

Anton replies that it was their combined responsibility to make certain other people fully understood the group's position, to which Maisie responds with another question. If they operate in secrecy, how can anyone else find out their intentions? A character named Athen patiently takes over Maisie's political education. With glowing eloquence he tells her that they have a sacred obligation to represent Communism to the outside world. Similarly, even if they are alone in a strange environment, even if they are alone in a prison cell waiting for death, they can take comfort in knowing they are not really alone because they have all of Communism behind them. This scene takes on a special poignancy when one realises its source.

Lessing modelled Athen on a man named Athen Gouliamis, who, despite her disdain for such classification, she sees as truly 'good.' She says she used his real name and exact language as a tribute to his purity of character. A Greek, Athen was nonetheless a member of the RAF and had come to Africa along with about twenty other young Greeks to train as pilots. All of them were Communists who had been in the resistance to the Nazi occupation of Greece. He had a strong political history that Lessing likened to the background of a poor black. What astonished her was that he had come out of a life of political and personal chaos as a supremely gentle person, filled with empathy for others. She never heard him express anger or bitterness.

Eventually Athen went back to Greece, to hide out in the mountains. Because of his politics he knew his life was in danger. Later, Lessing heard rumours that he had been arrested, and was shot trying to escape. But she also had indications that he was still alive and was even given an address for him.

She wrote several letters, she reported to Florence Howe, but they were never answered and, although she still had his address, she stopped trying to find him. Then, although Athen clearly touched a rare chord of sympathy in Lessing, her deeply ingrained fatalism attaches itself, as it so often seems to do, to this personal relationship, and her tone turns perfunctory. If she ever travelled to Greece, she said, she'd try to find him, but she had little doubt that what they both knew was going to happen, his death or imprisonment, had come to pass.

Doris Lessing begins a portrait of her own political evolution in the scene where Athen educates Maisie. The young Doris needed to believe that the collective's reasoning was sounder than any single member's doubts. The older Doris fiercely defends her individual thinking, and is convinced that any social institution, including those that run counter to the existing culture, will erase a person's essential singularity. In a 1992 attack on Communist influences on language and thinking, she reviled the notion of a writer's having to be 'committed.' She also condemns 'raising consciousness.' She grudgingly acknowledges that the use of such concepts can yield results, but claims the procedure invariably results in the pupil' s being given the teacher's propaganda, a variant of the former tyrant, the Party line.[4]

Becoming free from the bonds of political conditioning is part of Martha Quest's maturation in the Children of Violence series. Lessing has often called the last volume of this series, *The Four-Gated City*, a bildungsroman, translated by various scholars as a novel of education, of apprenticeship, of adolescence, of initiation. Popular in the nineteenth century, such works showed the young hero – for there were very few heroines in bildungsromans – moving gradually out into the world, confronting various aspects of society, and through these confrontations developing into a mature adult.

By calling only *The Four-Gated City* a bildungsroman, Lessing offers her own interpretation of the genre. The preceding four volumes of the series describe Martha Quest's development from childhood to adulthood – the traditional bildungsroman continuum. Thirty when *The Four-Gated City* opens, an age when the typical bildungsroman often concludes, Martha Quest in essence begins the journey again, for she recognises that the earlier stages of her life were not a voyage toward selfhood, but an escape from a self-destroying past. It seems that Lessing, the writer, was trying to make a break as well. The first three volumes of the Children of Violence series, and to a much lesser extent, the fourth, incorporates autobiographical fragments of Lessing's life. The *Four-Gated City* is not autobiographical in that sense as it does not use specific periods of her life. And no longer does Martha Quest serve as a sort of stand in for Doris Lessing. Instead, different sides of the author are, as Lessing herself has put it, 'parcelled out' to a number of characters.[5]

Lessing seems a to have employed this technique in earlier volumes in the series as well. In *Ripple from the Storm*, for instance, she could well be explaining her own life in the scene with Maisie. In writing about the girl's submission to a group's ideology, Lessing is showing the results of an imposed set of values that aim to make a person feel guilty if she doesn't adhere to them. Not surprisingly, she traces the phenomenon's roots back to her own childhood, and to the first institution that tried to entrap her, the family.

From their earliest days, children are taught to view themselves as good or bad by their parents' measure. It is extremely difficult to throw off the chains of this training. Constantly monitor a child's behaviour, often critically, and you raise a person unable not only to express independent ideas but to trust his or her own instinctive responses.

* * *

When Gottfried recalled his childhood, he would tell of a lonely, frightened little boy comforted by a protective nursemaid. *Come and cuddle me ... come and cuddle me ...* Doris Lessing could perhaps hear echoes of her own childhood voice in his recollection. What Gottfried Lessing needed, his ex-wife realised in retrospect, was a woman generous enough to give him the tender care she would give to an unhappy baby in the middle of a sleepless night.

Doris Tayler Wisdom Lessing was not that person. She was feeling too many emotions as it was, and was engaged in her own continuing struggle to break completely free of them. There was no room for Gottfried's needs when she felt entrapped by so many others.

Her parents continued to be a major drain on her energies. Maude Tayler had finally moved her husband into a small suburban house in Salisbury to be near the hospital. This also meant that she and Michael were nearer to Doris, surrounding her life with their complaints and reproaches. Now, added to their grievances about their daughter was the appalling fact that she had married a German, although Gottfried treated the Taylers with quiet respect.

The young couple came by the Taylers' house several times a week to give Maude some respite. She could dress up and visit a neighbour and try for an hour or so to escape the relentless misery that was her life: years of deprivation, no personal accomplishments, a beloved son at war, a dying husband, and a daughter who hated her. In conversations with her mother, Doris was coolly dutiful. She comments in her memoir on how Gottfried added his own ingredients to Maude's discomfort. Not only did she have to deal with her aloofly polite daughter, the remoteness seemed heightened by the presence of her reserved German husband.[6]

Even with Gottfried's support, Doris found it difficult to bear these visits with the dying man who was no longer recognisable as her father. Years afterward, she would still dream about his dying days, about the sad shell of a man that Michael became.

Her mother called Doris heartless, but Maude did not know how much this pillar of cold observation wished that charge were true. Many years later, in a short story, 'How I Finally Lost My Heart,' Lessing writes of a woman who actually opens her chest and removes her heart. After carrying it around for a while, she gives it to a girl she sees on the London subway. Unburdened, the heroine moves on, thinking, 'No heart. No heart at all. What bliss. What freedom.'[7]

Her heart still in place, Doris Lessing continued the journey for self as she tried to settle into her second marriage.

'Hello Tigger, How Are You?'

When she was a young woman, Doris Lessing's urgent quest for integration and connection took the form of seeking sexual union. The new Mrs Gottfried Lessing still believed she was justified in seeking sexual satisfaction outside her marriage. That Gottfried didn't know how to make satisfying love was sad, but she had no intention of being frustrated because of pity or compassion, and certainly not out of moral convention. Besides, she reassured herself, there were plenty of women in the Party who would put up with clumsy lovemaking in exchange for the cachet of having an affair with their political leader. Apparently, it never occurred to her to question whether he was more sexually compatible with other women.

Doris Lessing's sense of fragmentation started to intensify in this new phase of her life. It was impossible to reconcile the various aspects of her nature and experience, or to easily tolerate the powerful mix of her conflicting feelings and thoughts. She seemed to herself to be less a person than a collection of functions. In *Landlocked*, volume four of *Children of Violence*, Martha Quest, tormented by her feelings of division, thinks of herself as a house with half a dozen rooms, an analogy Lessing has often made about her own personality. Martha saw each room in the house as full of people who did not really connect to the people in the other rooms, but only to her. 'She had simply to accept, finally, that her role in life, for this period, was to walk like a housekeeper in and out of different rooms, but the people in the rooms could not meet each other or understand each other, and Martha must not expect them to.'[1]

Martha asks herself why she stays in this confusing house, What is it she is waiting for? The answer is quickly forthcoming. A man. A man who would connect all her separate parts, 'someone who would unify her elements, a man would be like a roof, or like a fire burning in the centre of the empty space.'[2] If love was not the only key to identity, it still promised a sense of unity to Doris Lessing, love coloured by intense romanticism and, most of all, by sexual satisfaction. Considering that she has mocked Freudian theory over the years, it is intriguing that as a young woman she pursued vaginal orgasm, as described by Freud, with an almost ideological fervour.

In later years, she expressed astonished contempt for feminists who politicised the idea of clitoral orgasm. She continued her paean to sex as liberator and integrator in *The Four-Gated City*:

> [W]hen the real high place of sex is reached, everything does move together ... Yet people regarded sex as the drainer, the emptier, instead of the maker of energy. They did not know.[3]

Lessing's concept of male-female relationships includes a surprising willingness to accept traditional views of masculinity. She has said more than once that she has sympathy for men, rather enjoys their swaggering, frontier-bashing ways. Perhaps her visits to her dying father further intensified her desire for a strong man. Each time she looked at that shrunken body, it must have been a powerful reminder of the price of weakness – a painful contrast to the lively young dad who had clasped her little body against his when they were on horseback and tickled her mercilessly in the spirit of fun. She had needed this man's love desperately in that household where the mother loved only her son, and gave her daughter an image of womanhood that was repellent in its cold need to consume and control. She was always certain that very little, if anything, was happening in her parents' sex life. She saw no intimacy even though her parents left their bedroom door open. And if her own eyes weren't evidence enough, Michael had told her as much in offhand remarks.

It was important to Doris that Michael had once been a different sort of man, a man who loved women and was confident in their company. She treasured his stories of his life in Luton before the war, where he danced every night with a string of lovely, lightfooted girls – just like his daughter, so deft on the dance floor – and had loved them all. Before going into the Army, Michael had been briefly involved with a married woman. Now he told Doris that he still thought of her. He acknowledged that they probably shouldn't have been together while she was married, but Doris felt he had no regrets about the affair.

Although Michael became critical of his daughter's life toward the end of his own, Lessing writes that shortly before he died, he told her of a dream he'd had the previous night. It was about someone he'd once been in love with, perhaps the married woman. In the dream he was standing in a kitchen on the crest of a towering mountain, with the lovely girl held fast in his arms. When he looked back at his life, he was consumed with regret. He had let conventional morals rob him of sensual pleasure, and he cautioned his daughter not to do the same, despite the fact that he himself was often one of the guardians of morality that Doris engaged in combat.

Most vocal of this shocked and outraged group was Maude. Although Doris did often see John and Jean, it was never often enough in Maude's eyes. Maude would often engineer situations to put her daughter into more contact with the children. Doris found these meetings under her mother's judgmental eyes unbearable. She much preferred it when kindly Dora Wisdom, Frank's sister-in-law, was able to stop by with the children at Doris's law office. When Lessing scholar Dee Seligman made her journey to Rhodesia in 1973, among the people she saw were two of Doris's friends from this period, Philippa Berlyn and Joan Falk. Berlyn, a co-worker at Howe-Ely, recalled in particular one of the children's visits to the office. Suddenly, she said, in marched John, about six years old, heading for his mother's desk.

'Hello, Tigger,' he said casually, watching her fingers move over the typewriter. 'How are you? I haven't seen you for a while.'

* * *

Berlyn had known Tigger Tayler since the late 1930s. When Tigger became involved with the Left Club, Berlyn had sometimes gone along with her to meetings. Berlyn's assessment of her unconventional former friend was sharply disapproving. Tigger's politics grew too extreme, and she was in general too 'emotionally volatile' and 'inward thinking.'[4]

Joan Falk was a Rhodesian who was intensely devoted to Doris in the early years of their friendship, which began in 1938. She had come to Rhodesia from England that year to work as a governess and the man she married, a Jewish German refugee, became friendly with Gottfried – indeed, Gottfried was best man at the wedding. Whatever strains there were in the relationship between the two couples primarily involved their political differences. Although the Falks were not conservative or racist, they were definitely not Communist sympathisers.

Also, Joan Falk was fond of Maude Tayler. Falk's aunt had known Maude in Persia, and had actually acted as a proxy – local godmother – to Doris when she was born. Falk fully recognised Maude's attempts to control, but she also admired her ability to cope with her unfortunate life. After Michael died, Maude became a sort of substitute grandmother to the Falks' children, staying with the family from time to time, visits Joan Falk remembered with sentimental warmth. While Falk understood how Doris's personality would clash with Maude's, her sympathies were at the very least divided between the two women.

Falk spoke of Gottfried's 'burning intelligence.' She also described him as virile, and saw her sexually charged friend Doris as being naturally drawn to his physical magnetism. Whatever the truth of Doris and Gottfried's sexual relationship, Joan Falk believed that the impetus for their marriage was based on physical attraction and desire. Falk saw the Lessings as trying to live like bohemians, a longing she linked to amorality. As an illustration, she described an evening when, during a dinner at the Falks' home, Gottfried nonchalantly followed her into the kitchen and asked her for a date.

During the interview Seligman sensed that Joan Falk's shock at the Lessings' style of marriage was tied to her disapproval of their revolutionary politics. This connection was definitely made by Harry Tayler when Seligman sought him out. If Harry needed more proof of his sister's moral descent – which had led to such depraved actions as disdaining her parents' needs and leaving her children – he found it in her reprehensible conversion to Communism through the conduit of Gottfried Lessing. Harry described Gottfried as 'a cold and ruthless man.' Together, he and Tigger led a 'decadent' life. But of course it would be so, Harry made clear. 'The two things go together after all – Communism and immorality.'[5]

Whatever other people said about them, Doris believed she and Gottfried were simply civilised people who harboured no illusions about their marriage. She told herself she had never loved Gottfried, and not for a moment did she consider that he might love her. As they went their separate sexual ways, they were for the most part polite to each other. There was no reason not to be, she believed, considering the basic unimportance and temporary nature of their marriage. When the war was over, they would part with hardly a ripple in the fabric of their individual lives.

In the late 1950s, the British painter and illustrator Paul Hogarth visited Germany after working on a project with Doris Lessing. By then, Gottfried Lessing had a relatively high post in the East German government. Hogarth tells how, to his surprise, a woman approached him at a party and said, 'Gottfried Lessing would very much like to meet with you.' Hogarth followed the woman to Gottfried's office, 'a huge space in one of those equally huge German buildings. I was sort of ushered in by several functionaries, passed from one to the other until I was standing before him. He was strikingly handsome, but with a very warm, engaging smile, not at all the forbidding, cold demeanour I would have expected from Doris's brief mentions of him.'

Hogarth reports being startled by Gottfried's eager questions about Doris. 'He wanted to know all about her, was she content with her life, was she physically well. It was clear to me that he was still very connected to her emotionally.'

* * *

Although to Doris's mind, she and her husband were primarily connected by their politics, she felt that he never thought her sufficiently committed to Communist principles. She furiously and sincerely argued against such judgement. She was as certain as Gottfried that the future of humanity lay in finally destroying a decaying capitalism and replacing it with a socialist paradise. Despite all her dissatisfaction with him, she respected Gottfried; she also had great feeling for Athen Gouliamis, and admired most of the fifty or so men and women who formed the core of their group. She still wanted to please these people who were so enviably certain about their beliefs.

Doris's political involvement did bring some personal rewards. Speaking out against the colour bar, distributing 'seditious' leaflets, satisfied her need for rebellion. Being out in the larger world allowed her to taste real freedom. Taking part in direct action liberated her from the fear that her life would become a facsimile of what she viewed as her mother's meaningless existence. What did it matter if she hardly slept or ate, or had any time to herself? Helping to create a perfect society would save her life along with everyone else's.

In retrospect, Lessing is awed by how much work the group did during this period of two or three years. They started and ran all sorts of societies and clubs, the Left Club, debating clubs, where they congregated and listened and talked. With great earnestness they fuelled themselves with political texts in preparation for the revolutionary tasks at hand, like trying to get the Salisbury housewives to buy the Communist newspaper. She is astonished to remember how she and an equally purposeful friend rode their bicycles up to posh homes in a Salisbury suburb and expected the woman of the house to be interested in their Communist sales pitch.

Lessing also recalls distributing her Communist newspapers to groups of blacks who lived in Salisbury's native community. But even as she passionately made her socialist case, many of the men were calling out to ask how they could get to America, where they believed they could make lots of money. Their eager questions elicited further lecturing about how it was more important to think of the group than your own self-interest.

Later Lessing would become embarrassed by the memory of that self-righteous young woman. And there is a refreshing earnestness to such self-deprecation. If Doris Lessing is always prepared to expose the imperfections and deficiencies in other people, she seems equally candid about her own flaws. But even as she pokes fun at herself, at some deep level she also seems contemptuous of her colleagues who remained loyal to the cause.

Her light-handed dismissal of the girl who once held these beliefs goes beyond bemusement, to the point where she is trivialising her youthful ideals. If she didn't realise her views were wrongheaded at the time, she certainly does now, Lessing impatiently makes clear. Perhaps it is because Lessing cannot really see herself in the young Rhodesian activist. The evolution of Doris Lessing has not been a linear process. There are a series of identities, embraced and then discarded. In her lifelong quest to find the real Doris, she seems to have unwittingly stumbled onto a number of Tiggers – personas who moved so effortlessly in a certain milieu that they dragged Lessing with them, away from finding her true identity herself. In looking back, she has little mercy for these traitors to her quest for self.

Breaking the Colour Bar

'Writers brought up in Africa have many advantages – being at the centre of a modern battlefield; part of a society in rapid, dramatic change,' says Doris Lessing. But it can also be limiting to be surrounded by organised oppression, no matter how hard you search for a different perspective. 'There are other things in living besides injustice, even for the victims of it.'[1] As a younger woman still living in an unjust society, Lessing may indeed have been frustrated at never being able to escape the effects of a segregated society. But going about her life after the Second World War, she thought of almost nothing else. Night and day, typing in her office, on the streets working for the Party, or at meetings in the flat she shared with Gottfried, breaking the colour bar was her major obsession.

Doris Lessing remembers their home as being constantly crowded with her revolutionary friends. Always a fine cook, she would some-times feed two dozen people a night, using only two hot plates in a tiny makeshift kitchen to turn out delicious meals. It was not unusual either for one or two visitors to spend the night, sleeping in the bathtub if no bed or sofa was available.

Most of these marathon meetings were taken up with discussions on how to penetrate the racism that encased Rhodesian life. They were sessions that Doris found immensely exciting, as were her forays into the black communities to distribute organising material, or to do her 'social work' by helping individuals deal with welfare problems. Lessing explains that until she joined the leftist group, she had never met blacks on an equal basis. Prior to that point in her life, she was either their employer or, despite her good intentions, a colonial superior. But no matter how wrong she felt the separation of the races was, she found no context to interact with black persons as equals.

Black Communist colleagues were usually unable to participate fully in ongoing strategy sessions because of an ugly body of Rhodesian laws. One immensely restrictive edict was a curfew which dictated that all blacks who did not live in Salisbury had to return to the native reserve outside the town by nine o'clock. Thus, late-evening meetings were conducted without them. Often the gathering would adjourn to a nearby restaurant that was whites-only even before nine. No ideology, no matter how heartfelt, was going to balance the relationship between blacks and whites. Other laws were repressive in different ways. It was terrible for Doris Lessing and her friends to observe the daily spectacle of the Salisbury streets. A line of Africans in handcuffs would be marching, flanked by police at each end. Behind the police would be a group of African women, following their husbands to court. For the most part, the offences were absurdly minor, such as not having a pass for a visit outside the native quarter, or riding a bicycle with a missing light.

A number of debates that took place around the issue of the colour bar threatened the solidarity of the Communist group. One was between essentially the welfare approach to the problem, which Lessing today sees as her only useful work of the time – calling up agencies to get a hungry black family food, or seeing that a black child got to school – and the political approach of trying to bring blacks fully into the political system.

Another area of difference grew out of this approach. The official Moscow line was that blacks should be led by blacks, not by whites. The problem with this theory, says Lessing, was that the native African population was not politically organised at the time. The only black person she had any substantive contact with at the time was a man named Charles Mzingele, who for years, she says, had been 'the old Left Book Club's 'token' African.'[2]

Mr Matushi in *A Ripple from the Storm*, may have been modelled on Charles Mzingele who, like his fictional counterpart, was repeatedly being punished for breaking the town's pass laws. Whenever Mzingele had to leave the Lessings and his other white comrades because of the curfew, they felt depressed at their own impotence. It took a commitment to Communism as intense as Gottfried's not to experience some waning of revolutionary energy and drive. For Doris Lessing herself, this erosion was linked to the first stirring of a familiar discontent.

Yet another path she had hoped would bring her to a feeling of connection and firm identity threatened to lead to a dead end.

* * *

The Reds were tolerated in Rhodesia after the Soviet Union became an ally during the war, but, as the war drew to an end, old antagonisms surfaced. Suspicions escalated about the group's subversiveness, particularly in relation to fuelling black demands for equal rights. Doris Lessing delighted in her role of provocateur. To openly defy authority was as thrilling – some who knew her would say even more thrilling – than what her actions achieved.

The group's principal accomplishment of this period was forming a black African branch of the Southern Rhodesia Labour Party under the guidance of a remarkable white woman, named Gladys Maasdorp, who was not a Communist, but a dedicated socialist. Middle-aged, conventionally married, and a mother, she was a member of the Salisbury town council, mayor of Salisbury in 1942-43 and general secretary of the Rhodesian Labour Party. Maasdorp, thinly disguised and sympathetically depicted as Mrs Van der Bylt in the Children of Violence series, was a close friend and supporter of Charles Mzingele. She was determined to create a black branch of the Labour Party, under Mzingele's leadership.

Despite the hostility of most Labour supporters toward the local Communists, and despite Maasdorp's own dislike of Communism, she managed to persuade the Lessings and all their cohorts to join the Labour Party so that they could cast their votes with her on the black African branch issue. The additional votes brought success, creating the African branch which satisfied Gladys Maasdorp's deep commitment to the concept of multiracialism.

Although that term would today strike Doris Lessing as abhorrent in its political correctness, she was a fervent supporter of Maasdorp's goals: easing the laws that made property ownership necessary for voting rights; changing discriminatory legislation such as that barring blacks from working in white districts; opening up civil service jobs to blacks; and improving health, welfare, and educational systems to serve the desperate needs of the black population.

Such goals are seen by some African scholars as falling into the welfare approach to apartheid, which would ease conditions but not create equality. In retrospect, it is questionable how much Gladys Maasdorp really wanted blacks to have autonomy inside the white political structure. Like many pragmatic politicians who champion idealistic causes, Maasdorp and her faction often hedged their bets. An unsigned article published in the Rhodesian journal *Labour Front* in 1944 is typical of the way progressive positions regarding black political participation are undercut to the point where one might wonder if they existed at all. In an attempt to relax white fears about black membership in the Labour Party the articles stated: 'For the information of the electorate,' the article stated, 'the National Executive Council desires to make its position with regard to African membership clear. It merely desires to provide a sympathetic channel through which the African's grievances and aspirations may be made known to those responsible for his welfare.'[3]

Later in 1944, Doris Lessing wrote an article for the same magazine about expanded opportunities for black farming. 'Collective farming would possibly provide a way of living more suitable to a people just emerging from primitive communalism than the jungle ethics of our capitalist world.'[4] That sentence seems typical of the dissonant combination of compassion and condescension that often seems to tinge early white radical rhetoric, including that spoken by Doris Lessing. Years before, Olive Schreiner also wrote in such contradictions.

'It would be a lie to say we love the black man,' Schreiner wrote,

> ... if by that is meant that we love him as we love the white. But we are resolved to deal with justice and mercy towards him. We will treat him as if we loved *him:* and in time, love may come ... We shall perhaps be able to look deep into each other's eyes and smile; as parent and child.[5]

There is little doubt that Doris Lessing understood early on how patronising the idea of parent and child is when describing relations between whites and blacks. And as time has gone on she has managed to find sympathy (and irritation) for both sides of Zimbabwe's racial divide. During Lessing's visits to Zimbabwe in late 1980s, she worried whether blacks would be able to make the land thrive now that they had begun to reclaim it. She told the South African journalist Fiammetta Rocco that over the generations of white rule, whites became highly accomplished farmers who cared deeply about their land. Lessing sadly notes that blacks don't recognise how much the whites care about Zimbabwe, how whites talk about how to improve the land all the time. 'Blacks don't know this, and they don't want to believe it.'[6]

One of the whites she included in this group was her son John, who was a coffee farmer in Zimbabwe until his death from a heart attack in 1992. In *African Laughter*, Lessing recalls listening to John and his friends as they sat talking on their verandas. Much of the conversation had to do with efforts to help the blacks, but the tone was familiarly paternalistic.

* * *

On February 12 and 13, 1944, a meeting of the black branch of the Southern Rhodesia Labour Party in Harare Hall in Salisbury provoked a national controversy. To the surprise of the white SRLP leadership, black members protested against the wartime compulsory labour and other harsh regulations. Spokesmen for white members of the SRLP who were present at the meeting urged the blacks to form their own trade unions. A sense of exhilaration surged through the hall, as blacks took heart at the sight of Europeans acting in sympathy with their grievances and sufferings. For Doris Lessing there was a deepening sense of futility, the beginning of her future disillusionment with all attempts at reform. Could these liberal, supportive whites, herself included, really do anything to alter the lives of the blacks in any concrete way?

The press made little effort to mask its hostility toward the meeting. As Gladys Maasdorp wrote to a friend overseas, 'Altogether it was an

unpleasant experience for all concerned – we were subjected, Europeans and Africans alike, to an intensive and venomous Press campaign.'[7]
Journalists accused the SLRP of that old colonial bugaboo – stirring up
the natives. But the attacks were filtered through the more current
hobgoblin of a post-war red scare. The SLRP was accused of being a
hotbed of subversive radicals whose foreign-born members were pushing their Marxist agenda by inciting the local black population in an
effort to weaken the Southern Rhodesian state.

The charges were in fact unfounded. While it is true that southern
Rhodesian Communists like Doris and her friends might have cheered
such activities, the same could not be said for either the SLRP as a
whole, or even the progressive faction of the SLRP led by Mrs Maasdorp. As for the meeting itself, it was a result of grievances from the
black community and not instigation by any white radicals of the SLRP.

The local Reds had now fully returned to the status of suspicious
troublemakers, determined to alter the white-dominated status quo. To
keep the SRLP from being further damaged, several 'aliens' offered to
resign from the Labour Party, including Doris herself, who had been
classified an alien because of her marriage to Gottfried, a German. The
party did not want to bow to outside pressure, and as a matter of
principle refused to accept these resignations. However, the climate had
sharply changed, and the black branch of the party continued to be the
victim of attack from inside and outside the SRLP membership.

As the war in Europe drew to an end, the Labour Party's influence
declined further and further, but Doris Lessing went on with what she
still called her welfare work. Perhaps the wounds of her life were being
eased by her seeing herself as a dedicated crusader against the injuries
a hostile world imposed on its most helpless members. When Lessing
looks back at this time, she herself questions – with great honesty –
what may have been the primary origin of her ambivalent activism.

'It could be said that in rebelling against my parents and what they
stood for, it was natural for me to use the inequities of white supremacy
against them.' She adds that she really doesn't believe this was the root
of her hatred of the colour bar. Still, 'if you are standing out against your
parents you pick up any stick at hand to beat them with.'[8]

Victory but not Liberation

In the concluding scene of the classic French film *Children of Paradise*, a grim-faced Jean-Louis Barrault struggles to push his way through a mad swirl of costumed Mardi Gras revellers clogging the streets of Paris. That image comes to mind when reading *Under My Skin's* account of Doris Lessing's trek through the streets of Salisbury on VE Day, May 8, 1945. Earlier that day, Lessing had visited her father, a man who had never recovered from the ravages of the previous World War. She was on her way home to see her husband who had spent a considerable part of the preceding weeks sitting by the radio listening to the reports of his homeland being devastated by the end results of the largest single invasion in the history of warfare.

That uneasy day of liberation can be seen as symbolic of her life at a post-war turning point, going from her troubled past in Rhodesia in the person of her dying, failed, father and progressing towards the uncertain future in Europe that Gottfried presented. This was not an association Lessing made then or later. But the concerns of her family and the changing world weighed on her. As men in uniform and women in party dresses spilled out onto the streets of Salisbury in a rush of ecstatic relief and unrestrained joy, she felt a complexity of emotion that prevented her from sharing the merry-making of the crowd.

* * *

The end of the War further altered the Communist group, injecting a note of uncertainty into Marxist rhetoric as political activity entered a new phase. New settlers started to arrive in the country who were not steeped in the ways of white Rhodesia and they were naive enough to question the mores and assumptions of the white culture.

As scores of black people also flocked to the cities and the process of urbanisation intensified, Salisbury's native reserves, always crowded, became hideously dense with people. Among the inhabitants was a young Lawrence Vambe, on his way to becoming a leading figure in the first generation of black African writers. Born in 1917, he was shaped by a close-knit, traditional native upbringing, and managed to surmount the restrictions on his educational opportunities. Although it was extremely difficult for blacks in Southern Rhodesia to obtain any education before and during World War II, Vambe did receive an advanced degree.

Vambe began his career as a journalist, covering the rising post-war African nationalism, which he vigorously championed. Like other African intellectuals, he was determined to achieve social progress for blacks in both the personal and working spheres. Only a fully multiracial society would be, to his mind, the basis for real equality and growth. In 1946, he began working for the African Newspapers Group. His news stories, written in Shona and in English, were vivid accounts of the life of Rhodesian blacks. He pressed white society to create better working opportunities for blacks, and cautioned his own people to hang on to their traditional values and moral standards.

Soon after the war ended, Vambe became involved with the Southern Rhodesia Labour Party, where he met Doris and Gottfried Lessing and the few other Communist and socialist whites who were members. Vambe remembers Doris Lessing both as a literary influence and as a strong supporter of his writing. He also credits her, along with Gottfried, Nathan and Dorothy Zelter, and a few other comrades, with openly campaigning 'for a common front between the working-class African and European in their struggle for economic justice .... Considering the force of reaction that confronted them,' he adds, 'I thought they were a brave group of people ... the anti-black elements in the Southern Rhodesia Labour Party and white trade unions were formidable.'[1]

Vambe's praise is tempered by an honest appraisal of the emotional power the colour bar had over even those, like himself or Doris Lessing, who intellectually wanted to shatter it. In comparing how he was influenced by radical whites and politically active blacks, he says: 'I do not deny that I learnt a great deal from whites with whom I associated. But their influence was not as profound as that of fellow black Africans. However, I will admit that by meeting these people and discussing our problems on equal terms, I began to rise above my then very robust racial prejudices against white people as a whole.'[2]

According to Vambe the rules against the races' mingling were, if anything, more strictly enforced after the war than before, as the colonial government tried to control the massive influx of blacks to white cities. Passes were needed to go anywhere, and fines were routinely ordered for showing up at any of the many places blacks were not allowed. Black businessmen were struggling to build careers in the new milieu, but prostitution and other illegal enterprises also emerged. Violence kept up with the changes as too many people tried to find work and found themselves in appalling conditions. In turn, police intervention escalated, keeping the blacks in a constant state of tension and paranoia. This combined with the post-war anti-red backlash made it difficult for Doris and her comrades to pursue their goals of helping their black fellow Southern Rhodesians achieve racial equality.

There is no denying that it took considerable courage and commitment to racial equality to stand up to the climate of the times. In this light it seems peculiar that Doris Lessing has often maintained a noticeable distance between herself and the people whose cause she championed. Phillippa Berlyn noted what she saw as Lessing's 'hypocrisy,' in this regard when she spoke to Dee Seligman in 1973. Berlyn believed that it was, and always had been possible to cross the colour line and form genuine friendships with blacks despite the physical restrictions blacks faced. She was critical of Lessing for not attempting to share in the African culture, for example by listening to native music, or, as she did, learning to speak Shona, and translating and reading Shona poetry.[3]

For her part Lessing, might see Berlyn's attitude as naïve. For much of Lessing's writing on black Africans suggests that the gulf that separates the races in a shared territory ensures that, even with good intentions, they will always be strangers to each other. In her story, 'Little Tembi,' a childless white woman becomes attached to one of the native piccanins. When she finally has her own child, her attention to the little black boy wanes. He responds by becoming increasingly troublesome and annoying. Finally he starts to steal, and when he is arrested, he refuses the woman's offer to help him evade the police. As he is led away, the woman is outraged.

'What did he *want*, Willie,' she asks her husband with frustrated confusion. 'What is it he was *wanting*, all this time?'[4]

Ironically, some readers have commented on a naiveté in Lessing's own work that stems from the very sense of disconnectness she has been so articulate in describing. One overall positive review of her autobiography in a Zimbabwean newspaper remarked on the absence of any attempts at close contact with African children or servants. The reviewer went on to make this criticism.: 'Perhaps this explains why so many black characters in her books, from King Lobengula to the fictional drummer Jim in *The Good Terrorist* come across as Paddington Bear: sugary sweet objects for her to cuddle. Had she known Africans as real people, in the context of their own culture, she would have known they loathe being thought of in those terms.'[5]

Lessing herself seems to acknowledge a past attitude to be overly kind to people of colour without engaging them in the type of direct interaction she has had with white acquaintances. In *Walking in the Shade*, the second volume of her autobiography, she recalls how she first perceived that she was escaping the restrictions of racial hypersensitivity. The event occurred in the 1950s in London. An Indian man whom she did not like showed up at her flat unexpectedly. Without hesitation she told him to leave. This was a transforming experience.

She no longer felt that she must be welcoming to a visitor simply on the basis of dark skin.

Shed of such restrictions she has applied the same – let the chips fall where they may – comments to race as she has to other socio-political issues such as feminism. When she was writing her space-fiction series, she became irritated with Robert Gottlieb because he objected to her mocking the phrase 'We Shall Overcome.' In correspondence with the editor, Lessing had no qualms about telling him that she considered the words empty and witless. Unlike herself, she says, Gottlieb was obviously clutched in a vise of misguided piety. When Fiammetta Rocco interviewed Doris Lessing after the publication of *African Laughter: Four Visits to Zimbabwe,* she was discomfited by some remarks that seemed to ascribe a collective identity to blacks.

'While she accuses the whites she met in Zimbabwe of being paternalistic, she is not above referring to black Zimbabweans as 'these people,' as in "they're so humorous, these people."' Rocco noted.[6]

But whether kindly or paternalistic, the distance is always there it seems. In her fiction Lessing often powerfully explores black peoples' external responses to white actions, but their inner thoughts and feelings are rarely touched upon. What does a worker think when he stands silently listening to the baas's abuse? What does the nursemaid to the white child feel when she suffers one humiliation after the other, when she is made to seem no more significant than a bothersome mosquito, which like her self esteem, is angrily swatted by the imperious child?

It is an intriguing paradox that although Doris Lessing has fought all her life against holding people back because of their skin colour, it is colour that appears to keep her from drawing seemingly obvious parallels between her life and theirs. In *Going Home*, Lessing's nonfiction account of her aborted return to Africa in 1956, she describes going food shopping and finding that despite many physical improvements in the shops during her seven-year absence, the way customers were dealt with remained unchanged.

At a vegetable market, she finds two white salespeople behind a counter. Two African men stand in front of the counter with baskets they have filled with their purchases. 'I waited my turn behind the two Africans to see what would happen. The woman behind the counter eyed the Africans coldly, and then, in the cool, curt voice I knew so well, said, 'Can't you see the white missus, boy? Get to the back.' The blacks did as they were told and Doris moved to the front and was waited on. Before the Africans could move up again, another white woman came in and once more usurped their turn.[7]

She writes that she tried to imagine what it would be like to suffer such treatment all of your life. Although she can grasp the pain of a single situation, she could not really fathom how the accumulated insults, disdain, and ridicule made a person feel. True enough, but it does seem odd that it she couldn't find some parallels in her own life that would offer some basis for empathy. The countless times her mother had favoured Harry over her, indeed the constant lack of affection she endured from Maude throughout her childhood, seems to stem from something as arbitrary as the men's colour – the simple fact that her brother had the good luck to be born the boy that Doris was intended to be.

One wonders whether she is even registering the emotions of the particular incident. The men's life-long suffering does not fill her with the same powerful outrage at unfairness that struck her when she was denied an evening of Sybil Thorndyke. Instead of suggesting that the men be served first, she simply observes the situation, and records 'the special tone of voice, the gesture of impatience, the contempt,' with which white Africans speak to black Africans.

In a curious way, that description sounds remarkably like a side of Doris Lessing that emerges when she is out of sorts with someone. British playwright Bernard Kops,who had shared some political interests with Lessing in the 1950s endured such an incident after her break with the left wing. After many years of not seeing her, Kops spotted Doris Lessing in the outdoor gardens at Hampstead Heath. Here is how he describes what happened next.

Kops, walking eagerly to her table: 'Doris, hello!'

Lessing looks up in icy silence.

Kops (growing uncomfortable): 'It's Bernard.' Lessing makes no sign of recognition, and so he says again, 'Bernard, Bernard Kops.'

Doris, staring coldly: 'I know.'

Lessing looks down at her teacup while Kops stands stiffly for a few moments, trying to understand what has just happened. He turns and leaves her table, going back to his own, where his wife waits, observing his bewildered embarrassment.

Kops feels that the resemblance between Lessing's occasional imperiousness and the attitude of the white colonial belittling the kaffir is more than a coincidence. 'Despite her rebellion against her colonial upbringing, I don't believe Doris has ever completely outgrown its influences. After all, metaphorically, mother's milk is a very potent brew.'

This is an appraisal that resonates for many other people who have observed Doris Lessing's flashes of arrogance, her rudeness, her sense of entitlement and occasional bursts of conformity. Without taking anything away from her battles against colonialist oppression, it seems that she is more a product of the British Empire than she allows herself to see.

* * *

Certainly, Doris Lessing, living in post-war Rhodesia, would never have considered that there was anything about the British empire she wished to absorb or emulate. Nonetheless, more and more, she was determined to escape Africa for England. And not the least of her reasons was the restrictions the issue of race relations placed on her writing.

Although she was drawing on the volatile race issue for material, most particularly for the novel she was trying to complete, *The Grass Is Singing*, she objected to the notion that just because this model shaped her life, she was obliged to write about it.

Lessing had filled journals with ideas for stories that she once had been determined to write. But the impulse had faded. She was frustrated at how the vastness of the race problem dominated every other plot she conceived. It was impossible to write honestly about Africa without writing about racism. Thus an impetus for working as hard as she did on *The Grass Is Singing* was that perhaps – as it had for Olive Schreiner – a novel about Africa would bring her success abroad, where she could escape the creative restrictions of racial inequity.

And then, even as she spun the familiar but now greatly intensified dream of freedom and flight from everything that interfered with her concentration on her work – her mother, her father, Gottfried, Africa, her children with Frank Wisdom – she became pregnant for the third time.

The Cape of Good Love

Why would she want to abandon two children and then start another family, her father demanded from his deathbed when she told him her news. Maude echoed Michael's reproach in harsh, accusing words. Their outrage made no mark on their newly lighthearted daughter. Indeed, she had spent remarkably little time reflecting on her choice. As with previous actions, she did not see the pregnancy *as* a choice. Some critics of Lessing's memoir have referred to her behaviour as careless and irresponsible. This, however, assumes the concept of free will, a belief Lessing does not share. Doris Lessing *had* to become pregnant. She was having a baby for the same reason she became pregnant with her first two children. Mother Nature had decided she should. Doris Lessing was a suitable candidate to help replenish the population that had been decimated by the war.

Once again one is startled by the contradictions in Lessing's personality. She was determined and fiercely rebellious, insisting on autonomy. At the same time, she seems to feel that her decision was driven by biological or even historical imperatives. Gottfried, though she still saw him as all icy logic, apparently also fell under these inexorable powers. He might have been expected to 'analyse' the wisdom of having a baby when, according to Doris, they both understood they would soon divorce. But, she explains, rationality had no bearing on their decision.

Although she would often regard herself as determinedly rational and attempt to battle emotion with logic, intellectual judgement was still far less important to Doris Lessing than the concept of destiny. Her belief that actions were guided by forces more powerful than consciousness precluded an inner search for reasons to explain a suddenly erupting wish for maternity. She craved a new child, she writes, and never attempted to answer her father's question.

Why *did* she want another child when she had abandoned two others? Did regret about her desertion fuel her new desire for a child? Was she seeking some emotional connection outside of her Communist circle? These are not questions Doris Lessing poses in her writings. The concept of an evolving self, equating growth with change, was still not her route to a sense of identity. Lessing does not build on former selves. She erases them, disowns them, and begins again.

Both before and after she decided to become pregnant, Doris and Gottfried were working at a furious pace. Gottfried held two jobs, one of which forced him to rise at dawn. She had left the law firm and was typing for three government commissions and trying in every spare moment to write. Husband and wife were both still politically active, despite Doris's secret knowledge that most of her excitement and sense of engagement with Communist ideals were gone. Gone, too, were many of the interesting people the war had brought to Salisbury. As Rhodesian soldiers in turn came home and picked up their old jobs, some of the comrades who had replaced them went on to other work, often in other cities.

Harry Tayler was one of the men whom the end of the War carried home. He had planned to study veterinary medicine in Edinburgh, but when he saw how ill his father was and how hard his mother's life was, caring for him while trying to make ends meet, he abandoned his plans and stayed in Salisbury, beginning a business career. In Harry's mind, families stuck together. His sister's disregard for that belief created an inevitable barrier to picking up the thread of sibling affection.

Frequent meetings between Harry and Doris at their father's bedside showed they had less than ever in common. They did not speak much – she knew how Harry hated her 'funny ideas,' and she found his stubborn colonialism enraging. However, there was some value to their shared vigil. Mentally, Doris was taking notes on the scene she tried to distance herself from emotionally. These encounters were more grist for her writing, and as such, she would put up with, even find some satisfaction in, their awkwardness.

Watching her brother across the bed that held their dying father's body, Doris Lessing saw an all too familiar breed, the mulish, narrow-minded colonial, tenaciously resistant to any change. As a sister she was tense, but the writer-observer was intrigued. Harry was quite fascinating under a sociological lens. He drank too much and sought out people who did not read serious literature out of a fear, she believed, that they might find ideas that contradict their smug self-satisfaction. She was already experimenting with capturing this kind of person in print as she worked on *The Grass Is Singing* and some short fiction, stories Harry Tayler would probably never read.

Many years after their father died, Lessing was outraged to learn of Harry's fondness for trashy popular literature. Didn't Harry remember all the 'good' books on their mother's shelves, or the intricate stories Maude told them before bed, Doris demanded, apparently seeing no irony in defending her mother's literary tastes despite the fact that Maude would have hardly included the Doris Lessing canon in her library.

Harry, on the other hand, was not at all critical of his sister for her bookishness. When Dee Seligman came to see him, a few of Lessing's books were on his shelves. Although he made a point of saying he had never read them, he saw her dedication to literature as neither foolish nor elitist. Harry seemed genuinely pleased to relate how much his sister always read, and proudly remembered how she could visualise the words on a page that she had studied the day before for a school examination.

* * *

Doris's routine work as a typist left her mind free for conceiving the poems and short stories she sent off to magazines such as the *Democrat* and *Trek*, published in Johannesburg, and to newspapers in England as well as Rhodesia. She has little respect now for these fledgling efforts, even though she rejoiced in their publication at the time. She believes that only a handful have any value, and would be delighted if no one remembered or spoke of them.

Playwriting was more interesting to the aspiring author than poetry. The little girl who had been bereft when she could not accompany her boarding school class to see Sybil Thorndike play Lady Macbeth had retained her love of drama. As often as possible, she and her Salisbury friends attended plays put on by local repertory groups. Over the years Doris Lessing would speak of being enchanted by the theatre, of being hopelessly captivated by the stage. Even if she suspects the play she is about to see is going to be disappointing, she gets an instinctive thrill when the curtain starts to rise, she says.

Still, *The Grass Is Singing* was the focus of most of her writing time. The first draft of the manuscript, three times the size of the novel it would eventually become, was sent off by ship to London. Lessing had no literary agent and her choice of publisher was random. The crossing took six weeks and months went by before the English publisher read it and sent it back to the unknown author without an offer of publication. Then the process was repeated, each time bringing her no closer to the success she wanted so desperately.

Never, however, would she allow herself to consider that she might be following an unrealistic path. Her determined blindness to the vagaries of artistic recognition was helped by Gottfried, who took her writing seriously, even if he didn't always approve of her themes. She found a similar mix of encouragement and disapproval from many of her comrades, particularly Nathan and Dorothy Zelter. Lessing attributes their negative response to a continued inability to detach from their own ideology. The Zelters disliked *The Grass Is Singing*, for example, because it seemed to say that relations between blacks and whites could never significantly change. Also a factor in the cool reception was that to the still dedicated Red, purely artistic goals were deemed trivial and bourgeois.

* * *

Much as Doris wanted to finish a new draft of *The Grass Is Singing*, and much as she claimed to be thrilled about her impending motherhood, in early 1946 she suddenly decided she needed to get away before the baby's arrival and ensuing demands. With Gottfried's blessing, when she was three months pregnant, Doris took a five-day train trip to Cape Town. The length of the trip did not bother her. She was on her own again, the state she loved most of all.

On her own, but not alone, for she had arranged to work for a few weeks at the offices of the *Guardian*, the Communist newspaper she so earnestly distributed up and down the streets of Salisbury. Her duties in Cape Town were in the subscription department, writing letters of solicitation and going to the industrial sections of town to sell papers. During these visits, needy residents of the 'Coloured' (mixed-race) and Indian quarters, who ostensibly came to purchase a newspaper, also sought help with housing, jobs, or medical needs. For them, and for the people she visited when she ventured into their own territory, she dispensed the kind of welfare she'd done so much of in Salisbury.

Interesting as it was to take on new social problems and to mingle with a new group of Communists, her primary goal was something quite different. Doris Lessing was determined to have a love affair. It was her right to have one, she felt; she was 'owed' one. Why was it her right? Because she had become pregnant? And owed by whom? Gottfried? Fate? Mother Nature? Although in *Under My Skin* she raises the question of why she felt so strongly that she deserved a love affair, she does not explore any answers.

The man she chose for a lover, after rejecting a couple of candidates, was like herself a person who mixed artistic ambition with radical politics. She has kept his real name to herself. In *Under My Skin*, where she describes him glowingly, he is René; In *Pursuit of the English*, an earlier autobiographical book, she refers to him as Piet. René/Piet had painted in Paris and in London, but he was struggling to make a living as an artist in South Africa, where he wanted to live. Tall and energetic, he dressed, spoke, and made love flamboyantly. Lessing moved into his cluttered studio. She left the *Guardian* to be always ready for his appearance, even when he travelled out of the city with another lover for several days.

It did not bother her that he was much sought after by other women and invariably encouraged their attention. So what if he never bothered to inform her of his impending marriage to a woman who was carrying his child? René loved women unabashedly – their faces, their scent, their voices – and when a woman recognises this response in a man, she is inevitably tantalised, Lessing writes in *Under My Skin,* hastening to instruct female readers that if they encounter such a man, they should not hold him to such artificial social ties as monogamy.[1] Lessing's attitude toward fidelity would change some when Clancy Sigal entered her life ten years later, in her twenties she demanded no such allegiance, from Gottfried or her lovers.

It seems that as a young woman her own desirability had a particular significance for Doris Lessing. It was another attempt at controlling her life, and also at self-definition. A good-looking woman needs to do nothing more than enter a room to find that she draws attention to herself, Lessing had remarked. It would be many years before Lessing recognised the fruitlessness of seeking a sense of identity through her physical appeal.

Lessing does not hold herself accountable for this misguided attempt to find completion. Rather, she sees it as inherent in the biological state of being a young woman. She is amazed that women go on believing that something special about them attracted the coveted attention. To Lessing's mind, this is a ridiculous assumption. The response a woman wants and receives has nothing to with anything she's said or done, but is simply the natural allure of youth.

After René returned from his wanderings, he took Lessing to live for a few days in a house borrowed from a friend. There he taught her to cook and enjoy spicy dishes despite her fear of gaining weight, while he in turn delighted in her swelling belly. She loved to pose for him, and watch his face as he studied her beautiful nakedness. 'I like to think,' Lessing writes, 'that my then Renoir-like body is on a wall somewhere.'[2]

They left the bed to do René's political work. Often this meant his standing on a soapbox in the coloured neighbourhood and making rousing speeches that elicited laughter and shouts from gathering crowds, Lessing among them, and from the dark faces leaning out the windows of shabby flats.

They rented a one-room shack by the sea outside Cape Town where they heard the waves crashing when they made love. It was a state of glorious hedonism, lived fully in the moment, but the clouds of depression were gathering in her, and internal voices insistently whispered that this rich present would soon become a lost and longed-for past.

* * *

After two months, she forced herself to leave him, and far more wrenchingly, leave the tantalising freedom she had found in Cape Town. As she lay on the narrow train berth, being carried back to the home she longed to permanently escape, Doris Lessing felt deeply distraught. Even though she still didn't regret being pregnant, she confronted how it was changing her future. What might her life have been if she weren't pregnant? She could have stayed in Cape Town, enjoyed René as long as he was available. More important, she could have booked herself passage on a boat to London or even Paris.

Instead, she was hurtling along on a noisy train, the sensuous smell of sea and sand steadily replaced by the murky dust that blew into the compartment. As awful as the trip was, she dreaded its conclusion. At journey's end, where would she be? With Gottfried, whom she did not love, engaged in the same old political activities, forced to the bedside of a father who tortured her with his slow dying.

Yet, sad as she was, disoriented as she felt, she still believed that she was helpless to have changed her situation, given the fate that governed her nature. Although years later Doris Lessing would briefly examine the ideas of Carl Jung, on this train ride carrying her in the wrong direction she would probably not have welcomed the Jungian perception 'When an inner situation is not made conscious, it happens outside, as fate.'[3]

A New Life

Gottfried Lessing was happy that his wife enjoyed her vacation. Perhaps it took some stress out of their relationship. Certainly Doris was feeling glum, no matter how healthy and happy she appeared. With the naïveté and emotional understatement that often startle people about Doris Lessing, she muses in her memoir how remarkable it is that a person may feel so different inside from how she appears on the surface. Lessing often presents as original thinking.

To combat her *ennui* Doris came up with a solution that artists have employed from time immemorial – create. During her final three and a half years in Southern Rhodesia, she produced short stories, drafts of the novel, *The Grass Is Singing* – and numerous poems, some of which she was able to publish. This allowed Doris to fulfil her crucial need to call herself a writer. Others have commented that her writing served as a psychological defence. 'I used to think of her as a depressive in a certain way,' says Stuart Hall, a writer and specialist in cultural studies who knew Doris Lessing in London in the 1950s. 'But a person who had learned to live with it … whose way of living with depression was to write.' The fierceness with which she applies herself to her work – no one and nothing come between Lessing and her writing – attests to the accuracy of this perception.

Lessing herself admits that every other aspect of her life fades when a new book takes hold of her attention. Although she loves the theatre and concerts, and enjoys parties if they include people who interest her, when she's writing she does very little reading, theatre-going, or visiting. Her prodigious output is proof of this ability to concentrate. 'Sometimes you wouldn't see her for days at a time,' recalls someone who shared her London home. 'You'd just see her remains … of her food or whatever else she left. She wrote all day.'

Although Lessing belittles the value of her poems, one magazine alone, the *New Rhodesia*, published fourteen of them between 1943 and 1949. Their themes ranged from nature to the fabulous, from satirical pieces to those more directly political. But as she grew to believe that poetry was not the best vehicle for her concerns, she turned ever more to the novel as her form of self-expression and self-preservation.

* * *

Doris Lessing had told herself that as soon as the war was over, she would leave Rhodesia. But Gottfried was hoping to become a British citizen, and he felt that his chances would be harmed if he were divorced. He had ignored the curbs on political activity by refugees while in Rhodesia and he worried that a divorce would be another mark against him. Consequently, he asked Doris to wait until he achieved citizenship to end the marriage. Doris herself also needed to reapply for British citizenship, since under the prevailing laws, marrying an enemy alien had meant that she had lost her citizenship.

In her memoir, where Lessing continually mocks her mother's reverence for England, she suddenly asserts a quite contradictory and unanticipated regret at the ending of her dual nationality. It seemed the greatest of losses to no longer have her British passport, and to have to actually petition to have it reinstated. This paradox is understandable if one considers how much England would be a stepping stone to a new life. As Lessing was well aware, many an artist has crossed the sea to find fame. And many a provincial has found success in the capitol of the Empire. Her future was tied to her having a British passport. Thus her feeling of entrapment grew overwhelming as it became clear she could not leave for a long time. Refugees were swamping government offices with applications for visas or attempts to gain British citizenship, and even with Gottfried's legal connections, there was no way they could speed up the process.

Gottfried planned to work as a business consultant in London, even though his belief in Communist ideology remained undiminished. Lessing is quite comfortable with the notion of separate selves residing in one body and this allowed her to see Gottfried's behaviour as perfectly reasonable. Gottfried could also be several selves just as Doris herself. The astute businessman who lived in one part of his mind would build a lucrative commercial career in London and easily coexist with the disdainful anticapitalist.

* * *

In October 1946, Peter Lessing was born. Gottfried was overjoyed about fatherhood, and visited his wife often, sometimes with the couple's friends, sometimes on his own. The nurses tried to limit the amount of time the baby spent with his mother, as before following the still prevailing rule of keeping infants isolated except when the mothers nursed them, but Gottfried commanded them to bring Peter to the room. Peter was the first baby born to a member of the Communist group, and amid the still optimistic response to the end of the War, he seemed a harbinger of promise for a better world. Even his mother felt such a sense of resurrection.

Gottfried's delight in his son made him a nurturing parent. He was perfectly comfortable taking physical care of Peter, bathing and feeding and dressing him. He did not share the fear of losing his masculinity that kept so many colonial fathers at a distance from their children.

Though motherhood interfered with Doris's writing, any misgivings about the baby she might have occasionally had disappeared as soon as he was born. She loved her son and enjoyed being with him. Often she took Peter to visit her father. She would lay the kicking little body next to the emaciated inertness of the old man. It is a striking image to think of the two lying together, the baby imbued with the endless potential of a new life and the grandfather whose whole existence had been reduced to waiting for his last breath. When that last breath came Doris refused to be there. She received word one day while bathing the baby, that her father was in the hospital, close to death. If she wanted to see him alive, she would have to leave immediately.

In *Under My Skin*, she explains why she did not go. In part, her refusal stemmed from distrust. Maude was forever histrionic, and Doris was all too familiar with the urgent summons to the dying man, who then continued to live. But the more compelling reason was that the alarm might be true. She felt herself exploding with rage, with a need to strike out in embittered frustration. She did not want to bring all that terrible pounding feeling to its source and make a scene at her father's bedside. But there is also something she doesn't say which bears pointing out. It's evident that Doris Lessing loved her father. It can be unbearable to watch someone you love die.

It was worse to deal with her mother after Michael's death than before. His illness, terribly restricting to her though it was, did fill Maude's time. Now alone, rootless, she hovered over her daughter's life, triggering all of Doris's old painful responses to her intrusiveness and disapproval.

Maude would appear at the Lessing flat, which was always filled with people she quickly realised were not the sort she would want to befriend. Her aggrieved disappointment enraged Doris. Nothing had erased Maude's indelible influence on her daughter. Not two marriages, not Doris's own motherhood, not her rebellious politics. Maude was always there, trying to fix Doris, like May Quest was always trying to adjust Martha, 'in a series of fussy little pushes, as a bad sculptor might ineffectually push and pat a botched piece of work.'[1] Doris responded by rejecting almost everything that Maude held sacred. Carl Jung captures this negative model of a daughter's dilemma in his idea of 'resistance.'

Anything, so long as it is not like Mother! ... This kind of daughter knows what she does *not* want, but is usually completely at sea as to what she would choose as her own fate. All her instincts are concentrated on the mother in the negative form of resistance and are therefore of no use to her in building her own life.[2]

The conflicts with her mother sharpened Doris's dreams of artistic success. Both drove her to the same course of action – flight to England. Lessing has never said that the desire to put a few thousand miles between herself and Maude was a motivation, but it must have occurred to her that she might be solving more than one problem. Gottfried was also eager to go. Their wait to leave Africa came to seem interminable.

Gottfried would spend his evenings talking to friends, or reading, or studying Russian, perhaps in preparation for his future life as an international businessman, or perhaps for the further development of his political activities. Doris would often go out by herself, walking up and down the dark streets, hearing music pouring out of radios inside the brightly lit houses. The songs were like the songs she had danced to, songs of love and possibility, and they fuelled her desire for romantic adventure and physical escape.

She answered the longing by taking a lover from among her wide circle of acquaintances. In the afternoons, he would come to the house in Salisbury where the Lessings had moved to have more space, while the neighbours watched his approach from their windows. The love-making was often interrupted by people dropping in, as Doris did not think or choose to lock the doors. In any case, it was exciting to have her lover hide in the bedroom closet laughing at her overheard lies.

With no attempt at analysing her contradictions, Lessing recalls that suddenly she fell in love with this quite comfortably married man. As if she were describing another person's mental and emotional processes, she reports that as a result of falling in love, all her desperate longings for flight evaporated. No more did she dream of living and writing in London. She wanted only for her new lover to divorce his wife and marry her, and they'd live happily ever after together in Rhodesia. He told her she was being absurd, that he had no intentions of doing anything of the kind, and had assumed she not only knew that all along, but shared his sentiments.

Once again Doris looked to biology for both the reason for her behaviour and its resolution. She had believed he would want to marry her because of nature's ruthless demands. The answer to biology's call, even if she did not marry the man who inspired it, was to have his baby.

Before acting on this increasingly urgent demand from nature, she visited a doctor because of back pains. He suggested that while he was performing minor surgery on her retroverted uterus, he could also tie up her fallopian tubes. Doris Lessing believes the doctor's suggestion, however kindly meant, was prompted by disapproval, since he knew her history. Whatever his reasons, she was ultimately grateful since, being a tool of nature, she knew that before she passed out of her childbearing years, she would fall in love countless more times, and would be compelled to have a baby with each lover. So, although Gottfried advised her against it, and her own body did the same, she forced herself to quiet her biological impulses, and agreed to the procedure.

The waiting to leave Rhodesia continued.

* * *

Sometimes now when the Lessings picnicked with Peter, which they often did, they were joined by Frank Wisdom, his second wife, and Jean and John, who watched the mother who had left them playing with her new baby. Maude was often present. Frank's sister-in-law, Dora, and her two children provided some respite from Maude's sniffing disapproval. Rounding out the group – Lessing acknowledges it was bizarre – were one or two flirtatious girls Gottfried had invited along to amuse him.

Lessing was ambivalent about her older children's presence on these outings, but she felt unable to put an end to the practice. In a rare moment of acknowledged guilt, she explains it is difficult to be assertive when you feel responsible for a problem. She remembers thinking, and it is a sentiment she sustained, that it would probably have been better not to have had any contact at all with her first son and daughter until she had achieved some status in the world. If she could know and respect who she was, she would feel justified in having left them. And they in turn, she suggests, would understand.

As 1948 came to an end, so, finally, did her life in Salisbury. Gottfried and Doris both became British citizens, started the process of divorce and eagerly made plans for their future. Doris would have custody of Peter until he was fifteen. Gottfried would then shepherd him through manhood. With all of them in London, Peter would be able to spend time with both parents even though they lived separately. Gottfried would pay a small sum to Doris for Peter's upkeep and she would supply the rest. Lessing still finds this arrangement sensible and condemns the punitive divorce conditions she believes many women demand in today's hostile climate between the genders.

The plan was for Doris and Peter to leave first for London. Gottfried would follow shortly. There is no mention in her memoir of bidding goodbye to her mother, her brother, or her two older children. Whatever her feelings about these farewells, she keeps them to herself, perhaps from herself.

After a short stay in Johannesburg as guests of wealthy friends of Gottfried's (Doris left their home when the wife became convinced her husband and Doris were having an affair), mother and two-year-old son set out for Cape Town to finish their wait for passage to England.

Doris had little money and she did not want to waste any of it before arriving in London, so she booked the cheapest room she could find. It was in a crowded, ramshackle boardinghouse, owned by a sullen, slovenly Afrikaner who made no secret of her dislike of her many English guests. Most of these were young women, reversing Doris's journey, war brides of South African soldiers waiting to find places to live in Cape Town.

Because of Peter, Doris was pretty well confined to the boarding-house. The only bright interlude was when her former lover 'René' came to see her, bearing flowers, fruit, and a huge fish, which he mistakenly thought the churlish boardinghouse owner would cook for Doris. René spun tales of his continuing conquests among women who flung them-selves at him in reaction to lesser men's impoverished lovemaking. He was appalled to hear that Doris was going to England, where women suffered such inadequacies most of all. Years later, Doris Lessing would accuse a British journalist of 'wanting me to say how I found English-men in bed; well they are not as bad as I'd been told.'[3]

At last, after more than a month, the Dutch ship that would take Doris and Peter to London arrived in Cape Town, and she walked up its ramp, a few short strides that would change her life forever. Once she was at sea, her exhilaration at escape began to subside. If the boarding-house had been confining, the four-week boat trip was exhausting. Two-year-old Peter, never a good sleeper, was enormously stimulated by the experience and ran around till nearly midnight, rising at dawn.

In Cape Town, Doris had realised how difficult it was to live life for herself when she had to take care of a child. She was without the Salisbury support network she had taken for granted – the husband, friends, grandmother, and servant who had helped her look after Peter. Now, as she pulled Peter from danger on the ship's deck, or desperately tried to get him to sleep, she wondered what lay ahead for her as a single mother in England.

There was one immensely important reason to be hopeful, to believe that her life would not evaporate into domestic drudgery, not be defined by motherhood. Her handbag might contain only twenty pounds, but in her suitcase was the manuscript of *The Grass Is Singing*. She had finally sold it to a publisher in Johannesburg, although she knew the contract was unfair – the publisher was to get 50 percent of her royalties. She worried that this agreement might prevent English publication, but she was going to find some way to solve this problem. Now that she was out of Africa, everything was possible.

Aside from having to be constantly alert to the antics of her son, Doris Lessing might have been Olive Schreiner sailing from Africa nearly seventy years before. She had cut and polished *The Grass Is Singing* to the point where she had reason to believe it would be as groundbreaking for her generation of readers as Schreiner's *Story of an African Farm* had been to hers. At fourteen, when Doris Tayler had first read Schreiner's book, she had found solace and hope through sharing the other woman's experiences in the African veld. Now, at twenty-nine, she was on her way to repeating Schreiner's triumphant conquest of London. Surely, the identity Doris had sought for so long, the identity that would make Jean and John understand her leaving, lay before her. In England she would find herself through success as an author.

In Pursuit of a Future

The warning to young colonial women about the 'Black Peril' had continued into Doris Lessing's adulthood: Savage black men lay in wait for white girls and women, ready to rape and slay them. One true story she had never forgotten was often cited to vivify the danger. A black manservant in Lomagundi had brutally murdered his white female employer. Lessing remembered another, related experience from her childhood: Men were gathered on the veranda, gossiping about a white woman, new to the area, who permitted her houseboy to help her button her clothes and brush her hair. The idea was so shocking that it shut down any other conversation. 'The tones of their voices went into that book.'[1]

Doris Lessing's first novel, *The Grass Is Singing*, draws on these memories. Lessing also turned to T.S. Eliot's 'Waste Land' for her novel's title, as well as for an evocative epigraph that began:

> In this decayed hole among the mountains
> In the faint moonlight, the grass is singing

And ended:

> ... The jungle crouched, humped in silence.
> Then spoke the thunder

Another, uncredited epigraph deepens the sense that Lessing's characters are fated for despair and destruction: 'It is by the failures and misfits of a civilisation that one can best judge its weaknesses.'

The Grass Is Singing evokes the physical and emotional terrain that shaped the young woman who wrote it. Its themes are embryonic versions of those that appear in later work. It opens with a (fictional) newspaper account of the murder of a white woman by her male servant. An inventory of valuables has revealed no theft, and nothing in terms of motive can be got out of Moses, the houseboy, other than an impassive confession to the crime.

The colonial African farm community displays almost more antipathy toward the victim than toward her killer who, after all, as a black

1. Doris Lessing in her early London flat

2. Doris Lessing in her Charrington Street home.

3. A debonair Gottfried Lessing.
Location and date unknown.

4. Cecil Rhodes, lover of England
and complex ex-Premier of Cape
Colony.

5. Doris Lessing in her thirties.

6. Writing in London as a well-known author.

7. Gottfried Lessing and Peter Lessing in a London Park, 1949.

8. Gottfried Lessing and an aide from his East German office, attending a trade fair in Djakarta.

9. Doris Lessing outside her home on Charrington Street, revered as the author of The Golden Notebook (mid 1960s).

10. Doris Lessing's kitchen on Charrington Street, the source of scores of coveted meals for her friends.

11. Doris Lessing playing with her adored cats.

12. Bertrand Russell at a mass rally in Trafalgar Square in the early 1960s, during his leadership of the Committee of 100.

13. A rare moment of rest from his gruelling work in a South Rhodesian diamond mine. (Paul Hogarth)

14. An afternoon at the exclusive Rhodes Club in Salisbury, which the artist called 'the inner sanctum of the colonial regime.' (Paul Hogarth)

15. Jenny Diski in her twenties, early in a distinguished writing career.

16. R.D. Laing in 1975. Brilliant and quixotic psychiatrist, existentialist philosopher and author. Still enjoying the celebrity that began in the 1960s.

17. Clancy Sigal in Los Angeles, California, 1992.

18. Doris Lessing in 1999.

19. Doris Lessing wearing a fabulous assortment of rings.

could only be expected to break the rules of civilised behaviour. The farmers whisper among themselves that the murdered woman, Mary Turner, probably deserved her death. After the initial chapter announcing the murder and the community's response to it, the novel flashes back to tell the story that inexorably led Mary Turner through the years to her life's final scene.

Mary Turner was inspired by a woman Lessing met when she first moved to Salisbury. Fresh off the farm, she encountered for the first time people who rarely left the town for the country. One woman, when she did go on a picnic in the bush, tried to cover every part of her body so as to avoid being touched by some flying insect. Very likely thinking of her mother's unhappy life on the veld, Doris began to speculate, What if that squeamish woman had married a farmer? Would she too become overwhelmed with raging self-pity, and even lose her mental balance, in the prison of farm life?

Mary Turner didn't socialise with her neighbours; she had an explosive temper; she couldn't manage her servants. Far worse, Mary Turner allowed a level of familiarity between herself and Moses that was completely forbidden. Indeed, when he is apprehended, Moses is put in another car from Mary's corpse because 'one could not put a black man close to a white woman, even though she were dead, and murdered by him.'[2]

If the colour bar made her society one of rigid oppression, Mary was also an emotionally repressed woman. Her childhood was lived in an atmosphere of continual chaos. Her father drank heavily, while Mary's heart raced with the excitement of fear, and her mother watched in helpless contempt.

As Doris Tayler had done, Mary escaped the family farm as soon as she could, finding a job as a stenographer in a small town. After the agitation of her childhood, she welcomed the orderly routine. At her parents' death, she felt nothing but relief.

Mary takes up residence in a girls' club rather than live by herself. There she can have the sort of superficial companionship she prefers. No one really matters enough to upset her, yet the mere presence of the other young women offers distraction from buried thoughts that try to work their way up to consciousness. Her days pass in such unruffled routine that at thirty, she dresses and looks much younger than she is.

One day, however, she overhears herself being discussed by some acquaintances. Apparently, rather than admiring her youthful approach to life, people consider her 'odd.' Why does she dress so girlishly? Why is she still not married at her age? Why isn't she interested in men? Suddenly Mary feels not fresh and free but like a silly, ageing old maid. The tension that this new perspective creates sends her into the embrace of the first available man who crosses her path.

Not only does Mary not love Dick Turner, she despises his cherished

veld where he takes her to live, especially when she realises that his
passion for the land doesn't translate into the skills needed to farm it.
Dick is a kind man but, like Michael Tayler, he is also a dabbler and an
ineffectual dreamer.

Mary tries to run Dick's depressingly inadequate house, but her
heart is not in it. As the home on the failing farm grows more and more
run-down, Mary peers anxiously at her life and is unable to maintain
the barriers against memory. As she unwillingly remembers her past,
she confronts her despair. Realising that it is unbearable, she takes out
her rage and frustration on the black workers. She is much harsher
than Dick when she angrily supervises them. Once she strikes Moses
in the face with a whip. At the time of the murder, his cheek still bears
the scar. Mary feels no remorse for her abuse. She has always regarded
blacks in full stereotype.

Later, after a succession of failed domestic arrangements, Dick loses
patience and shifts Moses from outdoor work to houseboy, making clear
to Mary that he does not want her to dismiss Moses as she has all his
predecessors.

As Dick struggles hopelessly to make his farm succeed, Mary re-
treats inside herself to a private world of dreams and fantasy. She
becomes increasingly alienated, and despite her racist sentiments,
finds herself turning to Moses for attention. She allows him to brush
her hair and assist her in dressing. He even helps her into her bed to
rest.

Moses is calm and stoic and, Lessing points out in panting prose,
magnificently proportioned.

Mary Turner also saw her houseboy bathing, paralleling an experience Lessing had as a young girl. Maude had told her to summon a
servant, and when Doris found the man under a tree, she saw that he
was naked. Because of the inhibitions of the Tayler home, this was the
first time she had ever seen a naked adult male, most particularly, a
naked penis.

Lessing has Moses remind Mary of her father in ways that are deeply
alarming. Indeed, Moses's body becomes Mary's father's. 'They advanced together, one person, and she could smell, not the native smell,
but the unwashed smell of her father.'[3]

'Unwashed smell' is the same description Lessing applied to her own
father in *Under My Skin*. Mary also dreams of an unpleasant tickling
game with her father that strongly resembles the one described in that
memoir. Though there are significant differences between the fathers
in the novel and the memoir (there is no physical resemblance for
instance), Lessing is clearly using details from her own life as part of
the mix.

Once, when Mary breaks down and weeps in front of Moses, she feels
her remaining power over him fully ebbing, almost reversing. Moses

has become the symbol of her repressed fantasies, and Mary cannot continue to live in their presence. In a flash of anger, she turns on Moses and orders him out of the house – out of her life – and as she does so, she knows he will return to kill her.

Struck by this sense of preordained doom, Mary is left wondering what she had done to bring herself to this fateful night, and she has no answer. She has always been, and is now, helpless to shape her destiny.

Lessing returns to her epigraph as she brings her novel to its close. As night falls, Mary waits on the veranda for Moses to emerge from the bush and complete her fate.

* * *

In the novel's earlier drafts, Doris had concentrated on a character named Tony Marston, an English émigré to Rhodesia who arrives during the period of Mary's murder. Marston is representative of the idealistic young Englishmen who regularly came to Rhodesia – Lessing says most never stayed for more than a year – and were shocked by their first view of overt racism. They would dash around for a while, condemning what they observed, then would either leave or adopt the repellent values, often becoming more rigid than the people who had lived there for a lifetime.

The political disenchantment Lessing was feeling when she wrote the book coloured her portrait with disdain. Tony Marston held superficial notions of liberalism, supposedly progressive views toward the colour bar; Lessing believed that unless such convictions are deeply and genuinely rooted, they seldom win out over self-interest. Lessing reduced the importance of the Marston character in later drafts as she abandoned her vision of the novel as a satire about the white community in Rhodesia. She realised after writing it this way that it couldn't have worked well because she had never been away from colonial Africa, and it was her conviction that in order to write satire, you had to draw on comparisons to other cultures.

Lessing has been faulted by some critics for not making Moses a fully realised person. She defends herself by saying she was trying through this anonymity to show how white people really view blacks: as having very little individuality. If she had made him a distinct personality, the balance of the novel would have been quite changed – and it would have been a completely different story.

For Dick Turner, Lessing draws on an idea that harks back to her feelings about her father: namely, how corrupting a man's weakness can be for the women around him. Mary despised her husband for seeming so impotent, and her anger contributed to her emotional collapse.

As Mary's condition degenerates, she hallucinates that Moses is a

grotesque version of her father making incestuous assaults, thus dem-
onstrating her difficulty in separating the past from the present, the
real from the imagined. This merging of perceptions took root for Doris
Lessing in the African environment of her childhood, where reality and
illusion are not as easily separated as they are in the West. Lessing
grew up in a world where witch doctors coexisted with university-
trained physicians. Her father believed in divination to find gold. Evil
spirits, fetishes, and magic, good and bad, were common phenomena to
the young girl on the veld, and she never abandoned her acceptance of
their validity.

In 'No Witchcraft for Sale,' one of the African stories that followed on
the heels of *The Grass Is Singing*, Gideon, a black cook uses the leaves
of a plant to save the eyesight of his employer's only son when the child's
eyes are bitten by a snake. Hearing about the miracle cure, a famous
scientist comes from the city to investigate. The family is proud to be
able to help the doctor, but Gideon refuses to cooperate. Stubbornly, he
insists he does not remember which plant he used. Although he eventually pretends to look for the plant, all the whites soon understand that
the real one will not be found.

> The magical drug would remain where it was, unknown and useless
> except for the tiny scattering of Africans who had the knowledge ....[4]

In an interview with Studs Terkel in 1969, Doris Lessing talked about
the different possibilities of experiencing. She was convinced it would
eventually be recognised that there are multiple ways of seeing the
world which are not all rational, but are equally valid. What we now call
superstition can simply be an alternate mode of perception.

She also told Terkel she believed in people's capacity to tune into
another's thoughts. It is a faculty that can be cultivated with patience
when you are not intimidated by scientific doctrine, she said. The other
faculty she believes a great many people have is seeing a play of
pictures behind their eyelids, a skill that usually operates on a separate
time wave than ordinary time.

The disintegration of Mary Turner was a product of forces Lessing
herself had been struggling against throughout her life so far: an inner
void overcoming a firm sense of self, and an outer world of imbalanced
oppositions – parents and children, men and women, blacks and whites,
rational and mystical thought.

One of the most important parallels between Lessing and her first
novel's protagonist is their sense of alienation. Perhaps Mary is the
person Lessing was afraid of becoming, so fragmented, so cut off from a
firm sense of identity that she is not only incapable of connection to
anyone else, she is detached from herself. As with the Martha Quest
novels, the power of *The Grass Is Singing* is due in large part to

Lessing's willingness to explore such fearful questions. We see that the void inside Mary was suddenly filled by an unexpected and enormous terror.

Later in her life critics would suggest that Lessing was influenced by the Scottish psychiatrist R.D. Laing. While their paths would later cross, and their ideas intersect, *The Grass Is Singing* explores concepts Laing would not write about for another decade. Mary Turner experiences what Laing called 'engulfment,' or 'implosion,' a state of feeling empty and fearing the effects of other people and the external world. In *The Divided Self*, Laing writes:

> Implosion involves the full terror of the experience of the world as liable at any moment to crash in and obliterate all identity as a gas will rush in and obliterate a vacuum. The individual feels that, like the vacuum, he is empty. But this emptiness is him. Although in other ways he longs for the emptiness to be filled, he dreads the possibility of this happening because he has come to feel that all he can be is the awful nothingness of just this very vacuum. Any 'contact' with reality is then in itself experienced as a dreadful threat ... Reality, as such, threatening engulfment or implosion, is the persecutor.[5]

Reality requires choice and decisions; no such action is necessary, however, if one delivers one's emptiness to the fates.

* * *

Doris Lessing has written a detailed account of her early life in London in a book titled *In Pursuit of the English*. Its subtitle is 'A Documentary' but she most certainly added an element of fiction to the mix. Lessing herself has acknowledged this to some degree, in her memoir *Walking in the Shade*. And indeed there are some differences in the events described in the two books.

According to *In Pursuit of the English*, upon their arrival in London in 1949, Doris and Peter stayed at the flat of an Australian woman who also had a small child, an arrangement made through a mutual acquaintance. It was apparent almost immediately that the situation was not going to work out. The woman did not want Peter to play with her daughter, because the little girl was too delicate. The woman herself, although substantially built, depended on Doris to do all the shopping and cleaning. In spite of her powerful girth, the woman cultivated an air of helplessness that Doris knew would make any kind of mutuality in their relationship impossible. But in Lessing's memoir *Walking in the Shade*, the flatmate is South African and it is the presence of two prostitutes in the building that makes the situation untenable.

Doris began looking for another place to live. Eager as she was to settle down somewhere, she had an even more pressing matter to contend with: publication of her book in England. She was still worried about the contract she had signed with the South African publisher. Nonetheless, she allowed no thoughts of failure. She had been calling herself a writer for years. In small ways she had made the title fit her. Now it would really be hers, and the entire world would know her by it.

'Then Spoke the Thunder'

Lessing sent some of her short stories to the Curtis Brown literary agency, and received a letter back from one of their agents, Juliet O'Hea, asking whether she had a novel written. Lessing told her that while she did indeed have one, she had sold it to a publisher in South Africa. O'Hea asked to see the contract and was horrified at its inequities. She threatened the publisher with legal action if he held Lessing to the terms, and he let her go, whereupon O'Hea sold *The Grass Is Singing* to a solid publishing house, Michael Joseph.

While all this was going on, Lessing was growing more desperate about her living arrangements. She had to feel at least relatively settled in order to look for the job she needed until *The Grass Is Singing* brought in some money. She would not be able to count on Gottfried for much financial assistance when he arrived in London. He had no position waiting for him either, and she had no idea how long it would take him to find suitable work.

Placing Peter in a nursery school, Doris applied herself to the steadily more depressing task of looking for lodgings. For six weeks she trudged up and down London's drab, war-scarred streets, consulting a guidebook for directions to the next rooming possibility. When, as inevitably seemed to happen, the space she found had something drastically wrong with it, or was already taken, she'd search out the nearest telephone booth. In this much damaged city, a great many people appeared to depend on public phones. There might be an extended wait in the long queue outside a booth before she was able to place a call to the next possibility checked off in her newspaper. The process was making her anxious and increasingly wary of agents and landlords, so that when she should have been trying to make a pleasant impression, she often greeted them with hostility.

Lessing's principal companions during this period were others like herself, men and women who for one reason or another found themselves domestic refugees. They were all desperate to find a spot in which to settle down. Yet despite, or perhaps because of, their sense of urgency, they regularly gathered together in tea shops where they told each other this new brand of war story. 'We could no longer face another long walk, another set of dingy lodgings, another refusal. We could not

face seeing our fantasies about what we hoped to find diminished to
what we knew we would have to take,' she wrote in her 1961 account of
that period, *In Pursuit of the English*.[1]

Despite such bleak moments, this book, written eleven years after
the fact, is more amusing than bitter as Lessing describes her attempts
to enter London's physical and emotional landscape. But in other
recollections of hers, that initial stay in England seems an unexpected
and painful variant of the estrangement that always haunted her life.
Lessing, who had come to London chasing romance and success, seems
to have felt lost in this foreign city. 'When I was first in England I was
disturbed all the time in my deepest sense of probability,' she mused in
her account of her 1956 return visit to the well-known, much beloved
landscape of Rhodesia.'[2]

That she had needed to escape Salisbury, because it was inbred and
culturally uninteresting, because anyone who wanted to be in the arts,
especially writing, came to London, didn't make the move any easier.
Even in 1992, more than four decades after she first arrived in England,
she admitted, 'There are times when I am surrounded by my country-
men and women and I think I will never, ever be part of this. But,' she
adds, typically, 'it is a great pleasure to me just to sit on a bench in the
park or in a café and watch what is going on.'[3] One of the most painful
differences Lessing had to overcome was simply her physical environment. London seemed horribly grey compared to the bright light and
intense colours of Africa.

Finding a place to live had become so consuming that Lessing asked
almost every person she met if he or she could expedite her quest. One
day, a laconic young woman who worked in a jeweller's shop where
Lessing had taken her watch to be repaired mentioned that there were
rooms to rent in the house she lived in. She invited Lessing to accompany her home so she might inspect the space and talk with the
landlords.

On the way they walked through acres of depressing debris. Matter-
of-factly, the girl explained that the damage was caused by bombs.
Pieces of what once were walls stuck up out of the rubble. Suddenly, in
the middle of the terrible waste, Lessing 'heard a sound which reminded
me of a cricket chirping with quiet persistence from sun-warmed
grasses in the veld.'[4]

Ironically, the sound that had brought a welcome vision of home to
her mind was coming from a typewriter. A man was sitting on a pile of
rubble and using a particularly large fragment as a makeshift table. If
such a scene was actually witnessed by Doris Lessing, it must have
seemed like a powerful omen considering her chosen career.

Finally, Doris and the girl she calls Rose arrived at a tall, narrow
house behind a loose wooden gate on Denbigh Road in the Westminster
section of London.

Memory flooded again. The wooden gate was moist and between the boards was a porous material that she remembered from Africa growing within a decaying tree. There was very little light in the hallway she entered with Rose. A stairway ascended in front of her, equally dark, ending at a closed door. But the landlady, named Flo in *The Pursuit of the English*, tempered her avidity with blustering warmth and her husband, Dan, whose sideline was stripping washbasins and baths from bombed houses and selling them to people rebuilding their own ravaged homes, was a hearty fellow, good-humouredly flirtatious toward his female boarders.

The rest of the lodgers were a mix of working-class Londoners who provided more than their fair share of action, some of it quite entertaining to Lessing. Love, hate, battles and reconciliations went on ceaselessly in the shabby, bomb-damaged house this motley group called home.

Lessing made friends with Rose and Flo, enjoying without condescension the differences in perspective between their working-class and her middle-class background. Lessing's curiosity about and concern for these people who lived at the lower end of the social ladder were natural outgrowths of her Rhodesian activities. When she observed her neighbours doing physical work for minimal wages, she could remember both her efforts on behalf of blacks and the ideology of her Communist mentors, who believed that truth lay in the minds and words of the working class.

Rose, however, was totally uninterested in Lessing's radical rhetoric. No matter who got elected, Labour or Tory, she didn't expect her life to get any better. Lessing observed that many of the workers she saw around London manifested the same sort of passive defiance she'd seen among Rhodesian blacks. Three white labourers invaded her room for a month to do repairs her landlady had ordered. The work could have been accomplished in a fraction of that time. The men's presence stole precious hours from Lessing's writing, but her irritation was softened by the memories of home their indolent behaviour evoked.

When one man took four days to replace two panes of glass in her French windows, instead of being angry she grew sentimentally nostalgic for the highly developed lethargy of African workers. She could see a black African farmhand in the Englishman's stead, ordered to plant some flowers. He ambles out to the land, making sluggish strikes at the ground with his hoe. There is a long pause before he brings the instrument up again and lets it drop once more. Then he stands silently, looking around, work, such it was, interrupted by his thoughts. In Lessing's ears ring angry shouts coming from the farmer's house. But the worker she recalls never seems to hear it. 'By the end of the day he has achieved the minimum amount of work.'[5]

Later, over tea, Lessing listens to the workman explain how the slow pace is a conscious response to the low wages and harsh life he endures as a member of part of the English working class.

This type of listening sets *In Pursuit of the English* off from other Lessing books in which she appears as herself, or through a surrogate such as Martha Quest, or Anna Wulf. The heroine of *In Pursuit of the English* does not strip away the conversational surface to expose the truth that lies underneath. Instead, she is a bemused observer whose subjects speak for themselves and frequently say things she could not anticipate. When Lessing asks another woman resident who makes her living as a prostitute if she ever enjoys sex, the woman responds irritatedly: 'If you're going to talk dirty, I'm not interested.'[6] The ironic humour in that exchange permeates the book, presenting a different side of Lessing from those in her other works.

* * *

Settled into their new home, Lessing transferred Peter to a private nursery, and looked for work herself, as a typist. Although Michael Joseph had paid her 150 pounds as an advance on *The Grass Is Singing*, she felt she had to get a job. London was a great deal more expensive than Salisbury.

Her days were long and exhausting. Peter, already an intensely active child who needed little sleep, was happily stimulated by the boardinghouse atmosphere. He would awake at five in the morning, and not go to bed until nearly ten P.M. She'd get up with him in the morning, give him some breakfast, take him to his nursery school, then go to work.

Gottfried Lessing arrived in London around the same time as their Salisbury comrade Dorothy Schwartz, who let him have one of the rooms in the apartment she rented. To his surprise, he could not find decent work. Then he suffered an attack of jaundice which kept him from job hunting and contributed to his flagging spirits.

It was not a good time for a German and a Communist to gain employment in a British organisation. For several months, Gottfried primarily filled his days working for the Society for Cultural Relations with the Soviet Union. For some unexplained reason – perhaps his emotional fatigue – he did not join the British Communist party for six months, although Schwartz did so almost immediately, and said that Doris also joined shortly after her arrival.

When he did join, however, Gottfried was an active member, and spent a great deal of his time in Party work. However, he worked mostly on his own, from his room, and so began to feel increasingly isolated and, without a decent salary, demoralised, personally and profession-ally. In a letter Schwartz lamented that he was 'fine material that had been trampled on. He had to be helped to find his feet, he had to be encouraged, he had to have his morale and self-respect restored.'

According to Schwartz's account of the period, Gottfried 'went back to Tigger on more than one occasion,' but Schwartz seems to think his ex-wife did not satisfy any of these needs.

These reunions were obviously abortive. Doris was actively involved with other men. On one occasion she left Peter with Gottfried and impulsively took off to Paris for a romantic fling with another émigré. Later in her life, when she looked back at Peter's childhood, she realised that his ever present needs saved her from dissipating her talents. Post-war London was a city whose morality was crumbling like its mortar. The writer John Mortimer tells of suddenly seeing used condoms littering streets, a symbol of the sexual abandon that seemed to pervade the atmosphere. The men were ready to consume young women like herself as if they were candy, and at the time Doris Lessing felt drawn to the hedonistic atmosphere of mid-century London that was headquartered in Soho. But with the burden of a small child it was simply impossible to embrace it fully.

Doris Lessing is not someone who bares her personal doubts in public. But in one interview given to a Spanish publication called *La Calle* she reflected on the difficulties of single parenthood, stressing that aspect of her parenting as an example of how the requirements of parent and child can run counter to each other. Children want a traditional relationship with their parents and an established routine in the family, Lessing says, and she advises parents who can't provide these resources not to have children, 'because the only thing they get, if they have them, their problem children, is mental turmoil, much sadness.' She adds that children who are raised by only one parent 'suffer indescribably.'[7]

Lessing's most reliable way of experiencing the freedom she craved was through Gottfried. Peter came to the flat Gottfried shared with Dorothy Schwartz nearly every weekend. 'In addition,' Schwartz wrote to a friend, Gottfried 'went there on at least two or three evenings during the week to look after him, and always, or nearly always, at 'madam's' bidding. Various other arrangements were made to suit Tigger as well.'

In *Under My Skin*, Doris Lessing suggests that Gottfried genuinely wanted continue to spend time with Peter, something that Gottfried's family and even Dorothy Schwartz attest to. Still, his frustration with life in London steadily increased, and as it did so, Germany began to loom large in his imagination. He obtained a visa to visit his sister and when he came back to London, it was to announce that he was going to return to Berlin as soon as possible. The wall between East and West Germany had not yet been erected, so he was able during his stay to visit his family house, where he was overwhelmed with memories.

Gottfried found the country of his youth exhilarating, and filled with hope. Out of a mix of idealism and homesickness, he became more animated and excited than he had been for months, afire with the idea of building on Germany's ruins. He would help construct the new Communist East Germany, a just and wonderful land.

After returning to London Gottfried applied for East German citizenship and prepared to return to his homeland. But when he received no response to his enthusiasm turned into intense frustration. Although he would have preferred straightforward reinstatement, he employed what he saw as an unpalatable but necessary subterfuge, and applied again for a temporary visitor's visa. Once in Berlin, he hoped to gain citizenship through his relatives, who were considered loyal and important German Communists.

Doris Lessing writes that she was frightened when Gottfried asked her to move with him to Germany. It had never occurred to her that their relationship would continue after their divorce except for meetings over their child, and she refused to go with him. On the day Gottfried left, she and Peter and Dorothy Schwartz saw him off at the railroad station. Gottfried had promised that Peter could come and visit him, although there were rumours that such visits from the West were not easy to arrange. In any case, now that he was gone, the full weight of child care would rest with Doris. Though she would soon have a boost that most single mothers only dream about – the reception for *The Grass Is Singing*.

* * *

'Outstanding,' 'remarkable,' 'astonishing' were adjectives that piled up alongside her name in reviews and newspaper articles, puzzling her boardinghouse neighbours. In the *New Statesman and Nation* of April 1, 1950, Antonia White wrote:

> It would be easy to write pages about *The Grass Is Singing* which besides being very well-written is an extremely mature psychological study. It is full of those terrifying touches of truth, seldom mentioned but instantly recognised. By any standards, this book shows remarkable power and imagination. As a first novel by a woman barely turned thirty, it excites great interest in her future.[8]

It was a propitious time for the novel to be published in England. The war had started a cultural and social upheaval, as well as a political one, and interest in new talent was keen. The subject of colonialism and class was as always fascinating to the British, particularly when it was linked in this book to an aspect they knew very little about: the abuses of apartheid.

The novel went into seven printings within five months. Lessing is modest about its success, saying that Alan Paton's novel *Cry, the Beloved Country* 'had just come out, and then came mine. I was just extremely lucky in my timing.'[9] She was so inexperienced then, and had so many troubles, that when the publishers called to tell her they had gone into another printing she took the news extremely casually. She imagines they thought she was being unduly blasé, but she really had no idea how remarkable a reception this was for a first novel.

Continued printings through the 1970s in England and throughout the world have made *The Grass Is Singing* one of Lessing's most successful books. But in 1950, money continued to be a serious problem. When she had planned her exodus to England, and anticipated her literary reception, she had imagined she would immediately be able to live on what she earned as a writer. It was shocking to face the reality of the writer's life. Nonetheless, she had no patience with indulging in self-pity.

Lessing recalls an incident after the reviews came out when everyone assumed she would naturally be ecstatically happy. One day, she went for a walk in her neighbourhood, and much to her surprise, she found herself weeping. She told a BBC interviewer that she was suddenly upset by being so short of funds. A man stopped her to ask her the source of her tears. When he heard about her lack of money he brusquely assured her everything would work out, that she would get some money the following week. Lessing's interviewer was appalled that the man hadn't offered her some money there and then. To which Lessing serenely responded that his attitude was exactly what she needed.

24

The Battle of Berlin

After *The Grass Is Singing* was published, Lessing's life expanded. She made new friends, some of whom would look after Peter and allow her to see the city after her day's work was done. Night time was probably the best way to see post-war London as the darkness covered up dingy decay. When she did find a babysitter, she would set off into the fog, marvelling at the way the light shimmered on the swirls of smoke. In a 1994 newspaper interview, she recalled 'the pleasure' of those walks and noted that 'London lost a lot of drama when they passed the Clean Air Act.'[1]

She also revelled in the city's cultural life. According to a 1950 newspaper article before Lessing arrived in London, she had never been to a concert or an art gallery, and aside from a road company of *Oklahoma*, the only theatre she had seen was provided by Salisbury's local amateur groups. It was thus extraordinary to visit the Old Vic, for example, where she was surprised by the raucous approach to Shakespearean humour.

Despite the strain the decision would put on her already meagre budget, Lessing quit her secretarial job when she received a contract and a modest new advance from Michael Joseph for a book of short stories. She was determinedly resourceful about making her money last and about finding ways to bring in some more. She reports that a prostitute who briefly shared her rooming house tried to give her some helpful advice, contrasting the risks of Lessing's occupation with her own secure profession: Even if a writer wasn't dependent on a job from which she could be fired, she could always hit a dry spell and have no one interested in buying her books. It was much more reliable to turn her own flat into a steady source of income. When Lessing politely replied that she really didn't think she was cut out for the work, her neighbour did not mask her irritation. 'You're a romantic,' she scoffed. 'That's your trouble. Well, I've no patience with those.'[2]

In the end, Lessing sold her clothing rather than her body, taking to the secondhand shop the evening dresses that had brightened her African nights. She didn't go dancing in London, so it seemed reasonable to trade the gowns for cash and get on with her writing. The meals she made for Peter and herself consisted largely of tinned soups and bread, supplemented for her by endless cups of hot tea and scores of cigarettes, and they were frequently invited to dine at Flo's rooming house table even though the rent didn't include meals. New clothes were completely out of the question for either mother or son.

What she heard from Gottfried about his ability to help out financially was not encouraging. As soon as he had arrived in East Berlin, he had petitioned to join the organisation Persecuted of the Nazi Regime (*Verfolgter des Nazi Regimes*), because he had been forced to emigrate from Germany and lost everything. Gaining this recognition would have given him credibility with East German authorities. However, his claim was refused and his Communist Party credentials were carefully scrutinised. Until they were accepted, he was not allowed to join the Socialist Unity Party (SED), which had been formed in 1946 by merging the Communists and Social Democrats.

The Communists who returned to East Germany after the war were roughly divided into two groups: those emigrants who had lived in the USSR and those who had been exiled in the 'West.' What Gottfried discovered was that the returnees from the Soviet Union were to a large degree Stalinists. They had survived the purges of the Communist ranks in the USSR because of their single-minded devotion to Stalin, and were tightly organised under the leadership of Walter Ulbricht.

The emigrants from the 'West' – Western Europe, South America – who returned in small numbers over the first post-war years were viewed with suspicion by the Ulbricht group. Until 1948, there had been a democratic atmosphere in the party, but from 1948 onward, the Stalinisation of the SED began in earnest. The party was 'cleaned' of 'unreliable elements,' many of them old Communists and Social Democrats. Suspicion, mistrust, and fear spread throughout the party, and for many became the main tenor of its existence.

When Gottfried returned to East Germany, these processes were already apparent, which accounts for his cool reception. His delay in being accepted into the SED – he was finally admitted in the second half of 1951 – and the fact that he never reached the heights his intelligence and commitment would have enabled him to achieve were typical of the suspicious attitudes generally applied to this group of returning comrades. For the better part of the period from his return to Germany in 1950 until he was accepted into the SED, Gottfried could not find full-time employment in or outside of government. Through his brother-in-law, Klaus Gysi, he did receive some freelance work for a publishing house owned by the communist Kulturbund, Aufban-Verlag, where Gysi was the managing director, but his income did not allow for child support contributions.

Undeterred, Doris was putting together a collection of Africa-based short stories as her next book. The more she wrote, the more she needed to keep writing, no matter what the financial strain. Much as she hated asking for money, she wrote to her Salisbury comrade Nathan Zelter to ask for a loan and he quickly responded with a hundred pounds.

She pulled her purse strings even tighter, spending less money on entertainment for herself and special treats for Peter. But all the while, she was certain that such self-denial was only temporary. One day she would have everything she needed or wanted. All she had to do was continue writing in explosive bursts of at least seven thousand words a day.

* * *

The rooming house where Doris Lessing and Peter had been living for a year was now scheduled to be repaired by the government's War Damage agency. After the structural work was finished, Flo and her husband began renovating the rooms, with the goal of asking considerably more rent from tenants. It was this plan that sent Lessing once again looking for living quarters. Except for the loss of writing time, the idea of moving did not bother her. As Flo put it to the other tenants during a farewell dinner – they would miss their strange intellectual friend – 'She has to go some time, it stands to reason. The way I look at it, some people have an itch in their feet, that moves them on from place to place.'[3]

Doris Lessing would agree. Even though she has lived in her current home for decades, she has always been 'a tent-dweller at heart ... I was never meant to settle.'[4] And some twenty years after leaving the rooming house, she told another interviewer, 'I don't quite know why ... surroundings don't seem to have much importance for me.' When it was pointed out that her novels are filled with minute descriptions of surroundings, she was briefly surprised, but after a moment agreed that in terms of her writing, place did matter to her very much. Waving her hand around the room she was receiving her visitor in, she mused, 'I suppose I'll write about ... this with passionate detail some day. Now I hardly notice it.'[5]

At a party in London given by the brother of a Southern Rhodesian farmer in the summer of 1950, Doris Lessing met Joan Rodker. At first she thought Joan was from France, dressed as she was in a white blouse, black skirt, and 'a cheeky black beret.'[6] But she was English, the daughter of a highly respected man of letters, John Rodker. Besides writing his own poetry, he headed a radically independent publishing house, The Imago Press, before and after the First World War. During his career, he published the works of T.S. Eliot, Ezra Pound, and James Joyce, among other 'moderns,' and his publishing house also issued the complete works of Sigmund Freud and the psychoanalytical writings of Marie Bonaparte.

Joan Rodker was an active Communist, a former actress, a woman with many talents who knew scores of people in politics and the arts. She was also a single mother of a son several years older than Peter. As such, she sympathised with Doris's housing problems which reminded her of her own troubles in New York a few years earlier. A friend had bailed her out by renting out an apartment in her house and Joan liked the idea of repaying the kindness by helping another young woman. After Joan gave the boot to a top-floor tenant she had become unhappy with, Doris and Peter moved in.

Joan Rodker liked Peter and she and Doris Lessing swiftly became inseparable friends. Lessing dedicated her 1957 collection of short stories, *The Habit of Loving*, 'To my friend Joan Rodker,' and modelled Anna Wulf's friend Molly in *The Golden Notebook* on her. Their relationship is also reflected in a few Lessing stories that show how women friends try to find relief from turbulence of male-female relationships.

Peter, now nearly four years old, was immediately very happy at Joan Rodker's house, but neither his sleeping pattern nor his energy level changed. He woke at 5 am and his mother would entertain him in her bed with stories and games, for Rodker's bedroom was right below their rooms, and Lessing was afraid she would be wakened if Peter ran around playing by himself. Lessing also had him listen to the radio turned low, dramatisations of adult plays that she believed held his attention despite his age. It is Lessing's opinion that until they reach about the age of seven, children are capable of understanding as much or more than most adults. After seven, they lose this capacity and have all the adult limitations on intellect and perception. 'At three or four, Peter understood everything, and at eight or nine read only comics.'[7]

Doris Lessing writes herself out of places and phases of her life. She would do this with feminism, with Communism, to a degree with male-female relationships. Part of her annoyance with being labelled as a writer about race relations, a feminist writer, or any other attempt at categorisation, is that by the time she has written her book, she is often no longer connected to its subject matter. Africa is the exception to this rule, since it remains part of her emotional inner life.

As Lessing sat writing in her new flat up under the eaves of Joan Rodker's house in Kensington, in the country that had launched her parents' exile, she reversed her recent journey, to return to the people, black and white, who would shape her stories – and thus allow her to better understand how they had shaped her life.

* * *

After Gottfried Lessing was admitted to the SED, he became actively involved in creating and leading the East German Committee for the Promotion of World Trade. This organisation then became the Chamber of Foreign Trade (Kammer für Aussenhandel), and Gottfried was its president from 1952 until 1957. At that time East Germany was not diplomatically recognised internationally, so that the Chamber carried out the functions of establishing foreign trade relations and foreign contacts. It served as a kind of political ministry of foreign affairs. 'I think,' said someone who knew Gottfried at the time, 'that almost single-handedly he formed the relationships with all the other countries, east or west. This was a relatively high-powered and certainly a very responsible position.'

In 1951, Gottfried invited Peter to come stay with him for the summer. Doris Lessing writes that she had some misgivings about sending a four-year-old child away for two months, but she felt there was no reason to distrust Gottfried's motives and agreed to the visit. Besides, it meant she would be free for eight wonderful weeks to write as long as she wanted to and follow her impulse for amusement wherever it took her.

Irene and Klaus Gysi remember Peter's stay as extremely pleasant, and found their British-speaking nephew an engaging little boy. When he returned to his mother, he was speaking German instead of English, but within a few weeks he dropped this vestige of his father's influence. When he arrived home – details of who supervised his journey are not clear – he carried with him a letter from Gottfried saying he would like the visit repeated every summer. 'And then – nothing, silence,' Doris Lessing writes. All contact ceased, and Peter cried himself to sleep over the break.[8]

Perhaps Doris Lessing recalled her own helplessness in the face of adult decisions that had nothing to do with her needs or wishes. In any case, she was outraged on Peter's behalf. She travelled to Berlin to investigate.

Her calls to Gottfried's office went unanswered and so after making it clear through an East German publishing emissary that she insisted on seeing him, she met Gottfried at his sister Irene's stylish new flat. Both Irene and Gottfried looked prosperous and untroubled. Gottfried was airily casual about her requests on Peter's behalf, completely ignoring the gravity of the situation. Only years later did Doris Lessing wonder whether perhaps Gottfried was afraid for his career, or even for his life, that some threat from above had influenced his cutting himself off from his son.

There is reason to believe that her belated assessment was an accurate one. As one intimate of Gottfried's family explained, 'Gottfried's generation of Communist adhered to Party discipline. The Party was always right. There was actually a song that was sung at any East German gathering, 'The Party, the Party, the Party is always right ....' As long as Stalinism ruled, even after his death in 1953, you weren't supposed to have contact with the West.' 'Gottfried believed that history followed its own rules,' another friend says, 'and the Party was just the representation of the iron laws of history. People like Gotti really believed in that. He was very intelligent, brilliant in many ways, but he was not scholarly in the sense of having a questioning mind, and no matter how high up he rose, there was really no free access to information. He was a conduit for the government, and there were always all these guys on the top controlling things.'

Some people believe that for a brief period, largely for Peter's sake, Doris Lessing considered moving to Germany, and that one reason for her visit to see Gottfried was to make up her mind about whether she could live there. It is, however, difficult to imagine her adapting to the oppressive political atmosphere of post-war Germany, even if she had not become so angry at Gottfried's behaviour.

That she perhaps cared more for Gottfried than she allows is another suspicion of some friends who knew her during this period. They point to her memoir and various interviews to substantiate their view. One says, 'The reason he appears in her writing again and again in whatever way means that he meant something to her … after all, her first husband disappears off the pages. And, remember too, she chose to keep his name.' Another friend reflects on Doris Lessing's extreme curiosity about Gottfried's two subsequent wives. 'I simply don't believe that level of interest is devoted to a man you have no feeling for.'

Whatever the truth of this, over the years Doris Lessing has occasionally reversed her antipathy toward Gottfried and has even seemed to share his affection for his homeland. In 1982, she was awarded the Shakespeare Prize in Hamburg, West Germany. Gregor Gysi, Irene's son and Gottfried's nephew, who was extremely important in East German Communist circles, was in the audience when she made her acceptance remarks. Never one to play up to an audience, she seemed genuine when she spoke of life with her then ex-husband during the war. She explained that because of Gottfried's homesickness, and his anguished concern for Germany, she had always felt a special relationship to the country that was giving her this prize, and that Gottfried had always believed the Germany he loved would be reborn. She also recalled how he had given her books by Thomas Mann to read when the war was still on. She doubted that many people were reading Mann as passionately as she was, she said, nor finding in it such a genuine source of home. She was trying to believe in Mann's spirit of empathy, humanity, and generosity. During the week that the Allies were destroying Hamburg with bombs, she was reading Mann and reflecting on the city and other great cities like it on both sides who were undergoing such agony.

Doris Lessing finished her talk by saying that along with her affection for Germany, she had some other feelings that she also borrowed from Mann. Her thoughts about the country were sometimes puzzling, intricate, and ambivalent.[9] This is a description that seems to go beyond her attitude toward Germany, and apply to her relationship with Gottfried; more important, as reflecting the ongoing contradictions of her emotional life.

Among the Believers

Doris Lessing's second book, *This Was the Old Chief's Country*, published in 1951, did not disappoint the readers and reviewers who had been
so impressed by *The Grass Is Singing*. The collection of ten short stories
set in Africa clearly reaffirmed her talent. This was a young writer who
deserved significant attention, something, explains the writer Elaine
Dundy, who knew Lessing in England, that the English were particularly ready to provide. 'England has always been very generous and
hospitable to new talent,' she says. 'They dislike professional slickness,
and love finding amateurs who have something new to say.'

There is little question that in these ten stories, Lessing presented a
fresh perspective on the fierce contrasts of colonial life: great wealth and
grinding poverty, endless labour and ceaseless boredom, astonishing
beauty and horrifying brutality. In an introduction to *African Stories*
(1964), which combined *This Was the Old Chief's Country*, four longer
stories that were published in *Five: Short Novels* (1953), plus stories
from *The Habit of Loving* (1957) and *A Man and Two Women* (1963),
Lessing recalls that when she wrote her first African books, reviewers
all concentrated predictably on 'the colour problem.'

A reviewer of *This Was the Old Chief's Country* saw in her exposure
of racism an admirable 'seriousness of purpose.' Over the years Lessing
has often been irritated with critics who call her writing style sombre.
She recognises, however – with some frustration – that when racism is
one of a story's themes, not only will it dominate attention, it usually
requires a solemn voice.

Lessing's own two favourites among her stories set in Africa reflect
her unhappiness over the way writing about the colour bar limited her
literary scope. These stories go beyond this theme, mirroring some of
her deepest emotional concerns, such as the knowledge that nature will
always win out over human desire. As 'A Sunrise on the Veld' opens, a
fifteen-year-old settler boy awakens in his bed before dawn. He is going
hunting, and anticipation of the kill mingles with pride of his body. He
'stretched his limbs, feeling the muscles tighten, and thought: Even my
brain – even that! I can control every part of myself.'[1]

Like Doris Tayler when adolescence released her from the restrictions of childhood, the boy rejoices in the idea of being on the brink of

manhood. Like generations of young men before him, he feels a surge
of power in his own potential. He will become anything he sets his mind
to, accomplish heroic feats, travel the world and make it a wondrous
place of his own design. Nothing will be allowed to stand in his way.

In the midst of his exultation, he hears a dreadful noise, a scream of
pain. A small buck, crippled with a broken leg, is being eaten alive by a
swarm of huge black ants. The boy thinks about shooting the animal to
end its misery, but before he can bring himself to pull the trigger he
realises that the deer is past feeling. He suddenly realises, and the
thought is punishing, that life may end randomly, in brutal agony.

The boy holds tightly to his gun, and feels for a terrible moment that
he is the dying, twitching animal. Then he watches the animal being
devoured, and grits his teeth, knowing that he was not powerful at all,
but utterly helpless to alter the terrible scene.

The other of Lessing's favourites is 'Winter in July.' In this tale of a
middle-aged woman who lives with her husband and his half-brother,
the veld's isolation both nurtures and exacerbates a person's inherent
lack of connection. Julia looks back at her youth as being alarmingly
rootless. She was considered brilliant and attractive; she had no short-
age of admiring men in her life. Many of them became her lovers – for
she lived almost as freely as a man – but she was unwilling to commit
herself.

Taking stock at twenty-eight, she though about her random moves
between jobs and men and apartments and even countries. 'She said to
herself that she was getting hard; yet she was not hard; she was
numbed and tired.'[2] In the midst of her ennui, she met two brothers,
Tom and Kenneth. She flirted with Kenneth, but was moved by Tom's
kindness and married him. When war came, Tom enlisted; Kenneth
was exempt from service because of weak lungs. Tom's absence awakened Julia's old feelings of uncertain identity. She realised that she had
not found identity in marriage; it had not provided her with a sense of
purpose and self. Nor has Africa made her feel grounded, even though
it was a country she had grown to love.

During the three years that Tom was away, Julia drifted into an
affair with Kenneth. They both missed Tom and 'they mistrusted the
destructive nihilism that they had in common.'[3] When Tom returned,
he was clearly aware of what had happened in his absence. But no one
dealt with emotions directly.

One July Kenneth tells them he is going to marry. Julia is swept
through with loneliness. July in Rhodesia is a winter month, the wind
is high, the nights are cold. During the day, Julia roams the still
beautiful veld, suffering from a feeling of intense dislocation. She feels
nothing and gives nothing to the life around her.

Later, as Julia anticipates meeting Kenneth's intended bride, she thinks finally that it is dreadful to not be able to articulate 'what we feel or what we are.'[4]

* * *

Although Lessing did write on topics other than racism, for the next decade, as she explored her African past in her books, this early identification as a writer on the colour bar – or, as she quoted a reviewer as calling it, 'the colour bore' – remained.[5] Her name was becoming well enough known for editors to send to her books to review, but invariably they were books about racism.

She had been categorised as a writer on apartheid, and while she had much to say on the subject, she resented being constrained within those boundaries. In the mid-sixties when a radio interviewer, Richard Kaufman brought up the name of James Baldwin, whose passionate attacks on racism were highly controversial at the time, she made some comments that seemed to reflect her own experience with the subject. Of Baldwin, she said, 'He's a fine man and a fine writer.' But, 'he's got all these labels stuck on him right now and he's going to find that a terrible handicap as an artist.'[6]

Through the 1950s Lessing continued to be engaged in the battle against British colonialism. There is much dispute about how political a person Lessing was in general, and in particular, how active she was in leftist politics once she arrived in England. One matter is clear, however. She remained committed to working against the effects and policies of colonialist government. In 1994, when asked by a reporter from the *London Observer* whether she believed she had influenced the world in some way, Lessing answered modestly, but firmly, 'Yes, I have had a small influence. Not enormous.' She gave herself some credit for altering the way men regard women, and was certain that 'I was one of the people who changed attitudes about what was going on in southern Africa.'[7]

In her introduction to *African Stories*, Lessing noted England's shock at what she already revealed about the colour bar in her first two books. 'Britain, who is responsible, became conscious of her responsibility too late; and now the tragedy must play itself slowly out.'[8]

Peter Worsley, an African scholar, recalled Lessing's accompanying him on a couple of occasions when he gave talks about colonialism. 'She did not speak as a social theorist,' he says, 'but simply as a literate woman on the left, who could talk about what kind of society Rhodesia was, what kind of culture it was. She could describe the living conditions very vividly, people living in shantytowns, matchbox houses. She didn't say anything ninety-nine out of a hundred other commentators wouldn't have said, although it certainly helped stir interest that she was both a white woman, and already a well-known writer.'

One of Lessing's comrades in the Communist Party, also a writer, who did see her as quite political, believes that the central element for her involvement with the Party was that 'to their credit it was absolutely foremost in fighting imperialist policy and apartheid. They weren't alone,' this colleague acknowledges. 'The left of the Labour Party and Christian groups and so on were also battling these issues. But the Communist Party really was the only party that was four square behind the issue of colonial liberation.' But committed though she was to fighting colonialist policy, Lessing engaged in Communist activities primarily as a writer. 'She wasn't a Party person in an organised, historical sense,' says the writer Stuart Hall. 'She always spoke as a writer first. She would write something about an issue rather than engage in planning or direct action.'

Her comrade on the *Going Home* journey Paul Hogarth recalls participating with Lessing in a cultural conference called by the Party leadership in London, in the early 1950s. 'She gave a very good speech ... She talked about problems of living in England and having a writing career. A lot of the writers and intellectuals at the conference applauded her, but her words weren't well received by the chairman of the conference. He thought it was the sort of speech that would be better at a writer's conference, not for a conference where aspiring housewives from the working classes had been invited.

'It was interesting for me personally as an artist,' Hogarth says, 'for it sort of reflected the gap between the Party's intelligentsia and the members of an organisation of that kind.' The gap became very clear as person after person got up to protest, in effect saying, 'It's all very well for you educated women,' an irony – but one no less distressing for this champion of the working class – considering that Lessing had probably left school at the same age they had or even younger.

Hogarth remembers Lessing as being shaken by the antagonism in the room, coming from both the participants and the leadership. Like many others who have heard her speak over the years, he found it difficult to decide whether her apparent insensitivity to her audience's expectations was conscious or simply an inability to recognise and empathise with other people's needs. 'The British Communist Party was really very insular, in a sense, when I look back on it,' Paul Hogarth says. 'It was a conspiratorial organisation. I think the Party principals were absolutely flabbergasted that it became an influential political party ... they hadn't bargained on it at all. They were uncomfortable with us who were articulate, even with someone like myself who had been a member since I was a student.'

Doris Lessing's future lover, Clancy Sigal would see her eventual break with Communism as primarily stemming from its unenlightened stance toward artists. He remembers her telling him to be careful when he was combining leftist politics with fledgling literary pursuits. The old left was miserable to writers and the New Left was likely to be the same, she said.

In 1952 Lessing was still a Party sympathiser, enough so that she welcomed the opportunity to join a group of six writers on a trip to the Soviet Union under the auspices of the Authors World Peace Appeal. The other writers were Naomi Mitchison, a novelist who, along with Alex Comfort, future author of *The Joy of Sex*, was one of the founders of the Authors World Peace organisation; a writer named Douglas Young who had the advantage of speaking Russian; Arnold Kettle, a prominent Marxist literary critic; a short story writer, A.E. Coppard; and another novelist, Richard Mason.

The group's mission was to convene with Soviet writers and discuss what they could do to lessen international tension. There was hope for candid exploration of how writers worked in both the USSR and England. Of particular interest was the concept of the writer's individual freedom, a premise the Russians did not adhere to.

The visitors were taken around Russia in between meetings, and one day in Moscow they stopped at a building where the enormous number of gifts presented to Stalin were displayed. From articles of clothing, to hand-sewn rugs, to paintings, Lessing was surrounded with symbols of Stalin's cult of personality. The ludicrously ugly art is described in *Walking in the Shade* along with other recollections of how the grotesque atmosphere of the Stalinist regime permeated the day-to-day experiences of the trip. These memories suggest that Lessing's political ideology in no way short-circuited her critical facilities – she would not be able to recall the paranoia, ugliness, and sinister hypocrisies of Stalinist society in such detail, had she not noted them at the time. In *Walking in the Shade*, Lessing also describes the British group's internal politics and her reactions to sights, such as Tolstoy's house. In all it is, however, a peculiarly passionless account. And it's difficult to understand how someone who spent almost all of her adult life up to that point, actively committed to the communist struggle, would not have a stronger emotional reaction to visiting Russia in 1952. Mixed emotions can be as powerful as pure ones, but here there seem to be hardly any emotions at all. Lessing's description of Russia doesn't read like one of Mecca written by a lapsed believer. Rather, it seems to be the work of a lifelong agnostic.

This was hardly the case. Lessing received her Communist Party card when she returned to Britain. And whatever her misgivings about the society she encountered, Lessing was still influenced by ideas she absorbed on her Russian trip. Indeed, she attributes the creation of a short story, 'Hunger,' to some reflections she had in Moscow about the way Russian Communist colleagues viewed literature.

They believed in a much simpler approach to writing, uncomplicated moral concepts, with clear demarcations of right and wrong. Although along with her British colleagues, she had been arguing against such simplistic thinking, now she thought about an author like Dickens, whom she believed to be a great writer. He wrote in that moralistic vein where good characters were saintly and bad ones villainous.

Coming from a country with social divisions as inequitable as any Dickens wrote about in England, she too could write a story with clearly honourable and dishonourable characters interacting. 'Hunger' became a favourite of readers and, although Lessing herself considered it unsuccessful, she won the 1954 Somerset Maugham Award for *Five*, the collection it appeared in.

In 'Hunger', for the first time, she used a black African as the main character, a poor boy, Jabavu, who yearns to go to the white man's city, a city like Salisbury, to make a new life. He teaches himself to read a bit before leaving, struggling to decipher words on scraps of wrapping paper from the native store, and walks miles to the next village to see a man who knows English and is willing to teach him to speak it. At sixteen, he makes the long journey to the city by foot, resisting attempts of drivers to trick him into taking a ride so that they could carry him to the mines and force him to work there.

One night he meets an educated black man named Mr Samu, a political radical who goes about with a briefcase filled with 'subversive' literature. Samu tries to enlighten the Africans about their exploitation at the white man's hands, and attempts to organise them against this oppression. He awakens in Jabavu a traditional conflict between self-interest and caring about other people's plight. Once Jabavu is in the city, self-interest wins out. He meets and is used by both good and bad people, black as well as white, for their own ends. Lessing shows how naïveté can turn to suspiciousness under corrupting influences such as urban life.

At the end of the story, when Jabavu is jailed for a crime he didn't commit, another African leader, Mr Mizi, comes to his aid, and revives the feeling of solidarity he had known with his tribe before leaving home. 'We, says Jabavu over and over again, We. And it is as if in his empty hands are the warm hands of brothers.'[9] Communist ideology influencing his healing response. Lessing considered 'Hunger' creatively unsatisfying precisely because it was of such simple moral construction. 'What is wrong with that tale is sentimentality, which is often the sign of an impure origin: in this case, to write a tale with a moral.'[10]

Mother of Violence

Lessing's happiness at her congenial new living arrangement received a powerful blow in 1951. About six months after the move to Joan Rodker's, a letter arrived from Africa from Maude, announcing that she was coming to London to stay with them and take care of Peter, so that Doris could write more freely.

The message literally caused Lessing to take to her bed, in hiding from what threatened to engulf her. She felt unable to avoid her mother's intrusion completely, but she knew she must defy her mother's wish to live with her. If Maude had to come to London, she would have to encroach on her daughter's life from some distance, although Lessing knew that any distance within the same continent was too close.

Primarily to help find the strength to resist her mother's plans, Lessing entered psychotherapy, an experience she drew on when she wrote *The Golden Notebook*. There, her therapist is called Mrs Marks. Anna also refers to her as 'Mother Sugar.' In real life she was a Jewish woman named Sussman who had converted to Roman Catholicism.

At first glance, healer and patient couldn't have been more incompatible. Mrs Sussman was in ways a person Doris Lessing would instinctively recoil from. She was a Roman Catholic, quite conservative, and a disciple of Carl Jung's school of analysis. Lessing was hostile toward all religion, revolutionary in her politics, and intellectual rather than emotional in her approach to life. Lessing discovered that these intellectual differences didn't affect Mrs Sussman's ability to help her, for she had a unique gift in knowing how to guide people through the shoals of unhappiness and discontent. Lessing went to see Mrs Sussman two or three times a week for three out of the four years that her mother stayed in London. Without these sessions, Lessing feels, she would have crumbled under the weight of her mother's unbearable presence.

The way Maude lived had not changed. Forlorn and needy, she exerted a kind of heart-rending pressure on her daughter. Mrs Sussman made it clear that Doris must resist that sort of blackmail if she and Peter were to survive.

One of the situations Maude disapproved of but could not alter was a child-care arrangement for Peter that competed with her own desire to be helpful. A refugee couple from Austria, the Eichners, who lived in the country, took in children over weekends and holidays to earn additional money. It was stiff competition for any grandmother. More summer camp than baby-sitting service, it was not unusual to see 20 children running around the Eichner's ramshackle house and the surrounding country side. Not surprisingly, Peter preferred the Eichners to spending time with Maude.

In the face of her mother's disapproval, Lessing was primarily purchasing a supporter with Mrs Sussman. Joan Rodker was sympathetic to her antipathy toward Maude, but she didn't find her so treacherous a figure. Lessing thought that Joan felt Maude was just a typical middle-class matron. Lessing's lover at the time was a man she calls Jack in *Walking in the Shade* and who may have served as a basis for Michael in *The Golden Notebook*. Although himself a psychiatrist, he gave Doris the pedestrian advice to resolutely stand up to her mother. No wonder, then, that Mrs Sussman was so important to her equilibrium. Lessing regarded the process as her salvation.

* * *

Lessing believes that emotional deprivation in childhood encourages men and women to repeatedly become infatuated with inappropriate, often impossible partners. Jack made it clear he was not going to divorce his wife and marry her. He never suggested their relationship would become permanent, or indicate that he would like it to be. But, she writes, she 'wasn't listening ... wasn't able to think at all.'[1]

She did listen, however, when Jack told her he thought she should find her own place and move from Joan's. Joan didn't like Jack very much, and he felt in competition with her. Lessing convinced herself that Jack wanted more time with her and that once she had her own flat, and he was with her more, she would inch closer to the goal she had resolutely held since they became lovers: to spend her life with him. Joan, who was already critical of the way Lessing was raising Peter – she found her too permissive and thought she responded to him more as another adult – tried to talk her out of the move. She upset Lessing when she told her that it was not a good idea to take Peter out of the Rodker home. Peter needed a father and Jack had no interest in assuming even a semblance of that role, and Lessing knew that he would miss the big-brother role that had been played by Joan's son Ernest.

It was while planning her move, that Lessing won the Maugham award, which came with four hundred pounds that she was to spend travelling outside England for at least three months. She used part of the money for a down payment on a flat, and went to Paris, leaving

Peter behind. The Eichners, Joan Rodker, and Maude would care for her son.

In order to afford her new apartment, Lessing had to take in boarders which Peter hated. He was used to the feeling of being part of a family at Joan's and now he was in the company of strangers. Lessing wanted to keep her boarders and she would often tell Peter to be quiet so as not to annoy them. Peter, aged eight, was placed in a new level at the school he had been happily attending but his behaviour and his work began to deteriorate. His mother removed him from the school and enrolled him elsewhere, and when that didn't work out, she repeated the process.

Although her tone in *Walking in the Shade* is reportorial rather than emotionally engaged, Lessing again does not spare herself in describing the effects of her new living arrangements on her son. She did not bring a television set into the flat despite Peter's fervent entreaties. And increasingly, mother and son were engaged in heated arguments over other views. There was a child in the downstairs flat for a while, a boy Peter's age, and Lessing hoped the children would be friends, but they didn't like each other. Peter had a stamp collection. Lessing recounts that the boy took the album and stole half the stamps. She describes Peter as feeling miserable and trapped, a fatherless child whom she finds it hard to support and encourage.

Jack would soon break off the relationship, leaving London to accept a hospital position abroad. Despite all the evidence that this ending was inevitable, Lessing was shocked and despondent for a long time afterward. Although some observers would assess this situation differently, in *Walking in the Shade* she called Jack 'the most serious love in my life.'[2]

Another relationship was coming to a turning point. After four years of a standoff with her daughter, Maude finally decided that her fantasy of making a new life with Doris and Peter would have to become yet another unfulfilled dream. She had spent the years in London living with a crotchety, ailing old man who was a distant cousin of Michael's. Her nine-year old grandson much preferred the Eichners to his grandmother's care when Lessing wasn't available, and Lessing made it chillingly clear that she wanted her mother gone.

Maude obliged her daughter. She left England in 1955, never to return, except on typewritten pages as a fictionalised maternal character (Mrs Quest) in Lessing's most ambitious undertaking – the Children of Violence series.

* * *

So we meet Martha Quest, the eponymous protagonist of Doris Lessing's third book – a British adolescent woman living in the 1940s, well before any sort of liberation. The novel was published in 1952, three years after Lessing's arrival in London. Although she is an extremely prolific and single-minded writer, when one considers that she was raising a child on her own, remained politically active, had a romantic life and was doing other writing, three books in as many years is an extraordinary output.

Lessing is a writer who can carry more than one project in her mind at the same time, and she had actually begun working on *Martha Quest* even before *The Grass Is Singing* was published in 1950. What is more, she knew from the very first moment of envisioning Martha that the character would appear in a series of books, to be called Children of Violence. Lessing knew the series would run to five books. She had the developing plotline in mind, with the exception of its ending. She also had not determined that the novels would become decreasingly realistic. It would take nearly twenty years to complete the series.

Judging by its impact on readers, the time Lessing spent on the Children of Violence series was justified. The playwright Arnold Wesker says he responded physically as well as intellectually and emotionally to her novels:

> Two novels by Doris Lessing stirred me at different times in my life to a kind of action. I can remember being on a 653 trolley bus returning from work and finishing one of the 'Martha Quest' books, *A Proper Marriage*, which affected me with such joy I bought flowers for my mother. Much later in life … in Wales, I became caught up in *The Four-Gated City* which I read through the night until dawn. When finished I decided to walk up Hay Bluff, the hill behind the house, and catch the sunrise. As I walked through the vast, empty landscape it seemed to me I heard voices, like the characters in the Lessing novel who were telepathic, echoing through the high grounds. At first I couldn't see anyone and then – there was a young couple running down the Bluff. They too had risen early to see the sunrise. A lyrical moment.[3]

Although most of the time hardly anything irritates Doris Lessing more than questions about the autobiographical aspects of her fiction, she acknowledges that much of *Martha Quest* is autobiographical. She postulates that a great many women begin to write out of a need for self-understanding.

Martha Quest was, Lessing says, like the youthful Doris Tayler an often belligerent, combative, uncharitable girl. Martha's surname which has obvious connotations, simply sprang to her mind, Lessing says, from a spontaneous source inside her own searching self. As for the series title, Children of Violence, the answer Lessing most often gives about its genesis is related to the two wars that framed her early life. She never forgets that she was born to a father who could not shake memories of the First World War from his ever disintegrating mind. This meant she was brought up with the rage of a man who felt that he had been betrayed by an ignoble war; his bitterness pervaded all of his daughter's life. Then, as a young woman, she witnessed the mass destruction of the Second World War. These wars predisposed her to a chronic sense of disaster, a feeling she thinks she shared with the youth culture of the 1960s. She told Studs Terkel in a 1969 interview that she was certain the young college student who is acting up on campus is showing the effects of the history of two world wars.[4]

In the more immediate years following the Second World War, when Lessing began her life in London, the social turmoil of the war's aftermath was ever present. English servicemen of all races and classes had fought, been maimed, and lost their lives in the name of their country's honour and survival. Those soldiers who returned were not ready to revert to the restrictive traditions of the Empire. Privilege and rights based on birth and social class were newly abhorrent to ex-military men from less elite origins. The war had also been fought alongside the great socialist power of Russia, and the great democratic power of America, providing the British soldier with a different perspective on class. Home again, the soldier challenged the social myths of his country.

Not all leadership or acts of heroism had been performed by graduates of Oxford or Cambridge. And if those institutions remained out of reach to most veterans, many insisted on some form of higher education, to further narrow the gap between the classes. Older generations who had stayed at home while the younger men fought for England believed that the ultimate reward of victory was restoring tradition. The younger generation was fed up with tradition's limitations. They were eager – and stubbornly determined – to build a new life, a new England.

Thus post-war Britain was feeling the pressure of widespread rebellion: social, sexual, political, and cultural. As Doris Lessing continued to fashion a writing, political, and personal life, she was heartened to see that other dissenters were finding their way through the cracks in the Establishment's facade.

The Happy Young Woman

One group that refused to maintain old mores was a fresh crop of youthful playwrights, brash newcomers to the arts, many of them from the working class. The West End was a bastion of the middle classes, mainly presenting the work of university-educated writers, or seasoned performers turned playwrights, to a relatively affluent audience. Now, there were dramatists who came from the poor, Jewish section of London's East End, such as Harold Pinter, Bernard Kops, and Arnold Wesker; or from working-class provinces, such as Shelagh Delaney, who quit school at sixteen. A few of the new crop of playwrights had a background in theatre, but even they had no connection to the West End establishment. For example, Pinter and John Osborne had acted professionally, but only as low-level actors in repertory companies far from London.

The new writing also began to develop a different style of performance: gritty and realistic rather than polished and mandarin. In the pre-War West End, young leads would serve tea, or saunter into a room asking: 'Tennis, anyone?' Actors like Albert Finney, Richard Burton, and Alan Bates were instead playing characters that drank pints of beer, and would sooner crack a tennis racket over someone's head than utter the cliché question of drawing room comedy.

Bernard Kops recalls that before these rebels arrived, an evening at the theatre seemed to be summed up by 'ordering tea for the interval which came to you on this nice tray with fruitcake on pretty china. Then along came the revolution that knocked all this politeness out the stage door.'

Only a few of the new crop of writers – John Mortimer and John Arden, for example – came from upper-middle-class, university-trained origins, but their politics and ambitions were the same as those of their less privileged peers. Their goal was to make the English theatre so that it presented far more diverse productions than in the past. They were not interested in following commercial tradition, turning out variations of some well-tested dramatic or comic formula.

This dynamic fusing of different cultures kicked off developments in fiction, poetry, music – jazz suddenly became immensely popular – and film. What kept the group cohesive was their shared sense of mission to change the polite status quo of British writing, perhaps particularly in drama.

Doris Lessing, while gaining fame for her fiction, was also starting to write plays, and she was excited about the possibilities of pursuing dramatic writing. Her love of the theatre and her dreams of being a playwright found sustenance in this bold, determined new circle. The group had already been labelled by the press department of the Royal Court Theatre – where many of the new plays would be produced – as the 'angry young men.' It was John Osborne's play *Look Back in Anger* that first inspired this appellation, which the writers themselves all mocked and rejected.

'I was never an angry young man,' says Arnold Wesker,

> ... none of us were, a silly journalistic misnomer. On the contrary, we were all very happy young men and women (let's not forget Doris Lessing, Ann Jellicoe, Shelagh Delaney). Who would *not* have been happy? Discovered, paid, applauded, made internationally famous overnight![1]

Look Back in Anger detonated on the Royal Court stage in May 1956, with what the theatre critic Kenneth Tynan called 'a considerable bang.'[2] Tynan warned citizens who believed the post-war world should go back to 'normal' that they had better stay away from Jimmy Porter, the play's hero, 'with his flair for introspection, his gift for ribald parody, his excoriating candour, his contempt for "phoneyness" ... and his desperate conviction that the time is out of joint.'[3]

* * *

Martha Quest was both similar to and very different from Jimmy Porter. She engaged in the same sort of rebellious behaviour as Porter, but she still had hopes of finding a purpose to her life. When Lessing wrote *Martha Quest*, she had strong feelings about the need for commitment, and believed that a writer could serve as a guide to the socially estranged. Her original affection for her short story 'Hunger' hovers behind this belief. As she explained, 'Hunger' failed not because it was trying to be socially responsible, but because it was too simplistic and sentimental. The more skilled she became as a writer, in plays or fiction, the better able she would be to combine commitment with creative accomplishment.

'Committed to what?' she would write in an essay titled 'The Small Personal Voice.' 'Not to being a propagandist for any political party,' but she soon adds an important personal caveat and goal 'unless their own private passionate need as writers makes them do so: in which case the passion might, if they have talent enough, make literature of the propaganda.'[4]

This essay was originally part of a 1957 collection called *Declaration*. The other contributors were John Osborne, Kenneth Tynan, Colin Wilson, Stuart Holroyd, Bill Hopkins, Lindsay Anderson, and John Wain. The energetic young publisher Tom Maschler assembled the group of writers to state their views on life and writing, explaining in his introduction,

> A number of young and widely opposed writers have burst upon the scene and are striving to change many of the values which have held good in recent years. No critic has yet succeeded in assessing them or correlating them *objectively* one to another. This volume aims at helping the public to understand what is happening while it is actually happening – at uncovering a certain pattern taking shape in British thought and literature.[5]

There was primarily one area of consensus among those who agreed to write for *Declaration*: the conviction that they were part of a new era in English literature and drama. Doris Lessing wrote that what separated current literature from past writings was ambivalent ideals and indeterminate values. Kenneth Tynan argued that: 'The mansion of drama is cluttered with debris, ancient assumptions that Shaw bashed and cracked but failed to dislodge. The job of new playwrights is to remove the rubble, to sweep the floor; to make room in a theatre which is as Arthur Miller has said, "hermetically sealed off from life."'[6] Tynan also suggested, that for the sake of a healthier theatre, dramatists should break down inhibitions about sex which is 'as various in its forms as … the postures that coalesce into male or female excitement.'[7]

John Osborne later regretted taking part in *Declaration* because he found it pretentious and amateurish, and believed that only Lessing and two other writers – Kenneth Tynan and filmmaker Lindsay Anderson – made any real contribution to readers' thinking. The main result of Osborne's own piece was to abort the party scheduled for the book's publication. It was to be held at the Royal Court Theatre, but was cancelled because of government pressure over Osborne's rude remarks about royalty. He had written, 'I have called Royalty Religion the 'national swill' because it is poisonous,'[8] along with other unflattering invective.

* * *

Lessing also talks in 'The Small Personal Voice' about 'a feeling of responsibility' toward her audiences. Focusing on her career as a fiction writer, she says that in publishing a story or novel a writer is asking the reader to see things through the writer's eyes. This places an obligation on the writer which, if he accepts it, makes him into 'an architect of the soul.'[9]

Lessing has come a long way from this sort of thinking. Today, for example, when she is asked about the multiple genres of her writing, and about how certain readers feel abandoned when she takes off in another literary direction, she waves away the issue as an irritating irrelevance. She has no duty to anyone or anything but herself and her work. Women who complained when she left realism for science fiction are not interested in serious writing, she says; they just want support for their own narrow concerns.

Reminded by an interviewer that she once thought she could change society through her writing, she answers with more repudiation of a former self: She was very young when she had such thoughts. No one changes anything in the world, no matter how rational one's arguments are. 'You can't be rational about life … We haven't got the right words; we are spiritual, even though the word is so debased.'[10]

Lessing's shedding of past beliefs coexists with her continued acceptance of the concept of multiple selves. She is extremely interested in the different kinds of people inside one skin. Her own sense of her 'real' self, she told an interviewer, is the one who is not only the 'observing' person she often speaks of, but a very isolated person even in the midst of a circle of people. What others call loneliness she sees as an ultimately private space that is necessary to keep hidden. It is the essential 'I' and no one must share it. She welcomes her seclusion and does not need to be with people much of the time. When asked whether she could go as long as a week without seeing or talking to another person, she replied, 'Good Lord, yes. Easily. If I spend too long with people, I can get quite hysterical for lack of solitude.'[11]

If no one is allowed to see the isolated observer, some are permitted to see the Hostess (a sort of grown-up Tigger), who continues to appear when Lessing needs protective cover. Out she comes, personable and proper and convivial. Another self who refuses to stay hidden is someone she has little use for, and does her best to suppress: the forlorn child, consumed with self-pity.

If there was ever a period when Lessing would be able to make use of one of her more social selves, it was during these early years in London, when sex, radical activism, and artistic rebirth intersected. For the first time in her life, cultural questions were being taken as seriously as political questions, and she had a growing circle of friends who were diversely engaged with both. It was a time of great change in England and the circles that Lessing moved in from politics to the arts all welcomed the culture's uncertainty. Its splintering walls offered them the opportunity to become both the recipients and instruments of further transformation.

Thoroughly Modern Mother

The hub of bohemian life in 1950s London was the Soho district, a neighbourhood Bernard Kops calls the 'furnace' around which they all gathered. 'It was pervasively cosmopolitan,' he says. 'A lot of dropouts, bohemians, intellectuals coming down from university would gravitate there, and soon, the new left would settle right into the heart of Soho.'

The area was an appropriate centre for Doris Lessing's polyglot bunch of friends. Early arrivals to Soho were the Huguenots in the seventeenth century, followed by Italians and Jews and Greeks, and later on, Americans who were relocating in London after the war. Some of the area's gathering places were already quite famous. Dylan Thomas and Stephen Spender once graced its French cafés. For Lessing's not quite so celebrated circle, there was no better place to congregate than in Soho's coffee bars, left political clubs, Italian or French cafés, literary pubs. or Jewish delicatessens.

Lessing did manage to join her friends when she could get time away from Peter, but, in the universally imbalanced equation between a mother and child, it was rarely too much time for Doris and often too much time for Peter. But she did not want to pack Peter off to boarding school at a premature age.

She is quick to tell journalists how much she deplores England's tradition of sending young children away from home. When he reached age twelve, however, she thought boarding school was in his best interests as well as hers. Though Peter's happiness was always an important factor in the decisions she made about life and work, she fervently believed it was a mistake to renounce all her own needs for his. A persistent criticism she made of her mother, and most women of Maude's generation, was their overidentification with their children. 'In moments of depression,' Lessing declared in 1994, 'when I think things are not improving, I remember they must be because you don't hear women saying, "I sacrificed myself for my children."'[1] Still it must have been difficult to strike a balance. As a single mother and artist living an unconventional life she was faced with a heightened version of the usual parental conflict – the challenge of loving and nurturing a child while pursuing a career and having a personal life.

In Clancy Sigal's novel *The Secret Defector* (1992), Rose O'Malley, who strongly resembles Doris Lessing, has a twelve-year-old son, Aly (short for Alastair). The narrator, Gus Black (Sigal's stand-in) comments frequently on the boy's precocious sophistication. At one point Aly shocks Gus by talking of his mother's former lovers. He also scolds Gus for having temper tantrums about Rose: 'You should let up on Ma, Gus. You're such a child – she isn't at her best with children.' When Gus accuses him of sounding too wise for his years, Aly demurs. 'Oh, I'm not .... It's just my pose, Ma says.'

'Blessed Rose was on to all our stratagems,' Sigal writes, 'including Aly's artificial composure, which was settling into a sort of detached scrutiny of the world, making him into an inside-out version of herself.'[2]

If Lessing didn't want to be overly limited by the traditional female role of mother, she still enjoyed male admiration. 'She was beautiful,' recalls the African scholar Peter Worsley, 'an absolute knockout ... very curvaceous, totally delightful.' Paul Hogarth recalls 'a cat-like kind of charm ... a wary, cool, feline sort of quality. She wasn't beautiful, but she drew men to her.' And the cultural studies specialist Stuart Hall found 'something very attractive and appealing about her face ... something rather maternal in its particular allure.'

When Mervyn Jones met her in 1952, they were both active Communist Party members, but she, like Jones, was 'a critical and independent-minded one. We had plenty to talk about, and the interest of a dinner with her was enhanced by the fact that she was a highly attractive young woman.'[3] In his memoir, Jones whimsically expressed regret over missed opportunities. 'An affair with Doris Lessing, as well as being a fascinating experience, would have made a good chapter in my autobiography.' But, for some undetermined reason, 'that didn't occur to me, and we became – as we have remained – friends.'[4]

According to Clancy Sigal, 'the sex life of the London literary scene was rife with androgyny, bisexuality, promiscuity, lots of timid (or perverse) experimenting.' Many of these people, he continues, 'called their behaviour all sorts of pretentious things, but straight fucking, it was not.' If *Walking in the Shade* is any gauge then Doris Lessing was more amused than shocked at these activities, even when they bordered on the perverse. For instance, the surprise of confronting drama critic, Ken Tynan's extensive whip collection, late one night, does not interrupt an enjoyable political discussion, or hinder the friendship between them. On the contrary, Lessing seems to appreciate such peccadilloes.

The only sexual experiences that seem to discomfort Lessing are homosexuality and lesbianism. One lesbian friend recalls that discomfort with a smile: 'She just pretended my partner and myself were only flatmates,' 'We had a silent agreement that I would not disabuse her of that belief.' Lessing's attitudes towards gay men, whose looks and manners she has mocked, seem even less comfortable. Perhaps because of her admiration of 'real men,' she is irritated when that conventional stereotype is abandoned.

In one letter to Robert Gottlieb she wickedly describes a gay couple who live in the flat above her own, and mocks the seemingly boundless energy of their noisy lovemaking. In a less humorous vein, she has linked homosexuality with misogyny in *The Golden Notebook*, where the gay couple in Anna's house indiscriminately dislike all women.

Lessing's ability not to refrain from moral judgements about human sexuality contributes to the power of her writings about it. All writers benefit from standing back from a situation to capture its entirety. 'Maybe the key to her strength as a writer,' says one old friend, 'is she'll be open to any experience, her own or other people's, and one eye is always taking notes.'

* * *

The fifties and sixties were busy times for the notetaker and observer, particularly on the political scene. The year 1956 is considered a watershed for the British left. The invasion of part of Egypt and the Suez Canal by the British and French was shocking to many English people, particularly those of leftist bent. Even more horrifying for the staunch Communist was the invasion of Hungary by the Soviet Union to quell a popular uprising.

Although his newspaper, the *Daily Worker*, did not print his reports, the paper's editor, Peter Fryer, in Hungary at the time, had witnessed both the popular uprising and the massacres in response. According to one of Lessing's comrades, Freyer said that when he saw the secret police shoot down the crowds he instantly lost all enthusiasm for the Communist Party.

Mervyn Jones remembers a lengthy night of discussion that took place at Lessing's flat. The conversation went on for hours until one of Lessing's African friends commented that it seemed to him everyone was so upset because they didn't believe white people should experience such horrors.

Hungary, says Mervyn Jones, was 'a body-blow to the Communist Party ... scores of comrades left who had never envisaged the possibility until 1956.'[5] According to one Communist Party contemporary, although Lessing would later make her defection public, she didn't then. She hated the idea of the press making too much of the gesture, as if it were some grand statement of mea culpa and renunciation. Instead, as a quiet first step, she simply neglected to renew her Party card for 1957.

Despite the added shock of the Communist Party's Twentieth Congress meeting in Moscow, where Khrushchev revealed Stalin's atrocities, the Communist Party in Britain, as well as in other countries, demanded total loyalty in all circumstances to the Soviet Union.

According to Raphael Samuel, an important voice of the New Left, who had been a Party member, the split in the Party broke along class lines, ...king class encouraging loyalty. Arguments were heated ...his period.

...be the intellectuals who left the Party, such ...P. Thompson. At first he tried to encourage ...munist Party to work, but when he saw that ...t. This situation suggests another reason for ...silently away from official Communism. She ...the polarisation of middle-class intellectuals ...

...n Jones jestingly says the largest party in ...munist Party. It was, I think, a valuable group ...e unflagging determination and the organisa- ...the submissiveness and the self-deception had ...ded that when creating ex-Communist charac- ...described 'a habit of sharpness and intensity in ...ss about ideas.'[6]

Doris Les... ...fested all of these qualities in the writing she was doing during this period. In 1956, she took time away from the Children of Violence series to write her fourth novel, *Retreat to Innocence*. Its cover copy paints a vivid picture of the attitude toward women's roles in the '50s. While announcing that 'Miss Lessing's credo was included in a recent book, *Declaration,* which contained the iconoclastic writings of the so-called Angry Young Men,' it adds what the publishers apparently view as a confusing contradiction: 'Although very much an attractive young woman, Miss Lessing's social views and her provocative novels mark her as one of the first among a rising generation of brilliant young social critics.'[7]

* * *

Retreat to Innocence was set in England, the first book Lessing didn't locate in Africa, and it deals directly with her Communist concerns at the time. While she was writing the novel, she was heavily influenced by readings in Lenin, Engels, and Marx.

The book's protagonist, a young English woman named Julia Barr, is wealthy, spoiled, and completely apolitical. She becomes involved with Jan Brod, a much older, leftist, Jewish writer, exiled from Czechoslovakia. Although she is a virgin when she meets Jan, and has an ineffectual but 'suitable' boyfriend, Julia is soon having an affair with Jan, who awakens her sexually as he attempts to educate her about the blessings of Communism. Once again, the Czech origins of Jan, echo Lessing's real life lover Jack.

Julia is affected, but not converted, by Jan's politics. Indeed, she

Reference to Doris' link of homosexuality w/ misogyny in Golden Notebook dislikes the changes in thinking he provokes in her. Eventually, they part. When he is forced to return to Eastern Europe, Julia marries her safe, comfortable civil servant.

Lessing captures the inconsistencies in Communist ideology even as she portrays the determined insularity of her characters' lives. Julia newly understands that she is trapped by the easy comforts of her upbringing. Jan told her that the calmness of her life would eventually be jarred, and now, no longer with him, Julia thinks perhaps she wishes it would. Like many another Lessing woman, she looks to someone or something beyond herself to release her from conditioned behaviour. 'I can't make a move out of all this for myself, but if something happened, I would be pushed out ... I'd understand it. I'd be part of it. Because of Jan Brod.'[8]

Julia is also in a way representative of the generation who would be born to Lessing's own Children of Violence generation. They are smugly secure, unwilling to ruffle the comfortable lives their parents built for them. At one point, Julia's father acknowledges that he might not have done her a favour by making her life so easy, by allowing her to feel she could have anything she wanted whenever she wanted it.

This naive, illusory mindset, Lessing suggests, keeps young people from understanding their own limitations in the face of fate's demands. Many years later, in 1971, Lessing would argue with Robert Gottlieb – who was her junior by more than a decade – for an early publication of her controversial novel about sanity and madness, *Briefing for a Descent into Hell*, because she felt that the political climate of America was about to change, perhaps making it less hospitable to what she had to say.

She wrote to Gottlieb to say that she did not share his sense of optimism or security. Her vision of the future was bleak. Lessing's belief in a capricious greater power infuses her reasoning. If there are battles which she cannot avoid she will stand fast and fight.

The Perils of Partnership

Lessing had been away from her homeland for seven years. Now efforts were ostensibly under way there to dismantle the wall of racism. Despite positive reports, Lessing and her friends in the African resistance in London were not convinced. They and her other colleagues from the League Against Imperialism often came to her flat to talk about African problems, and their pragmatic questioning reinforced her doubts.

In 1953, Britain had linked Southern Rhodesia (the future Zimbabwe), Northern Rhodesia (the future Zambia), and Nyasaland (the future Malawi) into the Central African Federation, also known as the Federation of Rhodesia and Nyasaland. Its stated goal was to achieve political and economic equilibrium and racial accord between a population that a contemporary *New York Times* account described as '200,000 whites, 6,000,000 blacks and about 18,000 Asiatics and mixed bloods.'[1]

However the same story noted that: 'British Central Africa was federated into a new state primarily to attract American capital for the development of its rich natural resources, but it is already being jarred by race politics.'[2]

The mechanism for healing the racial divide was a much ballyhooed but fundamentally obscure policy known as Partnership. Initially a term inserted by the British into the preamble of the Federation's constitution, against the wishes of Rhodesia's white elite, Partnership came to stand for an alternative policy to the rigorous segregation or apartheid, that had been instituted in neighbouring South Africa.

Under the banner of Partnership, provisions were made for African representation in the Federal Parliament and increased rights were extended to native peoples. (They would, for instance, be allowed to buy European liquor and join trade unions.) Such Partnership reforms were considered a radical step in the wrong direction by many white Rhodesians, who would have preferred to institute a strict form of South African style apartheid in the Federation. But to others, like T.R.M. Creighton, who in 1960 wrote a history of the Federation, Partnership was simply 'a narcotic, sedative word to quiet the objections of British opinion and the resentment of Federal Africans against a situation of racial domination by Federal Europeans.'[3]

Doris Lessing was an early proponent of this view. In *Going Home*, her 1957 book of reportage that came out of the return trip to Africa she had desperately wanted to make for several years, she explores the hypocrisy of Partnership and the continuing astonishing racial inequities in the country she loves and deplores. For behind the benevolent mask of Partnership lay the unrefined segregation of the Land Apportionment Act. This was the law instituted in the 1930s whereby territory was parcelled out into areas called Native and European, and scores of Africans were brutally moved off their land.

Noting that one white architect of Federation, with unwitting honesty, was said to have compared the new Partnership between blacks and whites to that of a horse and its rider, Lessing soon concluded that Partnership was a counterfeit program by whites to allow a small privileged class of blacks the appearance of equality in order to repress the protests of the larger body of Africans.

Lessing believed that because it was so basically fraudulent, the plan was doomed from its inception. Many Africans she spoke with even preferred the open discrimination of apartheid to the hypocrisy of Partnership. They disliked feeding into the colonialist's self-satisfied habit of saying one thing and doing another.

* * *

Certainly much of Lessing's sense of urgency about going home was to see for herself what was happening to Africa, and to write for a European audience about what she found. But there was an even more pressing internal demand. 'I had to go home, for emotional reasons .... I needed to feel and smell the place.'[4]

Lessing does not include among her emotional reasons the desire to see her two older children. In fact, she did not see them on this trip. She reports in *Walking in the Shade* that they were at boarding school at the time. Whatever she felt about this continued separation perhaps belongs to that self she refers to who lives in total isolation, the self no one else will ever be permitted to see.

It was apparently not the time to talk about it when she wrote *Going Home*. Although the book is filled with accounts of reunions, neither brother nor mother, son nor daughter is mentioned as Lessing revisits her African past. In *Walking in the Shade* she does note that she saw Harry for a couple of days and Maude for an afternoon during that 1956 visit. The meeting between mother and daughter was restrained and calm, belying 'worlds of grief.'[5]

Many of Lessing's friends had told her she would never be allowed back into Rhodesia because she was now a well-known writer whose Communist proclivities would make her pen seem too threatening. After all, Lord Malvern (Dr Godfrey Martin Huggins), the head of the

Federation (and Maude's former physician) had proclaimed, 'We cannot have the place full of agitators. There is no room for communists.'[6] But Lessing quickly dismissed such potential problems.

Nonetheless, there were several questions hanging over the proposed trip. One was just how safe it was to travel on her own through a country certain to be hostile to her presence. Another was financial. She was a successful writer, but her success was measured more in fame than money. Funds would have to be raised to finance the expedition. The airfare alone was 250 pounds, and her travels through the country would be a considerable expense.

She decided to look to benefactors who had a concern for Africa, both in and out of the Party. Other funds could be generated from magazines and newspapers that would commission her to write articles about her observations.

One day she boarded a bus to Fleet Street and marched into the office of Tass, the Soviet news agency, to propose that they pay her fare to Africa. In return, she would write reports on her findings for any newspaper of their choice in the Soviet Union. The Tass representative drove her to the Soviet embassy, where she presented her argument again, explaining why it made sense for someone outside the insular world of professional journalism to write about Africa.

She made it clear that she needed the money paid quickly, if she was going to board the plane two weeks hence. The Russians, operating with uncharacteristic efficiency, made the deadline. Although the money that arrived was somewhat less than she had asked for, with the other funds she had managed to raise it was enough to make the journey. (Only after she returned from Africa did she learn that the money was not intended for her airfare, but was back pay for Russian publication of a story or past USSR book royalties – Lessing's accounts differ.) She had also already arranged to pre-sell some articles to magazines in Moscow, another reason that she may have delayed resigning officially from the Communist Party. After her trip was over and paid for would be time enough to quit.

During this period, Doris Lessing was reportedly involved with John Berger, a man of extraordinary talent and energy who was seven years her junior. He was art critic for the *New Statesman*, and had been trained as a painter. He would go on to write fiction – his first novel, *A Painter of Our Time*, was published in 1958 – and he also became a filmmaker and a playwright.

Berger's brilliant, perceptive criticism and left-wing sympathies (he was not a Party member) made him a welcome and influential friend to the fellow-traveller cognoscenti and, according to Paul Hogarth, 'won him the respect of well-known writers and academics of the Communist Left, among them Doris Lessing.'

Berger and Hogarth were good friends, who often connected, as did

Lessing, through the Geneva Club, an invention of Berger, intended as a link between all the disillusioned leftist intellectuals. 'We were a bunch of Party members and fellow-travellers,' Hogarth explains. 'We created our own ethos in a sense outside of the Party. We just couldn't get on with the official leadership.'

* * *

Paul Hogarth and Doris Lessing were to collaborate on *Going Home*. In her memoirs Lessing writes that the collaboration was suggested to her by the Communist Party and she agreed to the idea despite ambivalent feelings. Hogarth remembers the situation differently. The Geneva Club served as a clearinghouse for members' projects. 'That's how I learned of Doris's interest in going to Africa,' Hogarth recalls. Whether or not Lessing had any reservations about making the trip alone, Berger, who like the London art scene admired Hogarth's work, suggested that he might be interested in collaborating with her on this project. At the same time, Berger talked to Lessing about the advantage of having Hogarth accompany her. Hogarth had already illustrated two travel books, one on China, another on Greece.

'Berger sold her on me as someone who could heighten the impact of the book she was planning to write through drawings that complemented the text,' Hogarth recalls. He was genuinely moved by her sense of mission as well as the prospect of southern Africa as a subject and agreed to go with her and provide the illustrations for her book, *Going Home*. Facing the same financial hurdles Lessing did, Hogarth had to 'beg, cajole, and borrow against the drawings I hoped to make. I sold a lot of drawings beforehand – as far as I know, half of the originals are still in the possession of a certain left-wing millionaire; they were left with his solicitors against a loan whose value has escalated to the point that I really can't repay it – and I arranged another advance or two from a left-wing lawyer.'

Hogarth remembers receiving Lessing's letters as their departure day – for which she made all the arrangements – approached, directing him to give up the idea of being given money. Instead, he should borrow it, and ask for large sums from a few rather than small funds from many. There was no time now to worry about running up debt.

Although Hogarth was excited by the opportunity to work with someone whose writing he admired, he did not feel any closeness toward, or from, his travelling companion. 'She was chilling, and self-absorbed. I always had found her quite intense, and the first Party intellectual who wasn't very kind and altruistic. All the other writers, the generation who'd been through the war, were very idealistic, but I didn't feel this from her at all.'

Hogarth and Lessing left London for Salisbury at 8:30 in the morning of Thursday, March 28, 1956, arriving Friday at 7:10 in the evening. Although she mentions Hogarth and his drawings on a few occasions in *Going Home*, he has an almost spectral presence in the book.

* * *

'Over the plains of Ethiopia the sun rose as I had not seen it in seven years,' Lessing happily writes.[7] The sky was vast over the tops of remembered mountains. She knew what the ground looked like below her, what the birds' songs sounded like as they nested in the tall trees, how the grass felt under one's naked feet.

Later, after settling into the home of her former comrades Nathan and Dorothy Zelter, she drove out of Salisbury to the bush. It was a beautiful African night, brightly lit by the moon and stars. She stood in the tall grass and heard the noise of the nesting crickets. Alone in the bush country where she grew up, beautifully at peace, she thought 'If I had to fly back to England the next day, I would have been given what I had gone home for.'[8]

Nathan Zelter was now a successful businessman and lived, Paul Hogarth recalls, 'in the protected isolation of a parklike suburb reserved for white settlers.' From this base, Lessing called upon her old comrades in a never ending cycle of cocktail and dinner parties. She was horrified by how many of her old Communist friends had been transformed by prosperity. She questioned their intentions, their scruples, and what seemed to her their liberal rationalisations. They in turn saw her as too quick to criticise a society they insisted was improving.

She also ran into old school friends whose politics had always been opposite from hers. Predictably, they were annoyed at the turn her life, and her pen, had taken since she'd left Rhodesia. They insisted that things had changed since she left and that it was unfair of her to be so critical of a way of a life she no longer knew. They hoped that after this visit, she would see the light and write something nice about Africa: it was certainly overdue.

Lessing paid little attention to comments like these, but some of her close friends were sufficiently enthusiastic about the effects of Federation that for about two weeks she was caught up in the plan's promise. The more she talked to people, however, wearing her mantle of investigative reporter, the more illusory the concept seemed.

* * *

Lessing talked to scores of people, black and white. She visited factories that employed black workers, black compounds on white farms, welfare workers and black schoolteachers, an adult education class for blacks who came to school at night after a day of hard work. With Hogarth at her side she drove into the countryside that had no proper roads, along stips, double lines of concrete slabs just wide enough to accommodate the wheels of an average-size car with great clumps of tufted grass growing in between. They passed rows of shops and farm buildings with corrugated iron roofs. Periodically, they stopped at tsetse-fly-eradication posts, where the car was sprayed before their pilgrimage was allowed to continue.

One day they drove to Umtali, the peaceful town on the border of what was then Portuguese East Africa (Mozambique). This was all excitingly new territory for Paul Hogarth, and a landscape of memory for Doris Lessing. She remembered three different stays in Umtali, the first when she was eleven and making an extended visit to a local family, the last when she was a young wife and mother at the beginning of the war, when Frank Wisdom was in soldier's training. They were there in her mind, that homesick little girl, that gaily laughing, bitterly unhappy wife, those baffling, entrapping times.

Lessing had suspected she was under surveillance by the police from the moment she arrived in Salisbury. One day, back in their own car, returning to Salisbury, they stopped at a Coca-Cola bar in the bush. Hogarth wanted to draw the scene 'because it seemed so incongruous to find such a place in the middle of the African bush.' Suddenly, he recalls, 'a big car drew up and a burly young man got out to make a note of our numberplate and watched me draw. After walking up and down for half an hour, he waited until I had packed my gear and placed it in the boot.'

There was no doubt now that they were being carefully watched by government agents. Lessing was to hear she had angered officialdom by mingling with the 'kaffirs', and continuing to, as Lord Malvern had put it years before, ask a lot of questions that were 'upsetting my natives.'[9]

Lessing was eager to visit the Union of South Africa. Although she had been assured by the South African embassy in London that she would be admitted without question, she had her doubts, particularly after seeing how closely she was scrutinised in less repressive Rhodesia. South Africa, she felt, could only be worse. It was.

She and Paul Hogarth had decided to sit separately on the plane to Johannesburg, thinking that they would be less conspicuous if they did not travel as a pair. Once again, although she mentions the scene in her memoir, in *Going Home* Hogarth disappears from Lessing's account of her entrance into the unwelcoming country.

He remembers it being 'very conspiratorial. I was watching her because she was ahead of me, and I saw her stopped.' Lessing was led away to a holding room. She felt the atmosphere was thick with suspicion, she wrote in *Going Home*, and that every employee, even the young woman selling cigarettes, was a member of the Special Branch of the police.

After a while a hostile official informed her she was not allowed into the country and must leave immediately on the plane she had just debarked from. A group of plainclothesmen moved her toward the aeroplane, where she was told to sit by herself, though not by the window. Mockingly she wondered whether they thought she might hurl a bomb through it. The whole episode is summed up in what seems an extraordinary understatement: 'It annoyed me.'[10]

What awaited her back in Salisbury did more than annoy her. She was invited to visit the office of Garfield Todd, Southern Rhodesia's prime minister, to interview him. With some reservations, she accepted. As the meeting progressed, Lessing finally realised that she has long since been secretly classified as a Prohibited Immigrant. And that her admission back to Rhodesia was made possible by the personal intervention of Garfield Todd. Todd had hoped that Lessing would write favourably about the new Partnership arrangement. She made it clear that she would not. Then for the rest of the trip she was followed around by government agents. After her return to England, a trip to Rhodesia House in London, confirmed her fears worst when a Rhodesian official told her she would not be allowed to visit her homeland again.

* * *

For years afterward Doris Lessing had vivid dreams about this expulsion. Asleep in her London bed, she is back in Africa, but suddenly with a wrench of anguish, she realises that she has no passport. White Rhodesians are coming for her to take her to the border and force her to leave. At the same time Black Rhodesians cannot see Lessing and go happily about their business, unaware of her plight.

Although her pain at being exiled intensified over time, in the beginning she was defiant. Writing about 'Being Prohibited' in the *New Statesman*, shortly after her return from Africa, she spoke of knowing many admirable people who were barred from their home countries, or locked into lands that they were not allowed to leave. Unhappy as she was with her own situation, she seemed pleased to join their ranks.

Lessing was capable of practising her own brand of lockout. Despite some warm letters about how much the editors at Michael Joseph liked Paul Hogarth's drawings, when *Going Home* was ready for publication only a few of his illustrations were used, truncated to the size of postage stamps, marking some chapter openings and not doing justice to the vivid renderings with their swirls of spiky lines.

'I reminded Doris that I had thought our mission to be a combined enterprise. But she blandly denied it had ever been thought of as such and told me that she had always intended the book to be more literary than journalistic. Moreover, it would be of interest to the public because *she* had written it, and because of her connections with Africa. Therefore, it could not be regarded as an equal effort,' Hogarth recalls.

She explained to Hogarth that artists and authors were supposed to make their own individual arrangements with a publisher and she saw no reason to change hers because he had neglected to take care of his interests, particularly – and, Hogarth says, 'this rubbed more salt in the wound' – since people don't purchase books because of its illustrations. Hogarth is still not quite clear about what happened. 'I had a most uncomfortable feeling that I had been used. She didn't want to go off to South Africa by herself, but she felt no real commitment to me or our collaboration. It rankled for a long time,' he admits.

Lessing ended the dispute curtly, she informed him that if he wasn't satisfied with the book as it was, she would be more than happy to publish *Going Home* with no illustrations at all. The drawings were a matter of supreme indifference to her. Years later Paul Hogarth saw Doris Lessing at a dinner of the Royal Academy of Art, the British society whose members are selected for a large body of achievement in the arts. Lessing was there as someone's guest. 'I went over after the banquet and I said, 'Doris, I haven't seen you for so many years.' And she said, 'What are you doing here?' and I said 'I'm a Royal Academician.' 'Oh, my God,' she said in horror, as if she was absolutely incredulous I had been given such an honour on my own.'

30

Red Sunset

In 1957 (the year *Going Home* was published) reports were given to the twenty fifth Congress of the British Communist Party about the decline in membership resulting from the outrage over Soviet suppression of the previous years Hungarian Revolution. While party leaders tried to dismiss the twenty per cent fall in membership from 34,000 to 27,000 as insignificant, dissidents berated the loss. An article in the *Daily Worker* specifically complained about the loss of leading intellectuals that the Party suffered; two were singled out, Doris Lessing and her friend the historian Edward Thompson.

In *The Golden Notebook*, Lessing conveys the painful confusion of breaking with Communism, a break encouraged by its failure to make Anna, the protagonist, feel whole. As Anna puts it to her comrade Jack, 'Alienation. Being split. It's the moral side, so to speak, of the communist message. And suddenly you shrug your shoulders and say because the mechanical basis of our lives is getting complicated, we must be content to not even try to understand things as a whole?'[1] Anna had hoped that by becoming a member of the Party, her sense of being split would heal. Instead, over time, it seemed to deepen.

For a substantial part of her life, Lessing did feel more whole through her Communist identification, so much so that before the horrifying events of 1956, she had been able to ignore signs that Russia was not living by its own creed. 'My own myth was that the things going on in the Soviet Union had nothing to do with true Communism,' she told an interviewer in 1985.[2]

Edward Thompson and his associate economist John Saville were departing from the party line even before the 1956 revelations, in a small, mimeographed news sheet called the *Reasoner*, in which they raised issues troubling them about the party and its activities. After publishing the second edition, they were told by Party hierarchy to abandon the activity or be subject to disciplinary action. There was much debate, but the decision to obey or not became academic because of Hungary. The *Reasoner* staff folded the paper not from Party pressure, but because they no longer felt the *Reasoner* served their purposes. The third and last issue of the *Reasoner* was printed, according to Thompson, 'through the smoke of Budapest' in which the distinguished intellectual begged the Party, 'my party,' to defend Hungarian workers. 'Shame on our leaders for their silence!'[3]

Thompson and Saville, while cheered by comrades like Lessing, were suspended from the Party for their protests, at which point they publicly resigned, and started a larger, independent journal called the *New Reasoner*. The journal's first issue laid out a vision of its mandate: 'We have no desire to break impetuously with the Marxist and Communist tradition in Britain. On the contrary, we believe that this tradition, which stems from such men as William Morris ... is in need of rediscovery and reaffirmation.'[4] The journal's masthead carried a quote from Marx: 'To leave error unrefuted is to encourage intellectual immorality.' The political scientist Ralph Miliband remembered that he 'was the only person on the board ... who had not been a member of the Communist Party.' Doris Lessing served on the editorial board of the *New Reasoner*. For some reason she tends to downplay her role, but her name is clearly printed on the masthead of early issues of the magazine. The other boardmembers were all ex-members and 'were in fact at the time still calling themselves Communists – free independent Communists.'

An open letter Lessing wrote to the original *Reasoner* in November 1956 is an indication of her continuing affection for Communism's ideology. Although she supported Edward Thompson's rebellion, she objected to his criticism of the Communists who kept silent when they should have spoken out about Russian persecution. 'We believed that Communism had a vitality and a moral vigour that would triumph,' she wrote, adding that if these comrades had spoken out, 'they would have been cast out by the party,' and so removed 'from a world movement in which we believed, and of which we wished to remain a part.'[5]

In 1958 the *New Reasoner* would join forces with another publication, begun in 1957 by Oxford undergraduates, called the *Universities and Left Review*. The average age of the *ULR*'s four editors, all Oxford educated, was twenty-four. They were from diverse ethnic and racial backgrounds, and not all were members of the Party. The *Reasoner* group, says Stuart Hall, one of the *ULR* editors, were on the other hand 'English to their fingertips.' Despite these and other differences – the *ULR* people were Londoners and cosmopolitan, the *Reasoner* editors lived in the country near the working-class provinces – the editors began to meet in order to determine whether it made sense to keep two journals of the same kind going, and eventually they decided to merge the two journals under the name *New Left Review*. Lessing became a member of this new editorial board.

This group and other people connected to the larger body of the *New Left Review* are considered architects of the important first New Left movement that would take hold of the Labour Party. Dorothy Thompson, widow of Edward and a historian in her own right, explains:

The Left movement which grew up around the journals and clubs in the fifties and early sixties was a coalition of people with varied religious and philosophical belief systems who were united around the political concept of a non-aligned European movement which would work out socialist policies independently of superpower influence and control. Not only did they not represent a single ideological position, they were by no means united in their definitions of socialism – only perhaps by the negative qualities of disillusion with Soviet-style communism and West-European, especially British, social democracy.'[6]

Several comrades – given her gradual retreat from the *New Left Review*, Lessing probably among them – preferred the *New Reasoner* to its reincarnation. A possible reason for Lessing's decreased involvement in the second journal, a friend speculates, was that she felt less important to it. Still another guess from a former colleague is that Lessing was involved with the poet Christopher Logue at the time. When Logue had some falling-out with the editorial board, he severed his relationship with the magazine, and Lessing's own withdrawal followed.

Whatever the cause, while she had attended *New Reasoner* board meetings regularly, she appeared at editorial sessions of the *New Left Review* only intermittently. When she did come, she almost never participated in the discussions. Stuart Hall remembers watching Lessing 'watching us. I would think, 'What are you seeing, what are you thinking, Doris?' She didn't put up a guard, it was just clear that what was going on in her mind wasn't any of our business. It would come out sometime soon in a story.' Nonetheless, Hall and Edward Thompson were always grateful to Lessing for contributing to its journal's literary content if not their political strategies. 'After all,' Hall reminds us, 'a short story by Doris Lessing would be published anywhere, so to give it to our little magazine was a big gesture ... that was her political gesture.'

In one of Lessing's much talked about stories of this period, 'The Day Stalin Died,' Stalin's death is handled with a surprisingly ironic touch. There are glimpses of the contempt Lessing would come to feel for all modes of political correctness.

At one point, the first-person narrator of the story visits with a comrade named Jean who chides her for having stated at a recent Communist Party meeting that the Soviet Union might be doing a certain amount of 'dirty work.' The two friends debate the influences of capitalist pressure, with the narrator taking the position that whether or not the thought was agreeable, capitalist interpretations were sometimes correct. Later the narrator catches sight of a newspaper headline that says Stalin is dying. The news doesn't tear a rent in her heart nor even in her afternoon.

Comrade Jean feels quite differently. She cries hysterically when she telephones the narrator and insists that Stalin's death must have been by assassination. The narrator objects that since Stalin was over seventy, it's quite possible his death was from natural causes. Jean will hear nothing of this. She knows in her Communist heart that the capitalists have murdered her leader. Lessing shows her disdain for naive ideological worship when she has the narrator, clearly only to humour her agitated friend, agree that they must redouble their efforts to be good Communists in the way their instantly deified leader would want:

'We will have to pledge ourselves to be worthy of him,' [Jean] said.
'Yes,' I said. 'I suppose we will.'[7]

* * *

Stuart Hall, the first, and long-standing, editor of the *New Left Review*, explains that the magazine 'was about making sense of the post-war culture. We did almost as much in the arts and architecture, the free cinema movement. It was a milieu that was interested in poetry, good writing.' New developments in capitalism were exploding in the fifties: television and mass consumerism chief among them. Economic lines were blurring, as working-class people bought television sets and shopped in the supermarkets that were beginning to open, stocked with some luxuries as well as staples. They were unknowingly involved in a cross-class experience, and their dreams and expectations became newly middle-class. Where was the old working-class culture? Where would this sense of classlessness lead?

The magazine raised issues of personal life, the way people live, culture, which weren't considered the stuff of politics on the left. *NLR*'s writers wanted to talk about the contradictions of this new kind of capitalist society in which people didn't have a language to express their private troubles, and didn't realise that these troubles reflected political and social questions.

The missionary impulse was strong at the New Left clubs, in London and throughout England, where diverse but sympathetic people came together. There might be visitors from the Labour Party, from the cinema, from music, from the universities.

The *New Left Review* crowd often met at a place converted just for their use by Joan Rodker's son Ernest who was, even at a young age, an accomplished carpenter. The club at 100 Oxford Street was the centre of the exciting new jazz movement. People could drink, listen to music, and talk, taking excited part in what are almost universally remembered as very convivial occasions. Doris Lessing often appeared. Even though she continued to watch more than speak, she still enjoyed being at the centre of radical politics.

William Phillips, of the *Partisan Review*, who briefly considered himself a (not very traditional) Communist, was attracted to Lessing precisely because she had left the Party but remained a radical. When they first met in the 1950s, he noticed that she seemed

> ... more like writers who came from the working ... and in her radical views, which were uncharacteristically lacking in ambiguity or irony. For a writer of her intelligence and independence, she was strangely literal-minded in her leftism.[8]

Early in their friendship, which was before Lessing's first visit to the United States, Phillips was also frequently annoyed by her anti-Americanism. Once, he recalls, they had 'a knockdown quarrel ... about McCarthyism, when she insisted that no one was safe from the witch hunt and that all intellectual and academic freedom in the United States was shut down. She made America seem like Russia under Stalin.'[9]

McCarthyism was indeed a major focus of Lessing's criticism of the United States. On her first visit to the United States in 1964, she harangued an interviewer: 'Sections of America seem absolutely hypnotised by the kind of propaganda that's fed to them .... Hasn't America been enfeebled by this hysterical fear of Communism?'[10] While William Phillips deplored the House Un-American Activities Committee's actions as much as Doris Lessing did, he tried to tell her that she was blowing up America's admittedly considerable shortcomings out of all proportion. But, like many other people who attempt to get Lessing to change her mind, 'I finally gave up, convinced it was hopeless.'[11]

Phillips believed that Lessing's revolutionary politics became a way for her to assert her 'individual purity,' an attitude he witnessed one evening when he took her, Alan Sillitoe and Sillitoe's wife to a reception at the American embassy given for Mary McCarthy. 'From the beginning, Doris could not contain her political hostility and contempt for the affair,' Phillips recalls though he admits that the gathering was 'a bit silly and pompous,' with a receiving line to meet McCarthy and the American ambassador, David Bruce. This setting of 'almost imperial splendour' seemed an improbable one for a person of Mary McCarthy's sensibilities.

> But McCarthy graciously accepted the formalities of the situation while Doris Lessing, I thought, overreacted by fuming against capitalism in general and American imperialism in particular. While all this invective of the class struggle was being delivered by the representative of the exploited masses, Mary McCarthy, the showpiece of the embassy, was greeting her guests, mostly liberal to leftist English writers, with a frozen smile, indicating her belief that on certain social occasions, gracious manners were more important than having the correct politics.

Phillips also felt – and he seemed in this assessment to be suggesting a sense of competition between Lessing and McCarthy – that 'underneath Lessing's politics and personal style was a powerful literary drive or, perhaps I should say, an enormous ambition.' 'Once,' he has explained, 'I asked, a bit foolishly ... what she wanted most to do. I had in mind the kind of book she saw as her ideal work or the sort of life she would like to live.' Her answer surprised him in its unexpected absence of social or artistic goal. 'She said she wanted to conquer England, and she had already accomplished that.'[12]

Chicago Blues

Today Molly rang up and said there was an American in town looking for a room,' Doris Lessing writes in *The Golden Notebook*.[1] And so begins the crucial union of Anna Wulf and Saul Green. They will fall in love but fear for their sanity before they finally help each other overcome the obstacles to their creative and emotional equilibrium.

'I remember how amused I always was to hear Doris introduce Clancy as "my lodger,"' a former friend recalls about the model for Sol Green – the man that he believed (contrary to Lessing's own statements) was the great love of her life.

As Clancy Sigal, an aspiring writer from Chicago's working class, recalls, he showed up on Lessing's doorstep in 1957, looking for lodgings. He was trying to find a place where he could escape from, and continue living, a most complicated life. Communism was the mother's milk his own mother had probably been too busy on picket lines to dispense. Jennie Sigal and Clancy's father both were factory workers and union organisers, and they imbued their son with the passion of political protest. In Sigal's novel, *The Secret Defector* (1992) – which many see as him taking his turn in the roman à clef match with Doris Lessing – he is ironic about the character based on himself. Gus Black describes himself as someone whose 'vital spark – Lenin called it *iskra* – glows brightest when fed certain cue lines. WORKERS OF THE WORLD UNITE. BAN THE BOMB. FREE THE ROSENBERGS. NO BLOOD FOR OIL.' Gus harbours 'an unsatisfied longing to be in the front line, anyone's front line.'[2]

As a boy, when Sigal wasn't distributing leaflets, or hanging out with his corner gang, he was reading authors like James T. Farrell, Thomas Wolfe, Ernest Hemingway, and Richard Wright, and he added the dream of becoming a writer to the one of saving the world. After serving in the Army during World War II, he made his way to the Westwood campus of the University of California. Three of his classmates were H.R. Haldeman, President Nixon's future chief of staff, Haldeman's protégé, John D. Erlichman, and Alexander Butterfield, who became an Air Force general and Nixon's personal aide. During the Watergate scandal, Sigal, as a journalist, would interview these three men whose college experience had been so different from his own.

Sigal's own campus persona was – in true family tradition – the agitator. He served as managing editor of the college newspaper, until he was 'hounded out' by students hostile to his Communist politics. The same Red sympathies led to his being blacklisted from graduate school by the dean of students, and he was beaten up by a bunch of fraternity boys for writing an editorial describing how the campus quad on sunny California afternoons was neatly divided between gentiles standing on one side and Jews on another. Sigal says that what he revealed was hardly shocking, he had merely voiced 'what everybody knew but didn't want to discuss.'[3]

'I think Doris really loved his brashness, that tough-guy arrogance he could put on,' Lessing's *New Reasoner* colleague social scientist, Ralph Miliband, recalled. 'He was so much the Brits' image of the American man, taken right out of their popular cinema; swaggeringly sexy, hard and insolent,' says another old colleague.

Lessing herself looks to American movies when she describes Saul Green as he seemed to Anna Wulf on their first meeting: 'He stood lounging, his thumbs hitched through his belt, fingers loose, but pointing as it were to his genitals – the pose that always amuses me when I see it on the films, because it goes with the young, unused, boyish American face – the boyish, disarming face, and the he-man's pose.'[4]

In the early fifties, after knocking about doing jobs like driving a taxi and sheet-welding to support himself while he tried to write, Sigal made contact with a Hollywood talent agency and was hired as an agent. It was the McCarthy era when people in Hollywood were naming Communists and fearing that someone else would name them. Although Sigal had quit the Communist Party, his politics were idealistic and strongly socialist. After a period of enjoying peddling talent, he found it increasingly difficult to breathe air that had turned thick with shame and fear. There were days when he felt perilously close to collapse. It suddenly was time to move away from a world that had no relation to his inner life. He quit his job, and because he still wanted to write, he applied for a fellowship given by the Boston publishing firm of Houghton Mifflin. To his surprise, he won the grant. He would use the money to go to Europe and write his novel.

Sigal's trip east on the first leg of his journey, driving in an unpainted Pontiac sedan, is the subject of *Going Away: A Report: A Memoir* which despite its subtitle and its autobiographical aspects, is a novel, the one he wrote for his fellowship, although it would take him longer to complete than he originally intended. It tells the story of a man tracing his past as he travels cross-country by car. The journey is punctuated by many stops to visit former friends and colleagues – from the trade unions, from college, from the Army, from Chicago, Sigal's hometown. It is a tale of some disillusionment, as he sees old comrades grown conventional and apolitical. Hellos are sometimes awkward rather than eager. When he says goodbye, it can be with sighs of relief on both sides as he climbs back into the Pontiac and moves on.

A classic tale of self-exile from a vividly rendered America that the author loves but can no longer bear to live in, the book ends with the protagonist on board a ship that will carry him and his dream of being a writer to Paris. Why Paris? Because two of his Chicago literary heroes, Nelson Algren and Richard Wright, had recently gone there, as had many other writers before them, in the 1920s. And much of Sigal's reading and ideas about writing had centred on the writers of the twenties.

Going Away, published in 1962, perfectly captured not only the dilemmas of midcentury life but the timeless, tortured ambivalence of the aspiring artist. Watching his boat pull out of New York harbour the narrator says:

> I leaned on the rail under the dark rain and ... thought of the book I was to write and that I did not feel I would write. I was committed to the writing of a book which was to be the sum and total of all that I knew of myself and the worlds in which I had grown up. How dare I? I write a book? ... I must be mad.[5]

Despite the Parisian literary history Sigal longed to be part of, in 1957 he could not get his novel under way. Reluctantly, he decided to change venues in hopes of finding more energy to write. He would go to London and look up a *Daily Worker* editor who might help him find a place to stay.

Lessing remembers being called by 'a comrade' about Sigal. He is certain he first phoned Joan Rodker, who said, 'Not me, buddy, but my friend, Doris Lessing, is always renting rooms.' Sigal knew Lessing was a writer, but had no idea what she wrote. When he knocked at her door, she told him he wouldn't like the room, because it wasn't luxurious enough for an American. When he heard the room cost only two pounds a week, he answered he would move in immediately. And so, he says, 'I took the room and that's how it all began.'

Clancy Sigal was seven years younger than Doris – in 1957, thirty-one to her thirty-eight – but 'I was older than her politically ... so we had an awful lot to talk about.' They became lovers immediately. Ralph Miliband appraised the affair as 'long and tortuous.' Sigal himself recalls it as a state of 'love and war.'

Many people were struck by what they saw as Clancy Sigal's audacity. One man recalls how Sigal made his way into New Left circles. 'Other people wait around to be asked. Clancy came right into the office of the magazine *New Left Review* and said in effect, 'Here I am,' as if we were all waiting for him.'

Lessing did not find his manner offensive. Indeed, he fit the ideal of the 'real man' that coexisted in her mind with the resentment she felt toward male chauvinism. In Hollywood, Sigal had often taken starlets in hand to craft a more glamorous image for them. He had a genuine interest in and talent for helping women make the most of their faces and bodies. He decided, he says, that Doris Lessing was 'in need of a makeover, because back in the fifties women dressed very badly in England. And I just couldn't bear it. And after a while, she couldn't bear it. There was never any suggestion of 'Why are you imposing your reaction and male will on me?' She said, 'Please, for God's sake, let's go shopping together' ... And it was fun.'

* * *

It is not likely Lessing would have been so amenable to another man's suggestions about changing her makeup, hairdo, and wardrobe. A major factor in her pulling away from the Left was what she perceived as their abysmal attitude toward women, particularly among many of the older men. She would complain bitterly to Sigal about a kind of Berlin Wall of Old Left males who consistently and cruelly put her down. According to Sigal, she'd rail, '"These men are driving me crazy. They don't take me seriously as a writer," which I think hurt her most of all, and "They tear me up as a woman."'

Sigal, by contrast, took Lessing and women in general, very seriously. Ralph Miliband remembers that Sigal spoke quite naturally to even the most beautiful woman as first a fellow human being. 'He never talked *at* them. But on the other hand,' Miliband adds, 'he could be quite promiscuous.' As a result, a series of jealous battles erupted between Sigal and Lessing and sometimes others were caught in the crossfire. The writer Ann Edwards, who had been a friend of Sigal's in Hollywood, is an example. She moved to London about a year after he did, but took less time establishing herself in their adopted city. Edwards soon found work in television and film and moved into a house that was quite posh compared to Lessing's flat. Her home became sort of a refuge for Sigal.

'Clancy would just turn up at my house after a fight with Doris. It could be any hour of the night. He would just show up and the maid would make up a room for him,' she recalls. Edwards was Sigal's age and very attractive, and Sigal told her that Lessing was certain they were having an affair. Edwards suspected Lessing of doing 'these girlish, silly things like telephoning in the middle of the night and then just being silent on the other end when I answered.'

To add insult to irritation, Edwards remembers Sigal informing her that she had been turned into a character in *The Golden Notebook*. Presumably he was referring to the interloping Jane Bond. If Sigal regretted this misuse of a friend, he envied Lessing's ability to write anything at all. He was suffering from writer's block, and although

Lessing claimed the same affliction, the pages continued to erupt from her typewriter.

'She's a ferocious worker,' Sigal says about Lessing. 'In the old Stalin regime, they would have called her a Stakhanovite. She goes down into the coal mines and she outproduces everybody .... It's a furious and almost cosmic creative energy.'

Because she *was* writing about Sigal, and male-female relationships, they fell into a baroque game that Sigal described in an article in the *New York Times Book Review* in 1992. She would leave new pages of *The Golden Notebook* lying around the flat for him to see. If he didn't like what he read about himself or their relationship, he would note in his journal changes for accuracy as he perceived it.

In turn, Lessing regularly leafed through his journal. He knew she was doing this not just because he read some of his own phrasing and thinking in the scattered *Notebook* pages, but because he laid a trap for his lover and co-conspirator. Imitating a technique he had seen in a spy film, *The House on 92nd Street,* he tied a thin black thread to the drawer in which he kept his diary. If the thread was broken at the end of the day, that meant she'd read it. It always was. Neither of them ever acknowledged the secret collaboration.

Sigal recognises that the arrangement might strike people as foolish, but he was moved by a desire to have Lessing see how he perceived their romantic dilemma. He thought some of the tensions between them would abate if she understood more about him. Their affair was greatly affected by Sigal's inability to surmount his writer's block. No wonder, then, that when he discovered she was coming to the end of *The Golden Notebook,* he exploded in fury.

He told her she must stop writing about him. She had no right to turn their intimate relationship into a story. '"Oh, can't I?" she shouted back. "Why not – it's my work, isn't it?"'[6] Her words struck a chord. Yes, that was what had brought them together, wasn't it? That they would help each other through a time of personal difficulty? He felt he could not suddenly change his mind about their earnest pact.

Lessing was more sympathetic to an innocent party who was tarred with the same literary brush as Sigal (and others). Her son Peter was mistakenly identified as the source for Molly's son Tommy who in *The Golden Notebook* is blinded during a suicide attempt. Peter was so troubled about being associated with Lessings characters that he objected to having her later novel *Landlocked* (1965) dedicated to him. As soon as she was made aware of Peter's wishes, Lessing acted on them, instructing her publishers that she no longer wanted the book to have any dedication.

If Sigal and Lessing's writings sometimes had them at each other's throats, they did have on less contentious point of common ground – difficult relationships with their mothers. Clancy tried to be of help during a period of intense stress for Lessing after her mother's death in 1957. At a robust seventy-three, Maude suffered a stroke and quickly died. Lessing believes her mother would have gone on for several more years if she had felt useful to someone. Sigal could understand some of what Lessing was feeling because of his complex relationship with his own mother. He introduced Lessing to the blues, sung by artists like Bessie Smith and Billie Holiday, as background music for her suffering.

Today, Lessing writes in *Walking in the Shade*, she cannot listen to such songs, with their moans of loss and grief, for they bring back too much remembered pain. But she also says that though she felt pity for Maude, their situation was inevitable. Were she to return to life, stoic, uncomprehending Maude, her daughter would still offer no welcome. 'So what use grief? Pain? Sorrow? Regret?'[7] No matter what unresolved, unexamined loss hovered around her determined, detached rationality the only thing to do was try to move on.

Thriving on Adversity

The atomic bomb that fell on Hiroshima and ended the war cast a shadow of horror over people's post-war lives. As nuclear weapons proliferated all over the world, the testing polluted the atmosphere, potentially causing cancer, leukaemia, and dreadful genetic mutations. Mervyn Jones expressed the situation's grim irony. 'There was something peculiarly odious about subjecting people to suffering and early death in peacetime to test the functioning of weapons that, in theory, were never to be used.'[1]

Despite rhetoric about the peaceful use of atomic energy, the cold war was sweeping the world, and announcements of the development of intercontinental missiles made the threat of massive destruction a horrible possibility. Various groups had already been objecting to the defence testing, but it seemed increasingly clear that the weapons themselves needed to be eliminated if any kind of moral equilibrium were to return to humanity.

In 1958, the Campaign for Nuclear Disarmament (CND) was founded to ward off the threat of nuclear annihilation. It was hoped that the urgency of the challenge would bring together people of all classes and political persuasions. In fact, the movement remained essentially middle-class throughout its several years of life, and the rank-and-file membership was heavily weighted to the left.

From the beginning, a host of actors and writers affiliated themselves with the organisation. Alan Bates, Peter O'Toole, Nicol Williamson, and Vanessa Redgrave, among others, joined forces with Doris Lessing, Arnold Wesker, Robert Bolt, John Osborne and other artistic members of the New Left. Canon John Collins of St. Paul's Cathedral was appointed chairman of the Campaign committee, and Bertrand Russell was named president. At eighty-five, Russell saw a commitment to world peace and the salvation of the human race from a nuclear holocaust as the last great concerns of his life.

Working for unilateral disarmament, the CND believed that if Great Britain gave up her part in the nuclear race, and encouraged the United States to do so, other countries might follow their example. The Campaign hoped to convert both the government and the general public to

its way of thinking. An initial public meeting was announced in small
ads in the *New Statesman* and other weekly magazines.

No one in charge would have been surprised if the two-thousand-seat
auditorium that had been booked for the occasion had remained nearly
empty on the appointed night. Instead, five thousand people arrived,
and impromptu sessions to handle the overflow had to be held in other
parts of the building. As Canon Collins brought the evening to a close,
a spontaneous cry of 'March to Downing Street' spread through the
halls. The throngs were so thick in front of the prime minister's home
at 10 Downing Street that the police had to use force to break up the
crowd and many, Mervyn Jones among them, were hauled off to jail.

The main result of the meeting was that it helped spread the word of
a four-day march from London to Aldermaston – site of the Atomic
Weapons Research Establishment – on Easter weekend (the future
Easter marches would reverse the route). The march had actually been
planned by another organisation – the Direct Action Committee
Against Nuclear War or DAC. It was the DAC that decided on the
unusually long distance. The usual distance of most protest marches
was from Marble Arch to Trafalgar Square, not this journey of forty-five
miles. Once again, no one could predict how many hardy souls would
show up for such a heroic trek. The newspapers reported that some
4000 people converged on Trafalgar Square for the beginning of the
march, but that only a few hundred actually began the trek to Aldermaston.

From that point on the march ebbed and flowed as people, left, joined,
and rejoined the crowd. Estimates vary as to the final number that
reached Aldermaston. While contemporary accounts run as low as 790,
participants such as Arnold Wesker recall that 4000 marchers arrived,
equalling the newspapers' estimates for the march's beginning.

The weather on Good Friday, the first day of the march, was dreadful, with a mix of rain and an out-of-season snowstorm, but it didn't stop
Doris Lessing from taking part. Indeed, according to Clancy Sigal's
rendition of the event in *The Secret Defector*, nature's obstacles only
spurred on Rose O'Malley, the Lessing character.

"'You just don't understand the left in Britain, darling," she muttered
grimly pulling on her Wellington boots. "Puritan Roundheads every
man jack of us. We positively thrive on adversity."'[2]

Sigal writes that because Rose was a successful author, she marched
in the front rows with the other celebrities from the arts and government and religion.

In the novel, Gus (the Sigal character) shares a poncho in the back
ranks with Rose's son Aly. They have formed an attachment to each
other – as Clancy Sigal and Peter Lessing did in real life – and they
enjoyed themselves immensely, with Gus feeling closer to Aly's age
than to Aly's mother's.

On the actual march, Lessing walked with Christopher Logue, and Mervyn Jones, and briefly with Kenneth Tynan who had taxied to Aldermaston and caught the tail end of the march. Kathleen Tynan reports that her husband, who was ambivalent about the theatrics of the situation, 'stepped out with a "Hello, hello, hello,"' and joined Logue and Lessing for a picnic.[3] Tynan had been at Trafalgar, but like many others had opted out of the march, until the final leg. They arrived to a fitting climax – a makeshift outdoor party. Many people, like Lessing and her friends, set up near the research centre. Some participants bought provisions from a travelling canteen that followed the marchers, others had brought food and wine from home to fuel themselves along the way or celebrate the walk's conclusion.

> 'In an astonishingly short time,' Mervyn Jones writes, 'ban the bomb' became the central, the most vibrant, the inescapable talking-point ... No one, the political professionals admitted with amazement, had ever seen anything quite like this campaign. It was at the same time a moral crusade, a wave of hopeful excitement, a social phenomenon and an intellectual trend.[4]

CND became the impetus for an infinite number of marches and demonstrations, often accompanied by poetry readings and jazz or rock music performances. At one weeklong nationwide demonstration in 1959, John Osborne, and his wife, the actress Mary Ure, along with other theatre people such as Constance Cummings, joined Doris Lessing in hitching up the ropes of their sandwich boards and marching past Downing Street, the Defence Ministry, and a Battle of Britain Remembrance Spitfire, while inside St. Paul's, Canon Collins was mellifluously preaching against the bomb.

Apparently, Lessing's vanity about her lovely legs won out over comfort when she dressed for the march. According to a newspaper account, as 'Canon Collins leant forward in his pulpit: 'There has been, both here and in America, a constant barrage of lies or semi lies, or half truths and evasions of the truth ...' novelist Doris Lessing, teetering on stiletto heels beneath her sandwich boards, cried: "Oh, my poor feet!"[5]

In 1959, a new group interested in more direct sorts of protest was put together. The Committee of 100, under the leadership of Bertrand Russell, espoused the idea of mass civil disobedience. Lessing was a member. The hope was that huge numbers of people – ideally some two thousand – would pledge themselves to stage sit-downs in public places, such as Trafalgar Square. *The Manchester Guardian* reported on the first meeting, 'Those present had responded to Lord Russell's invitation to come forward to form a committee that would sponsor acts of civil disobedience.' The story listed Doris Lessing among the people who were involved in discussing what contentious action to take. Some favoured storming government offices, others preferred interfering with official events like the opening of Parliament. Still others voted for disrupting broadcasts of the BBC and producing their own programs on pirate radio stations. Amid all the rhetoric, substantial amounts of money were raised.[6] And through demonstrations and public meetings, the group began to attract the attention of both grass roots supporters and the British authorities.

A crackdown on The Committee was launched a few days prior to a major demonstration scheduled for Sunday, September 17 1961, in Trafalgar Square. On the preceding Tuesday, twenty-nine members of the movement were brought up on charges of 'incitement to disorder' for being part of the organisation that was planning the protest. Although all the defendants were convicted and sent to prison (a fact reported differently by Doris Lessing, who was present), the demonstration went ahead as planned and the trial itself became a forum for the anti-nuclear movement. Bertrand Russell, the most prominent of the defendants, was able to make an impassioned declaration of purpose, which he read from a single, type-written page. 'We who are here accused are prepared to suffer imprisonment because we believe that this is the most effective way of working for salvation of our country and the world ... While life remains to us we will not cease to do what lies in our power to avert the greatest calamity that has ever threatened mankind.'[7] Immediately after his statement, the court broke out into roaring applause while angry ushers fought to restore order.

In *Walking in the Shade* Doris Lessing, who attended the Trafalgar Protest, dates it a year earlier and recalls seeing Russell there. Though he had been present at previous events, he was actually in Brixton Prison, serving a one-week prison sentence with Lady Russell. The elderly couple had got off relatively lightly due to age and infirmity. The others (including Robert Bolt, Christopher Logue, and Arnold Wesker) were sentenced to a month - the bulk of which was served at Drake Hall. Wesker remembers reading a great many books passed on to him by a sympathetic officer during his internment. The prison allowed some moving about within the building, and one evening, in the dining room, Christopher Logue jumped onto a table to announce that he was a poet and would be giving a reading that evening in the prison library. He played, Wesker recalls to a packed house.

After he was released from prison at the end of the month, Wesker resigned from the Committee of 100. He believed that the concept of civil disobedience called for new participants as each action took place. If the same people were always arrested, he reasoned, they would receive increasingly long prison terms, and so reduce the number of protesters at each ensuing event.[8]

Attrition was generally setting in to the campaign. Nuclear war had not broken out, and gradually people began to lose their sense of imminent danger. There was also a growing split between the broad movement of CND, which Canon Collins most represented, and the Committee of 100, the faction headed by Bertrand Russell, dedicated to the idea of civil disobedience. Many of the people in CND, like Mervyn Jones and Stuart Hall, were trying to prevent a situation where followers would have to choose between the two approaches. Younger people would adhere to direct action, the majority of the movement would not, and if the factions were asked to choose, they might well decide to get out of the movement altogether.

'We needed both wings, both tactics,' says Stuart Hall. Russell was obviously crucial because of his world stature and symbolic presence. Collins brought the ability to rally the churches, and having done important work in India and Africa he was admired by those constituencies. It was essential that these two wise, courageous men, who were also capable of being prima donnas, didn't skewer each other in public.

After a heated meeting with everyone offering opinions, Doris Lessing was nominated as the person to approach Russell to convince him of the wisdom of making peace with Collins. Her efforts were fruitless. Russell refused to relax his militant stance. Soon after, according to Ralph Miliband, Lessing got 'fed up with the theatrical kinds of activities,' and withdrew from both groups. The Aldermaston marches grew smaller and smaller. In January 1963, Bertrand Russell resigned, and to all intents and purposes, CND and the Committee of 100 were dead.

* * *

In his memoir, Mervyn Jones says that as the years passed CND was remembered reverently by many of his contemporaries. He quotes from a chapter he wrote about the campaign in a Festschrift for Canon Collins' seventieth birthday. 'There has been nothing quite like it in our times, and it is impossible to convey to younger people the nature of the experience that we – joyously, passionately, but also laboriously – went through.'[9]

Doris Lessing has no such affection for her days of protest. When the writer Lesley Hazleton engaged her in a discussion in 1982 about her new political attitudes, Lessing raged at the obstinacy of the peace lovers: When she attempts to argue for bomb shelters instead of romantic gestures, they don't even listen. And when Lessing recalls the Aldermaston marches, it is with some scorn. She was on six of them and, she says, unlike too many other people, understands that they were a failure. She feels it should be eminently clear to anyone living in this nuclear age that 'Ban the Bomb' was an empty cry.

Not content to snipe at the futility of the peace movement (as she saw it), in the early 1980s Lessing became an outspoken advocate for nuclear preparedness. In interviews, letters to the editor, and other writing, she advocated the expenditure of billions of pounds for the production of 'large communal shelters' to be used in the event of nuclear conflicts.[10]

As she erased her old image of Communist radical, Doris Lessing also abandoned her sympathies for the working classes. In 1992, she told journalist Jane Kelly that when she first came to England, 'I thought the British working class were prisoners, but now I see that they don't want to get out of it, which is even more horrifying and it does this country a great deal of harm ... The cleverest of your people go abroad.'[11]

By the end of the fifties, Clancy Sigal was writing a wide range of articles for various periodicals; what he wanted to write about was working-class life, and preferably in a longer form than magazines allowed. Through Lessing, he had met Edward Thompson, who had a network of people who had been in the Party or in Popular Front type of activities, peace committees, friendly trade unionists, even people on the left of the Labour Party. Many were ordinary workers who weren't intellectuals in the traditional sense, but self-made, working-class autodidacts. Through Thompson Signal met one such man named Doherty, who was a coal miner in the village of Thurcroft. Doherty also wrote novels.

Sigal would write his first published novel, *Weekend in Dinlock*, about life in a working-class mining village. Before he left England in 1989, he gave Doherty credit for making the book possible. 'I wrote it,' Sigal says, 'but he opened his village, his pit, and himself to me.' When Doherty read the book in manuscript, he said he was sure the novel would bring Sigal fame, but in the long run, it wouldn't be able to help 'the likes of us.'

The 'them' that the 'us' of Len and Clancy stood against, Sigal says, was not just the upper class, but 'a whole world of cosmopolitan sophisticates, centred in London, who drove us mad with their double signals of praise and patronisation.'[12]

To some degree, Sigal always felt outside Doris's literary life. People didn't see them together very often, not enough to form a sense of what the bond between them really consisted of, which was in fact very primitive and basic. On some deep level they 'knew' each other when they met.

'We were terribly supportive of each other,' says Sigal. 'I would support her in her fiercest denunciations, including her friends and publishers ... And she would support me.' When he was fighting his writer's block she'd tell him to stop complaining and feeling sorry for himself. Maybe that's what artists did in America, but in England, she said, they just got down to work, without gratuitous agonising.

'And I think her saying it's not that big a deal was hugely liberating,' he says. Just as it was liberating when 'after the worst fight, she would just go light up a cigarette, sit down and go to work, the way my mother went to work on a machine. That I understood ... that no matter what happens, after all the Sturm und Drang you go to work on a machine .... My mother did it, and Doris did it. I said, 'Well, I can do it.' And so I think in that sense we gave each other a hundred percent support.

'And I think we both knew ... that whatever the troubles, we were very good for each other at that particular time. And she would put up with a lot and I would put up with a lot.'

Lessing fiercely supported Sigal when *Weekend in Dinlock* was published, in 1960. Edward Thompson and several others, particularly the older people with long connections to the Communist Party, still felt proprietary toward the working classes, and didn't fully agree with Sigal's bleak portrait of their lives. Also, Thompson had been studying the working class for decades. That a young American could come in and, on the basis of brief visits, try to present a picture of the miner's life was apparently irksome.

In fact, the book is vividly written and does not condescend to its subjects either by treating them as sociological symbols or by making them 'noble savages.' Many miners who read it generally seemed content with the book's depiction of their world, finding it honest and empathetic. Critical praise, as Len Doherty had predicted, also was high.

Whatever threads of anger, chaos, deception were woven into their relationship, Doris Lessing and Clancy Sigal, and literature, were well served by their union, for during their time together, they both wrote the books that launched them into new levels of their careers.

Playing with a Golden Tiger

In 1962, *The Golden Notebook* was published, and Lessing's *Play with a Tiger* received a full-scale West End production. The characters in the play were born in the novel. Dave Miller and Anna Freeman, the protagonists of *Play with a Tiger*, are nearly twinned figures to *The Golden Notebook*'s Saul Green and Anna Wulf (whose maiden, name, not coincidentally, is Freeman). Both couples share the same emotional turmoil in their relationships: 'Sometimes the flat is an oasis of loving affection,' Anna Wulf says in *The Golden Notebook*, 'then suddenly it's a battleground, even the walls vibrate with hate, we circle around each other like two animals.'[1]

The play's central image and theme are actually mentioned in the novel. At one dramatic point in the novel. when Anna feels fragmented to the point of madness, she lies on her bed gazing at light flickering across her ceiling. Suddenly the light turns into two enormous eyes watching her. She fantasises being inside a cage with a great tiger lying on top that could jump into the cage at any moment. Unexpectedly, she hears people coming to capture the tiger and her fear for her own safety is replaced by concern for the animal. She tells the tiger to flee, and he follows her command. Anna is grateful, for she knows that the tiger represents Saul, and she wants him to be unfettered, to roam freely through the world. At this point in her reverie, she thinks about writing a play herself, about Saul and the tiger.

Play with a Tiger takes place between nine in the evening and four o' clock the following morning, 'and the subject of the piece,' wrote theatre critic Kenneth A. Hurren, 'if I am not underlining the obvious, is sex ... The trouble with Dave, a Chicago boy, is that he is unusually and indiscriminately randy.'[2]

Doris Lessing's continuing conflict over the promiscuous instincts of 'real men' and her own need for emotional security are integral to the play's story. Ostensibly, Anna Freeman is willing to accept men's polygamous nature and she tries to be sophisticated and casual about it, but she rebels at the idea when her own feelings are at stake.

As she does in *The Golden Notebook*, Lessing experiments with form in her play. At the end of act one, the walls of Anna's bed-sitting room disappear so that the room seems part of the street. As the room's boundaries disappear, so does the reality of Anna and Dave as they are now. We move into their minds as they recall their pasts – Anna, a young girl in Australia, Dave, the street-smart boy in the slums of Chicago – before they began their loving assaults on each other. Lessing had already undergone psychotherapy when she wrote the play and she uncovers early psychological bruises that explain the lovers' behaviour, such as inadequate nurturing from their mothers. Lessing talked to Clancy Sigal a good deal about his mother, and she sensed in him a deprivation she knew all too well. It was part of the bond between them.

* * *

Most of the critics had misgivings about *Play with a Tiger*. Kenneth Tynan felt it was overlong and underdeveloped. Only the second act captured his imagination, when 'Anna and her runaway lover' take part in a 'prolonged duet ... They are subject and object in a human sentence of which the verb (they sometimes persuade themselves) is love.'[3] The play would run only two months, a great disappointment to Lessing who had been waiting four years to see it put on. The reason for the delay in production, she explained to journalist Donald Gomery, was that the producer, Oscar Lewenstein, wanted the lead role to be played by Siobhan McKenna, and he was waiting for her to be available.

As Lessing discussed the upcoming premiere with Gomery, who was interviewing her at her flat for a story about a playwright's anticipation of opening night, she smoked incessantly. '"When I'm tense," she said, "I smoke 50 a day; 30 if I'm not so tense."' The reporter was surprised at her quiet, modulated tone of voice, for, as he explained to his readers, since Doris Lessing had arrived in London, she has 'won for herself the reputation of one of the angriest young women of today.'[4]

Lessing would be very angry about the play's misfiring. McKenna received some negative criticism that the playwright agreed with, and Lessing fumed that she had been forced to wait so long for someone she had never wanted at all. But an equally infuriating aspect of the experience was that cast opposite McKenna was Alex Vespi, a young American actor who Lessing considered blatantly and grossly 'a sexist stud.' (Such a feminist-tinged reaction didn't keep Lessing from also criticising a revival of the play by 'feminists,' who 'played it as a great blast against men ... as a shriek of hysteria.')[5]

If Lessing found the male lead disturbing, Clancy Sigal was apoplectic. He watched the play from a seat in the balcony for which he had been given a complimentary ticket. Sigal told her he wanted to rewrite some of the dialogue, but Doris had passed the point of letting him 'correct' her writing. Her version of Clancy Sigal would remain between book covers and behind footlights.

So confident was she of her creation that sometime later, at a party,

she suddenly embraced her lover, and told the assembled guests –
Henry Kissinger unaccountably among them, Sigal remembers – 'I
invented Clancy!' Sigal objected, declaring 'My mother, Jennie, did that
by giving birth to me.' Lessing waved away the response. Jennie had,
Lessing said, getting the last word, 'the easy part.'⁶

* * *

If Lessing was surprised by the disappointing response to *Play with a
Tiger*, she was totally unprepared for the powerful reaction to *The
Golden Notebook*. Although the book did not initially enjoy gigantic
sales, it received immense and important critical attention.

The novel deals with several experiences that describe the social
climate of its time: Communism and its turning point in 1956, the
acknowledgement and rise of sexual politics, personal and intellectual
upheaval and breakdown, the conflicts of contemporary motherhood,
and the relationship between historical time and the individual life.

Anna Wulf, is the narrator-protagonist of the novel, is a writer whose
first book, *Frontiers of War,* was a more than modest success. In part
because of that success, she is suffering from writer's block as she tries
to work on a second novel. Anna is approaching forty. Her lover of
several years, Michael, has recently left her. She is a single mother,
does volunteer work for the Communist Party, and is in analysis with
a therapist she calls Mother Sugar.

Almost all the reviewers commented on the book's daring new form,
long excerpts from four notebooks that Anna keeps, black, red, yellow,
and blue. They are used to show the divisions in her life. Anna's black
notebook details her early life in Africa. The red notebook describes her
changing engagement with Communism. The yellow notebook holds
parts of the novel she is struggling unsuccessfully to write, plus notes
for other stories. The blue notebook is more like a conventional diary,
including much detail about her sexual life and her experience with
psychoanalysis.

These notebooks also contain sections of a short novel called *Free
Women*, which explores the important friendship between Anna and
Molly, another divorced mother, who has a troubled son. At the end of
the novel, Anna owns a golden notebook in which she hopes to record
an integration of her separate experiences. The last section of the blue
notebook begins with Anna saying that her daughter, Janet, is her
anchor to normality. Now that Janet has gone off to boarding school,
Anna's hold on sanity wavers. While this is happening, in the last one
hundred pages of *The Golden Notebook*, Saul Green arrives at Anna's
flat, the Communist from America who needs a place to stay. Anna is
instantly aware of a parallel to her own mental state, and, like Doris

Lessing, she is also able to use fiction as a way of accepting truths she avoids in real life.

In the yellow notebook she creates a story outline: 'A woman, starved for love, meets a man rather younger than herself, younger perhaps in emotional experience than in years; or perhaps in the depth of his emotional experience. She deludes herself about the nature of the man; for him, another love affair merely.'[7]

Saul and Anna come together in a mix of irritation and affection. She accuses him of turning her into a mother figure, something that further complicates her ambivalence about the mother role. Anna and Saul both project aspects of themselves onto each other. Recalling a dream which is a paradigm of their relationship, Anna says, 'I was playing roles, one after another, against Saul, who was playing roles.'[8] Together they go through a wide range of ways to behave as man and woman. At the same time, Anna is amazed at the number of female roles she had never played, either because she rejected them or had never had the opportunity to embrace them.

As the novel ends, Anna's writer's block is broken, and Saul gives her the first line for her new novel, which she inscribes in the golden notebook: 'The two women were alone in the London flat.'[9]

It was one of Lessing's goals to show the effects of twentieth-century experience on the individual – in particular, on the artist. She had never lost her Communist-inspired interest in the relationship between the individual and the larger cultural collective.

A statement, which Lessing had originally written as a letter to her English publisher, appeared on the dustjacket of *The Golden Notebook* explaining her creative process. She says she had long considered writing a novel about being a writer, but decided the subject had been used already. She was also interested in the artist's self-absorption and how that affects her work. Finally, she thought that the way to approach the subject of a writer's life was to have the writer be suffering from writer's block. Showing how Anna's block came about, she would also show the problems in the larger culture. She saw the splintering of Anna Wulf as a phenomenon that was not unique to writers and artists, but rather grew out of the conditions of everyday life.

In a 1971 introduction for the Bantam paperback edition, Lessing recalled that at the same time that she was considering writing a novel about a writer's conflicted life, she was thinking of making a statement about the conventional novel by breaking away from traditional form. But her most important goal was to 'shape a book which would ... talk through the way it was shaped.'[10]

* * *

Stuart Hall, speaking as a cultural theorist as well as one of Lessing's former comrades, recalls: '*The Golden Notebook* was a very important book for all of us … we liked her earlier books very much, but they were still moving on the ground. *The Golden Notebook* starts to soar. It had another dimension. Its experimental qualities made her a novelist of really important stature.'

For many former Communists, the red notebook was particularly rich in shared meaning. Just as Doris Lessing could describe segregation and racism to audiences in highly personal terms, speaking from her own experience, she captured, in this part of the novel, the individual's dilemma about the collapse of a passionate political dream. To leave the Communist Party in the 1950s, to relinquish the glorious vision, was to become terribly afraid of turning into an isolated, bourgeois, apolitical pessimist.

Women did not read *The Golden Notebook* simply as literature. The book was personally and politically enlightening about what it meant to be a woman in the larger world. They read it, too, to learn about love and its discontents. Indeed, it was perhaps in the sphere of love and emotions and male-female roles that, much to Lessing's increasing dismay, *The Golden Notebook* made its biggest impact of all.

Emerging from the straight-jacket of the 1950s, women were ready to read about the struggle to live a complex, meaningful life outside of the rigidly defined roles of previous generations. Anna understood that she would face internal as well as external obstacles in her attempts to create a new design for her female experience.

Like it or not – and although Lessing welcomed the fame that came from admiring female readers, she doesn't like it at all – *The Golden Notebook* was one of the first feminist texts. Remembering what it was like to read the novel as a young woman in 1962, the writer Vivian Gornick calls it a book that 'embodies the history of the contemporary feminist movement, in some ways more than *The Second Sex*. It is an essence of the gestalt that finally became the contemporary feminist movement.'[11]

Gornick grew up with a mother who said that love was the most important element of a woman's life. Doris Lessing was saying that work was equally necessary. While many, like Gornick, found that duality romantic, Lessing seemed more embittered by the problems these coupled needs engendered. Gornick also remembered being overcome by Lessing's descriptions of sex, which are both celebratory and tinged with depression. Lessing makes clear that the intelligent woman who desires a rewarding sex life must fight the repressive aspects of sexual submission.

Men also reacted powerfully to this window into women's inner lives. Irving Howe confessed to particularly enjoying the conversations between Anna and her friend and intellectual cohort, Molly. 'My own curiosity, as a masculine outsider, was enormous, for here, I felt, was the way intellectual women really talk to one another when they felt free and unobserved.'[12]

Howe cheered the arrival of what at the time was uncommon in contemporary literature, an intellectually mature and sophisticated female protagonist. Anna Wulf's observations were barbed, and she made no secret of her many emotional problems that resulted in large part from her attempts to be a 'free woman.'

The critic John Leonard captured the astonishment of many men who read the novel. For the first time, he said, he felt he understood what women really thought about the men in their lives. 'She saw me under my sheet, she knew my wicked heart ... In my vanity and petulant neediness, *I had been found out* ... I sought to modify my swinish swagger. Henceforth, at least in public, I would try to behave as if Anna Wulf were watching and reporting me to Molly.'[13]

In terms of literary value, Leonard has said that the book 'didn't bear any resemblance to what other women were writing and I don't recall anything like it in terms of ambition, either male or female, on the contemporary scene.'

To read *The Golden Notebook* was to 'rethink everything,' all the 'isms, all your experience, everything in the labyrinth.' In his excitement of discovery, Leonard tried to get his wife of that time, who was a scientist, to read it, but she quickly lost interest. He sought out a close friend, a professor at Berkeley, 'and I couldn't get her to read it either. I kept saying, "you are an intelligent woman, this has to be the writer for you. She comes out of colonialism, she comes out of racism, she comes out of Marxism, she comes out of psychology, but I couldn't get them to read it."'

Doris Lessing would not be surprised at this resistance. Although the book would become a sacred text for several generations of women, the admiration was not universal. 'A lot of women were angry about *The Golden Notebook*,' Lessing recalled in 1981. 'The number of women prepared to stand up for what they really think, feel, experience with a man they are in love with is still small.'[14]

Around the same time, Lessing told the BBC that a great many women had been extremely indignant and had no qualms about letting her know their feelings. They acted as if she had given away some deep female truth, and demanded to know why she had turned on them in this way. Lessing claimed this discomfort arose from the fact that the majority of women would still run like frightened animals having stones thrown at them if a man called them castrating or unfeminine. In Lessing's opinion, if a woman becomes involved with a man who would use these terms, she has earned the abuse she receives.

Infinitely more women, however, lauded the book than attacked it, a situation that continued to rankle the reluctant icon.

On a visit to America in 1969, Lessing gave a reading at the Poetry

Center of the 92nd Street YMHA. The feminist writer Susan Brownmiller attended the event and asked the question in her follow-up
Village Voice article, 'When a cult writer is introduced to her cult, is it
necessarily a painful encounter?'

This one, Brownmiller wrote, indeed was, for it turned out to be a
meeting 'full of surprise and misunderstanding.' Efforts to get Lessing
to talk about feminist issues were turned aside, often quite rudely. She
made no pretence of hiding her impatience with these reverential
acolytes. Finally, after flippantly dismissing of several questioners,
Lessing did make some attempt at apology. 'I'm sorry there are so many
unhappy women. But there are a lot more important battles than the
sex war.'[15]

Lessing's irritation with the tenacious hold *The Golden Notebook* had
on women's psyches increased with time. In response to my author's
query in the *New York Times Book Review*, one avid fan wrote back:

> Some years ago I went to hear Lessing read at the 92nd Street Y.M.H.A.
> in New York City. A woman in the audience asked her a question ... about
> ... *The Golden Notebook*. But Lessing answered in a way I had never
> heard another author do. She paused for a moment and said, 'That's the
> stupidest question anyone has ever asked me.'

Another enthusiast waited after a Lessing reading of another book to
have her sign a well-thumbed copy of *The Golden Notebook*.

> As I waited in line, I inwardly told myself not to say a word to her ... I'm
> well aware that Lessing hates the fact that she has a cult following ... But
> despite this awareness and my intentions, when I handed her my book to
> sign, these words fell out of my mouth: 'This is the happiest day of my life.'
> 'Oh, don't exaggerate!' exclaimed Ms Lessing, waving her hand in
> dismissal. As I shrivelled inside, she handed me my book. Her eyes met
> mine. I looked at her with true regret and helplessness, knowing there
> was nothing I could say under the circumstances that would convey what
> her work meant to me without sounding idiotic.

In 1982 when Lesley Hazleton interviewed her for the *New York Times
Magazine*, she explored Lessing's feelings about the women's movement and women's continued response to *The Golden Notebook*. Lessing
insisted that the novel was not meant as a call to arms for women's
liberation. In fact, none of her books had been written from a specifically
feminist perspective. She felt that the women's movement had latched
on to the book because it was a new kind of writing about women, but
she never intended it to be interpreted as a diatribe against men.
Indeed, the book was intended to show the evils of all kinds of categorisation, and seeing people in opposition to each other.

Hazleton told Lessing that many women believed she had abandoned
their concerns in the years since *The Golden Notebook*. Speaking very

sternly and deliberately, Lessing told her visitor that she had been writing for thirty years and a great number of her books deal with issues that concern women. What women want from her is not literary work but a kind of religious testimonial. She should decry the beastly actions of men and stand by her sisters in their holy cause. Well, she would not play to that irritating need. 'They want slogans and nonsense ... Everything I dislike about politics is enshrined in the women's movement ... It's just petty and stupid.'[16]

Hazleton remembers the daylong conversation as 'fascinating because you don't really talk with her, you get talked at by her.' As Lessing delivered her 'tirade,' her thermal underwear peeked out of her skirt, and it had a little lacy edge. The contrast between the harsh diatribe and the soft lace created a paradoxical impression often associated with her. This is a woman who can seem both frightening and vulnerable , and for Hazleton – as for others who have crossed Lessing's path – it was a strangely appealing combination.

It does please Lessing that *The Golden Notebook* is being taught in some history and political science courses rather than only in women's studies or even literature classes. The book has sold over a million copies all over the world, and currently averages sales in the United States of about five thousand copies a year. She continues to receive passionate letters from admirers. Their worship still gets short shrift from the self she is now. Feminism 'was a movement with so much energy it could have changed society, and now they've blown it,' she told a reporter for the London *Telegraph*. 'Thank God, I'm not a part of it.'[17]

The Madness of Wisdom

Clancy Sigal's writer's block produced physical symptoms as well as mental turmoil. Headaches, stomach pains, icy sweats, and even sudden fevers attacked his exhausted body. Nights were often battles against the rising fear of an approaching new day, when again he would be unable to write. Lessing would hold his cold, clammy body in her arms, trying to break through his terror with sex and love he says.

Lessing told Sigal that some of his panic had nothing to do with writing. It was unfocused, nameless, to her thinking, the result of his childhood, his parents, especially his mother. In his novel *The Secret Defector*, Sigal has Rose constantly telling Gus that many of his painful feelings and destructive habits have oedipal roots. Lessing also blamed the prevailing culture for her lover's despair, just as she had always found it culpable for her own sense of fragmentation. Knowing how much she had been helped by therapy, she urged Sigal to see a psychiatrist, but he was resolutely hostile to the idea. In *The Secret Defector*, Gus dismisses similar entreaties that he see a shrink with, 'Rose, just shut the fuck up, okay?'[1]

But Clancy Sigal, at least, would eventually see an extraordinary shrink, the Scottish psychiatrist R.D. Laing, a poet and iconoclast who for many years was 'the best-known psychoanalyst in the world,' according to a 1989 obituary by Anthony Storr, himself an eminent, far more traditional psychiatrist.[2]

Laing was a product of the 1960s, making the most of a cultural moment when strong convergence between radical politics and radical psychoanalysis took place. He was particularly popular with the New Left, who found his iconoclasm sympathetic. The staff of the *New Left Review* regularly met with 'Ronnie' Laing to talk about social and political issues from a personal perspective. 'It sort of forced people to be self-aware because there were a lot of intellectuals who had read a lot of Sartre, Engel, and I don't know what, history and economics,' says Robin Blackburn, a very young staffer at the time, and now the editor of the *New Left Review*. 'He was really obliging people to connect the theory with their own experience, which is a very New Left Idea.'

By the time he was in treatment with Laing, Sigal had moved out of Lessing's flat. 'We had been living in each other's pockets for a long time,' he explains. 'We both had been successful, we did have some money. And I thought, 'Well, now's the time for me to get my own place.' It had been love and war, and maybe the balance just tipped a little bit more to the war than the love.' But they continued to meet all the time, even though they were also seeing other people. When asked if something finally happened that caused a more decisive parting, Sigal responded, 'Yeah, something certainly happened with me. I became a nut and began to detach from everybody and anybody.'

That he was pulling away did not alter Lessing's concern for his mental state. Sigal does not remember her directly recommending that he see Laing, but he indicates she was drawn to the man in part because of a shared interest in expanding consciousness.' She was experimenting with morning glories during this period .... she was very engaged with the higher consciousness ... And somehow or other, she put me on to Alan Sillitoe, who was a friend of Laing, and the connection was made.'

The writer Elaine Showalter is quoted as saying, 'In London in the late 1950s, Doris Lessing, Ronald Laing and Clancy Sigal formed a circle of almost incestuous mutual influence.' The three principals have never affirmed this assessment of their relationship. Laing argued that while he and Sigal became colleagues and good friends, Sigal primarily saw him professionally. 'Although he didn't want to regard himself as a patient ... he wanted to consult someone about his life and he thought I might be able to do that. So I agreed to that and he saw me for about once a week for two years.'[3]

Lessing felt a broad-based affinity for R.D. Laing. It would have been difficult for her *not* to relate to a man who declared, 'The initial act of brutality against the average child is the mother's first kiss.'[4] Laing believed that even with the best of intentions, parents corrupt a child's natural growth by carrying out the imperatives of their own conditioning. Sounding remarkably like Doris Lessing, he writes:

> From the moment of birth, when the Stone Age baby confronts the twentieth-century mother, the baby is subjected to these forces of violence, called love, as its mother and father, and their parents and their parents before them, have been. These forces are mainly concerned with destroying most of its potentialities, and on the whole this enterprise is successful. By the time the new human being is fifteen or so, we are left with a being like ourselves, a half-crazed creature more or less adjusted to a mad world. This is normality.[5]

Both Laing and Lessing were deeply interested in the definitions of madness and reality. Lessing was sympathetic to Laing's belief that the insane person is simultaneously victim and symbol of a sick society. In Laing's view, the schizophrenic person is protecting himself from life's assaults, much as we all try to do every day, in a less dramatic fashion.

In *The Divided Self*, the 1960 book that catapulted him to fame, Laing says that 'there is a comprehensible transition from the sane schizoid way of being-in-the-world to a psychotic way of being-in-the-world.'[6]

One of Laing's most controversial and fundamental precepts was that 'madness need not be all breakdown ... It may also be breakthrough.' Given this mindset, he did not believe in trying to prevent or stop psychotic episodes. Rather, he would respect them, and even try to expedite their course. The schizoid personality may be a prophet, Laing came to feel, showing us the way to a new and more unified way of life:

> If the human race survives, future men will, I suspect, look back on our enlightened epoch as a veritable Age of Darkness ... They will see that what we call 'schizophrenia' was one of the forms in which, often through quite ordinary people, the light began to break through the cracks in our all-too-closed minds.[7]

Thus when Sigal complained to Laing about Lessing using his life in her writing, the two men discussed the significance of a severed self being increasingly split by someone writing about him. Laing was intrigued with the idea and argued jubilantly, 'That woman stealing your soul was the luckiest thing that ever happened to you .... She's emptied you for the Great Task ahead ... the schizoid voyage.'[8]

Laing was fiercely opposed to the kind of treatment offered by most mental hospitals: confinement, shock treatments, tranquillising drugs to quiet the chaotic brain. In his view, these hospitals were prisons, and the psychiatrists who prescribed the treatments, cruel agents of the repressive culture. Clancy Sigal remembers that Laing 'related with unusually relaxed humanity to patients who early in his career he saw bludgeoned with ECT and insulin shocks.'[9]

Laing had formed his attitudes about therapy early in his career. As a medical officer in the British Army, he treated a catatonic young private. Instead of administering the usual treatments, he spent hours with the troubled soldier, going so far as to take him home on leave to shield him from other doctors prescribing insulin and electric shock. 'He swallowed tea and chocolates that my mother put in his mouth,' Laing recalled in his memoir, *Wisdom, Madness and Folly*. After returning to base, Laing explained to the private that all he had to do was to continue to walk, sit, stand, and lie down in a normal way, to obey orders and speak (a few words would do) when spoken to, and he would be out of the Army for good in a few weeks.

Without any treatment besides Laing's comforting presence and friendship, the soldier was able to return to normal life. 'Years later, he became the director of a well-known college of dance and drama. He would have stood no chance whatsoever if he had gone through the usual psychiatric mill,'[10] Laing wrote.

Laing believed that if he could heal one person this way, he could do it for others as well. In the 1960s treatment with R.D. Laing often meant taking the new mind-expanding drug, LSD. Laing was given his first dose of LSD in 1960, for experimental purposes, and soon after, he was given permission by the British government to use it in treating his clients. Although he personally had experienced no alarming effects from the drug, he was aware of its potential problems for certain people, and did not dispense it casually.

His method of treatment was to dilute a small amount of LSD in a glass of water, and drink the mixture along with his patient over sessions that lasted no less than six hours, sometimes considerably more. Laing's son Adrian, who wrote a biography of his, father spoke to former patients who said that 'dropping acid' with R.D. Laing was both 'exhilarating and liberating.'[11] Many people believed that one six-hour LSD session with Laing was more helpful than years of traditional psychoanalysis. For some patients, however, the experience was overwhelming, so Laing was reluctant to have anyone take the drug without supervision.

Laing told Dr Bob Mullan, a friend who has edited several books about the Scottish analyst, in addition to a 1999 biography, that he had given the drug to Doris Lessing over a series of six visits, but she fell into the category of client who received no visible benefit from the experience. Their sessions ended, he said, because Lessing felt she should not be charged for them, since they were colleagues as professional writers. Laing argued that she had come to him as a patient, not as a writer, and that he expected to be paid for his efforts. For her part, Lessing has never publicly acknowledged such treatments, or any use of LSD.

* * *

While Laing worked to change social conditions for those diagnosed as mentally ill, his main goal was to alter individual consciousness. As the years progressed, Doris Lessing moved farther and farther away from her own belief in social change, toward the conviction that only individual, internal transformation mattered.

In 1964, Laing wrote: 'We are socially conditioned to regard total immersion in outer space and time as normal and healthy. Immersion in inner space and time tends to be regarded as anti-social withdrawal, a deviancy, invalid, pathological *per se*, in some sense discreditable. We are far more out of touch with even the nearest approaches of the infinite reaches of inner space than we now are with the reaches of outer space.'[12]

This was a provocative stimulus for Lessing's 1971 novel, *Briefing for a Descent into Hell*, which she begins by announcing, 'Category: Inner-space fiction – For there is never anywhere to go but in.'

By the mid-sixties Laing was in great demand as a lecturer, and the darling of a burgeoning television industry. Invitations poured in from other countries, especially America, where the student movement found excitement and validation in his philosophical and political radicalism, not to mention his acceptance of drug use as a tool for the examined life.

But fascinated as Doris Lessing was with Laing's theories, she worried about Sigal's deteriorating condition. 'I was totally nuts,' he says, 'and I remember her saying to me very clearly, "You be very careful of what you're doing, because I think you're getting caught in something so dark and so powerful that you want to be extremely careful."'

In 1964, Laing founded the Philadelphia Association, a registered charity aiming to set up a network of homes where mental patients could live together without oppressive institutional treatment. Clancy Sigal was on the association's board, whose members he labelled 'the brothers.'

Laing's most famous and infamous creation was a therapeutic community called Kingsley Hall. It was housed in a former community centre in London's East End. Several physicians lived together with a group of extremely disturbed men and women who would otherwise have been sent to asylums or isolated units in hospitals. In both of those environments their movements would be monitored and greatly curtailed. At Kingsley Hall, there was no distinction between the freedoms of staff and those of patients, and anyone could walk through any door.

Laing told an interviewer that he had established an environment where people who were considered schizophrenic did not have to receive treatment if they objected to it. He saw the issue as centred in human rights. His primary conviction was that people who don't hurt themselves or other people should be allowed to live according to their own wishes, even if they would be diagnosed as psychotic. 'I don't think that being psychotic should be against the law.'[13]

Although traditional psychiatrists deplored Kingsley Hall, some of Laing's theories generated a surprising amount of respect within a wide swath of the psychiatric community. In his obituary of Laing, Anthony Storr talked of the distance a psychiatrist places between himself and the patient when he labels the patient mad and himself sane, compounding

> ... the patient's sense of being alienated and misunderstood ... There is a great deal of truth in what Laing had to say. Psychiatrists need to be able to understand the schizophrenic experience from the inside as well as recognise it as an illness. *The Divided Self* is a masterpiece; and I still

recommend it to psychiatrists in training as the book most likely to help them understand the subjective experience of being schizophrenic.[14]

Clancy Sigal spent considerable time at Kingsley Hall, as did a number of other people less troubled than those residents who had previously been captives of mental hospitals. Adrian Laing says Kingsley Hall 'became one of the 'in' places in London – a refuge for left-wingers, radicals, poets, philosophers and people who fell under the all embracing-term, 'artists.' Self-awareness and self-discovery was all.'[15]

Clancy Sigal describes Kingsley Hall in his artful comic novel, *Zone of the Interior* (1976). The protagonist, Sid Bell, is an American novelist of working-class background who moves to London and has an affair with a novelist named Coral who has written a novel in which Bell is a character, called *Loose Leaves from a Random Life* (the same title Sigal gave *The Golden Notebook* in *The Secret Defector*). Bell begins to suffer a whole catalogue of ailments and finally, when conventional psychiatrists fail to help him, he turns to a thick-brogued Scottish therapist named Willie Last, and Bell's life is irrevocably altered. Last enthusiastically dispenses LSD and recruits Bell as one of the organisers of his commune of doctors and schizophrenics, a uniquely socialist loony bin. It will be a place where 'class doesn't matter.' As one resident puts it, 'It's what's insane in a man that counts.'[16]

Patients at Kingsley Hall were allowed to act out, whether slamming doors for hours on end, or going outside on a bitterly cold winter day without shoes and socks something sure to bring a response from the already unhappy neighbours. Laing recalled, 'I did my best to say to people ... you know for fuck's sake, you are going to blow it for everyone if you walk out in this street without putting your fucking shoes and socks on.' He also laughingly recalled a patient who 'went out on the roof once covered in shit and danced, she did a sundance, naked, and someone phoned up the local fire brigade: Take this woman off the roof.'[17]

The only restrictions at Kingsley Hall were on what Laing called 'transgressive behaviour.' 'You could be in any state of mind you liked,' he said, 'but you had to behave in a certain way ... Just because you are fucking out of your mind doesn't mean you can take a hammer and bash someone's skull in ... I don't care what world you're in or whether you're in the sixth dimension or the twenty-seventh dimension, *don't do that!* I wasn't encouraging people to walk over each other and make a mess.' On this, or any other issue, he said 'we took our chances together.'[18]

Perhaps not surprisingly, Kingsley Hall did not last more than a few years, in part because Laing himself ceased to be very active in its operation. But he remained defensive about its purpose and accomplishments.

It was not a failure in this respect. That for the time it went on people lived there who would have been living nowhere else – except in a mental hospital – who were not on drugs, not getting electric shocks ... who came and went as they pleased. There were no suicides, there were no murders, no one died there ... no one got pregnant there and there was no forbidding of anything ... You might have thought that everyone would have died of starvation or pneumonia or by killing themselves or raping each other or beating each other up or wasting away on drugs or overdoses. But people didn't do that.'[19]

In *R.D. Laing: Creative Destroyer*, an anthology edited by Bob Mullan, Sigal writes that he eventually became part of a program called Villa 21, an experimental unit in a traditional mental hospital, run by a colleague of Laing's, David Cooper. By this time Sigal had moved from being – at least nominally – a patient to something like a "writer in residence" among the schizophrenics and their fevered doctors.' Laing encouraged Sigal to write about his experiences at Kingsley Hall and Villa 21. Sigal says he stopped taking notes on his observations 'when the other patients insisted on seeing my obsessive scribbling as a symptom of craziness, which it was.'[20]

* * *

One night at Kingsley Hall, Laing and some of his colleagues became concerned about Sigal's mood and shifting behaviour. Their story is that he appeared to be suicidal. Sigal was angered by their intrusiveness, brushed them aside, and fled to the flat he kept in London. The doctors followed him there, and before he could shut the door, they jumped on him and jabbed a syringe filled with a powerful tranquilliser into his thigh. When he had passed out, they carried him back to Kingsley Hall.

R.D. Laing always maintained that out of love for the man, he was saving Clancy Sigal's life. Sigal denied he was suicidal, and instead accused Laing of being hypocritical, pointing out that his actions belied the philosophy of Kingsley Hall, which was to 'let someone go through their craziness without forcible intervention.'[21]

After two days, Sigal managed to escape from the watch of the staff at Kingsley Hall and never returned or spoke to R.D. Laing ever again, despite Laing's entreaties. In 1994, Sigal told Adrian Laing that he 'believes to this day, and without reservation, that Ronnie and the others "tried to kill me and almost succeeded."'[22]

According to Sigal, Laing would later block publication of *Zone of the Interior* in the UK because he was furious with its descriptions of his activities. Similarly, Sigal believes Doris Lessing spoke to at least one British publisher in an attempt to prevent UK publication of *The Secret Defector*, because of its alleged portrayal of her personal life.

R.D. Laing's career began to slide in the 1980s. Fame had taken an even greater toll than criticism from the governing medical community. His own personal life was tumultuous, reportedly including drinking that was out of control. He died at sixty one, playing tennis in St. Tropez.

Clancy Sigal, perhaps less enraged than he had been while Laing was alive, wrote a remembrance of his former friend and therapist:

> If we stopped thinking in terms of madmen and madwomen and started participating more joyfully in the unhappiness (called madness) of others there was some possibility ... that people in trouble might be helped. To his dying day, R.D. Laing probably got his greatest kicks from seeing the lost walk out of the woods.

About Laing's last day, Sigal adds:

> In the heaven he did not believe in, or in the hell he thought he existed in only on this despised earth, I hope he is wryly amused as I am that he should have passed away while playing tennis in St. Tropez. He always told me normal life was the most dangerous.[23]

A Brilliant Mutation

'I think Doris always felt the educational system failed Peter,' her former assistant says of Peter Lessing, who never attended university and had a rocky path through secondary education.

When Peter was twelve years old, his mother sent him to St. Christopher's, a progressive boarding school, located not far from London which she had chosen very carefully. Ostensibly, it would be everything her own boarding school experience was not. St. Christopher's was coeducational, there were no school uniforms, and teachers as well as students were called by their first names. It would not turn out to be an idyllic experience for those students who found a dissonance between the school's theory and practice. For some boys and girls, the lack of structure was confusing, while others sensed a reverse sort of rigidity in the determinedly 'open' atmosphere.

In Peter's class was a young girl named Jennifer Simmonds, who came from a severely dysfunctional home. Her father was a con-man, her mother a tormented hysteric who used to tell her daughter, 'I wish you'd never been born. You're useless, you should have been strangled at birth.'[1] In 1961, when Jennifer Simmonds and Peter Lessing were fourteen years old, she was expelled from St. Christopher's. Wryly, she recalls that because it was a progressive school they 'asked' her to leave. Once home, she became distraught and was taken to a mental hospital in Brighton. Doris Lessing heard that one of Peter's classmates was in 'the loony bin,' says Jennifer, who is now the fine novelist Jenny Diski.

Remarkably, never having met the girl, Lessing wrote her a letter asking if she would like to leave the hospital and come to stay in Lessing's home. Jenny Diski lived with Doris Lessing for the next four years, and intermittently after that. Lessing sent her to another school, took her on holidays, and encouraged her to write. Just before Diski was to sit for her A-level exams for college admission, her father died, sending her into a bout of self-destructive behaviour. She would experience other times of severe stress and depression before finally achieving psychological equilibrium.

While she was trying to help Diski, Lessing encountered another young woman in psychological trauma. In January 1963, Lessing's very close friend Suzette Macedo took another friend, Sylvia Plath, to meet

Doris Lessing. It was a few weeks before Plath committed suicide. While Plath was extremely voluble and clearly enjoyed the experience, Lessing became increasingly disturbed by it. As Plath biographer Anne Stevenson reports, Lessing recoiled from what she saw as an 'incandescent desperation' about Sylvia Plath, 'a total *demand*' directed at herself. Lessing drew back from it. Her hands were more than full at the time, and she had not found Sylvia sympathetic.' She said to Macedo after their meeting, 'I just couldn't cope with her.'[2]

Peter related to Jenny as though she were a sister, at times aligning himself with her against his mother, at other times competing with Jenny for Lessing's attention. Lessing spoke of Jenny as if she were a daughter, and behaved toward Jenny's daughter Chloe as if she were a cherished grandchild. When Doris Lessing set up trust funds for her three children, she was said to have established a trust for Diski as well.

Jenny Diski does not often speak publicly about Doris Lessing, except to reveal Lessing's extraordinary rescue of her. However, in 1991, Diski told journalist Suzie MacKenzie of the *Guardian* that her relationship with Lessing 'was wonderful, but difficult in some ways ... And now you're going to ask me if I loved her, and I'll say yes. But if you ask me what I mean, I've got no answer.'[3]

* * *

Two volumes of books of short stories (*A Man and Two Women* and *African Stories*) *Landlocked* (volume 4 of Children of Violence), and a memoir, *Particularly Cats* – all well received – followed *The Golden Notebook* in the 1960s. The final volume of the Children of Violence series, *The Four-Gated City* (1969), veers from the realism of the rest of the cycle, and creates a bizarre landscape of social and personal breakdown.

The novel is full of harrowing descriptions of what appear to be an imagined far-off future. On closer analysis however we see that much of what is described could be current reality viewed through a subjective lens.

> But the most frightening thing about them was this: that they walked and moved and went about their lives in a condition of sleepwalking ... they stood with the masses of the pelt hanging around their faces, and the slits in their faces stretched in the sounds they made to communicate ... each seemed locked in an invisible cage.[4]

Lessing is not describing a bunch of drooling lunatics shuffling about a grotesque insane asylum, but rather, what 'normal' citizens look like in a psychotic contemporary world.

John Leonard reviewed the novel for the *New York Times*. An editor at Knopf, her U.S. publisher, remembers, 'I kept reading the reviews and I said 'No one has understood you, Doris. 'No one understands this. Then John wrote ... in the *New York Times*, and I said, 'Finally, someone has understood what this book is.' The only review that did.' Leonard describes the world Martha Quest observes when she arrives in London as one 'in which technology and fascism have triumphed; a world in which sex and imagination and intelligence have been brutalised, a world of figurative and literal plague and a world for which the only hope is drastic biological mutation.'

What makes Lessing's black vision so compelling, Leonard explains, is that it rings so true. It is not some demonic literary grandstanding, but a clear-eyed look at modern life. 'It is the inevitable terminal point toward which the modern mind is monorailing.'[5]

Martha Quest wanders around bomb-ravaged post-war London and thinks, 'Yes, the price you paid for being awake, for being received into that grace, was this, that when you walked among your kind you had to see them, and yourself, as they, we are.'[6]

She goes to work as a combination nursemaid, housekeeper, and editorial researcher for a writer named Mark Coldridge. He has written a novel about an ancient city, a four-gated golden city, which was betrayed by its avaricious citizens, sending a kind, clairvoyant ruling priesthood underground. This aspect of Coldrige's novel reflects Lessing's own interest in the unrecognised potential of the human brain.

Lessing told Joyce Carol Oates in a 1972 interview that both she and R.D. Laing were 'exploring the phenomenon of the unclassifiable experience, the psychological 'breaking-through' that the conventional world judges as mad.'[7]

* * *

In *The Four-Gated City*, Martha Quest truly 'grows up' when she understands that her madness is part of the world's madness, and only by recognising the insanity around her can she find the truth about herself. Lessing was fascinated with madness, so much so that she experimented with trying to deliberately induce a shattering of sanity (which Martha Quest does in *The Four-Gated City*).

'It's very easy to send oneself round the bend for a couple of days,' she told Josephine Hendin in a 1972 radio interview. 'I did it once, out of curiosity.'[8] She had known a number of 'mad people' and felt she understood quite a lot about the condition. In any case, she used a technique medicine men and witch doctors were quite familiar with, going without eating or sleeping for several days. Lessing explained that such mental dislocations could also be observed in prisoners-of-war, for example, deprived of food and sleep. It is common for these victims to hallucinate and become bizarrely disassociated.

The difference to her mind between how a mad person is treated in Western society and other cultures when he hears voices or hallucinates is that we immediately label the person insane and lock him away to receive massive drugs or shock therapy. In other cultures, the person's experiences are taken seriously, and he is not considered a threat to normal society.

But Lessing, she is cautious about suggesting that other people emulate her experiment. It is often difficult to come back from the experience and its manifestations. It took her several weeks to shake free of the experiment's effects, not all of which were pleasant. The most unpleasant was the figure she calls the 'self-hater.' The voice repeatedly listed her weaknesses and sins in sharp accusatory tones.[9]

Lessing explains the self-hater by reiterating the belief, which she shared with R.D. Laing, that a child is damaged when brought up by a mother who makes her love conditional in relation to the child being 'good.' So, Lessing observes, people can become delusional, certain that they are disliked or the objects of cruel malice.

Sometimes when Lessing tells the story of trying to replicate insanity, she says she didn't eat or sleep for a week; at other times, the period is two or three days. Whatever the duration of the experiment, however, her experience with the self-hater remains constant. A horrifying encounter, being told over and over again how dreadful a person she was, not worthy of being alive.

At times Lessing shrugs off the similarity in thinking between herself and Laing. An editor at Knopf remembers that 'when she did *The Four-Gated City* she was quite friendly with Ronnie Laing. And I suspect some of the book was based on discussions with him, although she never talked about it.'

Even when she admires someone, Lessing does not enjoy being identified with that person's thinking. However, the connection between Lessing and Laing continued to manifest itself in her writing after *The Four-Gated City*. Her powerful piece of 'space fiction' *Briefing for a Descent into Hell* (1971) bears a strong resemblance to a case written up in Laing's 1962 book, *The Politics of Experience* (1967).

The psychotic voyages on which *Briefing*'s central character, a classics professor named Dr Charles Watkins, and a patient that Laing discusses in his psychological study embark are similar. They even have the last name. In the novel, Charles Watkins is found in a state of disorientation, wandering around London, and is taken to a hospital. The confinement doesn't halt his psychic journey through the sea and sky to a foreign world filled with both hideous and lovely creatures.

He comes upon a group of godlike messengers who are being instructed on their descent into earth (hell) to rescue humanity from destroying itself. In *The Politics of Experience*, the real-life Jesse Watkins, a sculptor, believes that there are gods present, 'beings which are far above us capable of ... dealing with the situation that I was incapable of dealing with, that were in charge and were running things.'[10]

Doris Lessing is intrigued by the infinite but meagrely used capacity of the mind. She explained to Studs Terkel that most of us don't ordinarily use our full sensory capacity. But she believes that many people can hear another person's thoughts, and other people could develop the ability if they tried hard enough. As she told Lesley Hazleton, she believes humanity is evolving to that point.

She also seems to feel that certain people are facilitating that process. Lessing told National Public Radio interviewer Susan Stamberg in 1984 that writers and artists are part of a higher evolution. The ability to notice opens the mind and thus frees creativity. Lessing believes there are many layers of thought that a writer has access to, tapping in to them at different times for different needs. When Lessing is ready to write, she opens herself to these collective influences. She wanders around her house, brews tea or coffee, gazes unfocusedly out her window, until she feels the first happy stirrings of work.

* * *

Lessing's openness to different wavelengths has allowed her to connect easily with people – beginning with her father – whom others might call mad. In 1992 she told broadcaster Eleanor Wachtel that she had known and been around mad people since childhood. After a while she began to wonder why this was, and decided that she must be projecting her own madness onto others.

Lessing may not have been completely serious about this self-assessment, but it's one that has some resonance. In many ways she seems a woman who has been able to channel her psychic pain into creativity. She is a fantasist, and the strength of her work comes from allowing herself to project her fantasies and fears into a story. Those forces that threaten to overwhelm her rationality are muted and even dissolved when she begins to write.

Lessing contends that she has had telepathic experiences and believes that many other people do as well. In 1980, she told interviewer Christopher Bigsby that she thinks we probably experience telepathy without realising it because we are programmed to renounce such ideas. She does not employ the paranormal as parlour tricks; rather, she is very serious about recognising and applying the phenomena. She keeps a diary of unusual coincidences and events that she believes will happen long before there is practical evidence to support the prophecy.

Similarly, dreams are a vital tool and companion. Since childhood, Lessing has looked to dreams as a source of ideas, or as a way to recapture the past, or as cautionary tales. They also have become an integral part of her writing methodology. She thinks about a new book in great detail before going to sleep, and very often finds the answer to some writing problem in her dream. She has trained herself to wake from dreams and take notes for the next day's writing, keeping a dream diary at her bedside all of her life, recording the night's stories as soon as she awakens. This is a process that has become progressively possible as she grows older and finds it easier to wake herself from sleep.

She told Studs Terkel how the title, *The Four-Gated City* came about in this way. Although she knew the phrase existed in mythology and the Bible, it had not presented itself to her as a title. Then she had a dream in brilliant colour of a sacred cow standing on four huge white legs. The animal's hind legs were the people of the city. When she woke, she knew the name of her novel.

Many of her dreams have consistently been of Africa. A dream that evolved over a period of months was of the family house on the kopje. In real life after Maude and Michael went to live in town the house was eventually destroyed by decay and brushfire. Its demise haunted Lessing for many years and she purposefully willed herself to dream it all back, directing herself as she fell into sleep to reclaim every room in all its details. Night after night she restored her home until it stood as it once had with sharp and moving clarity.

For many years, Lessing hoped to be able to write her autobiography through her accumulated dreams, but eventually gave the project up in frustration. The atmosphere of her dreams was too elusive to capture in words, and, intriguing as each dream was, it became difficult to string them together into a coherent story. She did try to do this with her 1974 novel, *The Memoirs of a Survivor*. The narrator looks through a wall into a dream world in which she also sees the reality of her own childhood. When the book was published it bore the subtitle 'An Attempt at Autobiography,' but no one else saw it that way and the phrase was deleted from foreign editions and reprints. This lapse seems to have annoyed her considerably.

Dreams figure prominently throughout Lessing's fiction. In *The Golden Notebook*, Anna's dreams contain important symbolic images of her life: a clump of African earth, metal from a gun that was used in Indochina, human flesh from victims of the Korean War, a Communist Party badge taken from a man who went to his death in a Soviet prison. Lessing uses the dream symbol as a narrative tool to vivify what she is telling us about Anna's past and her concerns for her future.

Lessing's writings about sleeping and wakefulness explore the same ground as her reflections on madness and sanity. In the land of Doris Lessing, states of being often seem to be reversed. Her characters are most aware of their feelings when asleep; conscious, they see their lives as a dark, confusing dream.

Pen Pals

In a 1969 memorandum, Juliet O'Hea, Lessing's British literary agent wrote to John Cushman, Lessing's new American agent, briefing him on his illustrious client. Describing the relationship between Lessing and her editor at Knopf, Robert Gottlieb, her American publisher, O'Hea wrote, 'She and Bob Gottlieb are bosom friends and she trusts him completely.' In tight coordination with Tom Maschler, Lessing's British editor, Gottlieb oversaw production of Lessing's work through 1987 when he became the editor of *The New Yorker*. During Gottlieb's reign, Lessing evolved from a force to be reckoned with to a venerable figure in English literature.

Robert Gottlieb was born in 1931, the only child of intellectually inclined parents. He attended private schools and graduated from Columbia University. From there he went to England for two years of postgraduate work at Cambridge. Gottlieb grew up reading Henry James, Jane Austen, and, as Lessing did, the great moral novelists, George Eliot and Proust. He did not share Lessing's early penchant for Russian literature. 'Of course,' he says, 'I admired the Russians tremendously, but I didn't feel that I had learned anything from them personally. I learned how to behave from *Emma,* not from *The Brothers Karamazov.*'[1]

Gottlieb went to work for Simon & Schuster as an editorial assistant to Jack Goodman, the editor-in-chief in 1955. 'I came into this out of my insane passion for books,' Gottlieb said of his career choice. 'I had a vast love for literature, and I had a great curiosity about what people were reading, whether it was literature or not.'[2] To this end, he made it a point to read books from every best-seller list that appeared since the list's inception in 1895.

'What makes Bob a great editor,' said Doris Lessing in 1994, 'probably the best of his time, is that he has read everything.'[3] She feels this background is put into play when he edits one of his authors. She adds with her customary derision of contemporary publishing that such a background is no longer taken for granted among even top editors at established houses.

In 1957, Jack Goodman suddenly died, and Simon & Schuster was coincidentally sold back by its owners, the Marshall Field estate, to two of the firm's founders, Max Schuster and Leon Simkin. There was considerable acrimony between the two men, and many people in high positions left the company because it seemed so unstable. When replacements weren't brought in at the same mature level, Gottlieb explains, soon 'the kids were running the store.'[4]

Gottlieb rose in a short time to become managing editor, and within a few years he was appointed editor-in-chief. His concern for his writers and his gifts as an editor quickly placed him in the elevated category of a Maxwell Perkins. He paid meticulous attention to every detail that went into writing and publishing a book he felt a passion for. A book, to his mind, is where all knowledge begins. It is a tangible entity that can affect and even change our lives.

Gottlieb and Lessing had worked together for two years before they finally met in 1964. 'I remember going round to her then-house and eating some kind of – it wasn't couscous, it was in that neighbourhood – and, of course being immediately struck by her, and quite unnerved by her, because Doris at that time was not only very beautiful and very articulate, but also had, let us say, quite an edge and was very imposing.'[5] By this time she had begun to wear her hair in a loose bun at the nape of her neck. At age forty-five, her skin was still clear, and, she had taken to wearing exotic fabrics such as tapestry and Indian prints. In 1968, Gottlieb moved to Alfred A. Knopf as editor-in-chief and publisher, taking Lessing along with him. At the same time, Lessing left her American agent, Elizabeth Otis, for John Cushman.

Although she has followed some suggestions, Doris Lessing really does not want to be edited. 'For years, I wondered why Doris was so eager to hear my opinions and suggestions and so reluctant to act on them,' Gottlieb said in a BBC documentary about her. 'We must never forget that Doris, among her many virtues, wilfulness and stubbornness are not the least ...'[6] He told another writer that Lessing would often listen very agreeably to what he had to say about changes he had in mind for her manuscripts, not because she was going to follow his advice but because she felt it was kinder to hear him out.

'I cut a bit out of *The Four-Gated City* at his suggestion, which perhaps was a mistake. Bob has made mistakes. But, nearly always, he is right.' She considers Bob Gottlieb 'an authoritarian personality,' something she has told him directly, something too, his great affection for her notwithstanding, he feels about her.[7]

At the same time that he was forthright in his criticisms, Gottlieb' could be almost seductive in his manner toward her. In his letters to her while serving as her editor he declared how brilliant she was, how much he cared about her, how proud he was of her work. When she sent him some photographs that Peter took of her to select for a book jacket, Gottlieb told her his choice, then added it is a lovely picture of a person who is also so exceptionally lovely.

*   *   *

Gottlieb is considered a man of large ego, and he readily acknowledges that in large part because of his analysis, he is objective about his strengths. He knows he is a forceful man, a good administrator, and that he makes a strong impression on people. He once commented that he married his wife, the highly regarded actress Maria Tucci, because she was the only woman he had ever met who was so strong that nothing he could do would seriously hurt her. Something of this is at play in his relationship with Lessing. She is so fiercely inner-directed and emotionally detached that his criticisms will never faze her.

He could be totally honest with her without worrying that he will upset her or excessively affect her writing decisions. He recalled that when he published Lessing's tenth, best-selling novel *The Summer Before the Dark* in 1973, they were walking together in London and he told her he thought the book would be her most successful so far. She found the prediction interesting because in her opinion, it was not the best book she'd ever written. It is the rare author, Gottlieb believes, who could be so uninvolved with their most current creation.

Doris Lessing has her own goals for her writing, and perfectly polished prose is not always one of them. At one point Gottlieb called some of the writing in *The Four-Gated City* clumsy, and in a letter Lessing calmly agreed with the charge. It was a deliberate clumsiness, she explained. She intended to disturb people. She wanted to make them irritable.

Similarly, Lessing is often described as pedantic, her voice more preachy than one might prefer in a novelist. One publishing colleague of Gottlieb's recalls that in *Briefing for a Descent into Hell*, 'he told her to tone things down a bit so the writing didn't seem so didactic, that a particular argument of hers stuck out like a sore thumb. And she wrote back and said, she was glad it was sticking out because the sentiments were important to her, and if it was that noticeable, maybe some reviewer would pick up on it and quote it.' Her reasoning was based on her belief that most critics were sluggish frauds who always took the easiest way out when writing a review.

An issue Lessing and Gottlieb did cross swords over was the increasing practice of authors giving interviews to publicise a new book. It is a custom Lessing continues to deplore with her new publisher HarperCollins. After the publication of the first volume of her autobiography in 1994, she went on a fourteen-week worldwide tour. She complained to her publishers that it made much more sense for her to stay at home and begin writing another book, but they did not take her objection to heart.

When she did write her next book, the novel *Love, Again*, 'This time round I stamped my little foot and said I would not move from my house and would do only one interview.'[8]

The reason for her antipathy is that she believes that, as with critics, 'only a minority of journalists are any good.' There must be something amiss, she says, 'when, meeting a friend after a profile of me appeared in a serious newspaper, he remarked how much he enjoyed it, while knowing that half the facts were wrong.' When she protested the situation, the man laughingly assured her that he knew 'profiles, interviews, news about the famous and the infamous are taken as entertainment, not as fact.'[9]

On that autobiography tour, Lessing spoke at Rutgers University's Newark campus. The audience was largely composed of African American students, many of whom were the first generation of their family to attend college. The talk had been billed as one that would cover how literature could unite the world. After a fulsome introduction by an African American professor, stressing this theme, Lessing came to the podium and, without acknowledging the man's remarks, said she was going to talk instead about what it was like to have to go out and sell your book. Many members of the faculty were astonished that she would so cavalierly abandon a topic people had come to hear, and that she did not perceive that this body of students would not consider it a hardship to appear on national television or have their picture in the newspaper.

Lessing would heatedly write to Gottlieb how it enraged her that despite Knopf's having a publicity department whose job was to sell books, it was the *author* who was really doing the selling. She, Doris Lessing, had to exhibit her personality and be interviewed about irrelevant matters that would generate letters from people and groups she had no interest in hearing from, let alone feel obligated to answer. If she did not answer an interviewer's stupid questions, she complained, he or she would make up her answers.

Robert Gottlieb tried to defend the practice of book promotion. He expressed distress at Lessing's notion that somehow it was improper for an author to try and sell her books. It was not, in his opinion, base to enter the marketplace, particularly, he pointed out mildly, when publishers pay authors large advances that they would like to recoup.

If Lessing did not take readily to such arguments, it was in part because of two particularly unwelcome experiences she and Gottlieb had shared.

One involved Joyce Carol Oates, who came to London in the spring of 1972 and wanted to meet Lessing. Gottlieb encouraged Lessing to see her, overcoming her considerable reluctance. The two writers met at Lessing's home and engaged in what Lessing considered a private conversation. She was outraged to discover some time later that Oates had considered the meeting an interview, one that was published in the *Southern Review*.

Writing to Gottlieb in the early 1970s about an upcoming visit to the States, Lessing made it clear she was not interested in his arranging a social gathering in her honour, because she was still feeling agitated over 'Joyce Carol Thingummy,' who came to see her under what Doris Lessing saw as such shamelessly false pretences. (Oates denies the accusation of deception.)

An interview that inspired even greater wrath was the one conducted by Lesley Hazleton for the *New York Times* in 1982. It was to be the cover story in the paper's Sunday magazine section, and Gottlieb argued Hazleton's case. Once again, Lessing unwillingly consented to the meeting. To Hazleton's amazement – because she had heard of Lessing's aversion to being interviewed – their talk lasted seven hours, albeit uncomfortable ones. Lessing was often 'preachy and bitchy. "If you really wanted to know you would ask me *this*, not *that* ...."' Hazleton recalls.

When the article appeared, severely cut to almost half its original length, and no longer the cover story, Lessing hated it. She resented its reference to the influence of R.D. Laing as if he were her 'guru,' and she was enraged at mentions of Clancy Sigal. To Lessing's mind, the piece was salacious and rude. Nothing Gottlieb could say would soothe her ire. She had wanted to vet the article before it was submitted to the *Times*. Why had he not let her do that? Lessing seemed to be unaware, or unbelieving, that newspapers such as the *New York Times* have policies against the type of approval process she sought.

According to Hazleton, who was personally unhappy with the abbreviation, the article would have been longer if it had run as a cover story. 'Which it nearly was,' she wrote to Gottlieb, 'except the *New York Times* got quite a shock when they called Doris in London ... and told her they wanted to photograph her for the cover. She said, it seems, 'I've already been photographed once this year, and that was quite enough. Call that photographer, not me.'

'If anyone else had done me out of a cover story, my journalistic instincts would have been aroused to sheer indignation,' Hazleton says. 'But the fact that it was Doris – and the way she did it – simply made me laugh.' She added that the newspaper people were 'even more disconcerted when they called me to ask if I could 'do something' about Lessing's lack of cooperation.' Remembering Lessing's frigid irritation during their time together, the idea that she would listen to a plea from Hazleton struck the journalist as absurd and once again, undoubtedly to the caller's confusion, she could only laugh.

Lessing's wrath did upset Robert Gottlieb enough so that when Lesley Hazleton called him after the article appeared, she recalls, he snapped at her and hung up the phone. Lessing wrote a short, nasty letter to Hazleton accusing her of shoddy journalism, and a letter of protest to the *New York Times* that they did not print presumably because Lessing had been travelling for a while before writing to the paper, and too much time had elapsed since the article's appearance. This only added to her simmering resentment.

* * *

Briefing for a Descent into Hell (1971) was Lessing's first book to be issued by her new British publisher, Jonathan Cape, headed by Tom Maschler. Maschler was, like Gottlieb, a man whose talent had launched him on a precocious publishing career. At twenty-two, he was an editor at MacGibbon and Kee, where he put together *Declaration*, the 1959 Angry Young Man (and Woman) anthology. The book did very well in England and America, both critically and financially, and Maschler's name became prominent in the publishing world.

A year later, he was fiction director at Penguin Books, and less than two years later, at the age of twenty-six, he became the literary editor at Jonathan Cape. Maschler's ego was vast, and matched, many felt, by a massive self-absorption. He could, however, be immensely charming and attentive to people he was interested in.

He was very interested in Doris Lessing. According to some former publishing associates of Maschler they had a very close personal relationship early on, but that had nothing to do with Maschler's desire to sign Lessing as one of his authors. He had enormous respect for her writing, and although he paid a great deal of attention to merchandising his books, it was her quality rather than the money she generated that made him covet her for Cape.

Their friendship extended well beyond their business relationship, and according to observers, Lessing delighted in being at the centre of the triangle with Robert Gottlieb and Maschler. Correspondence between the two men shows a personal relationship developed from working closely when they brought out one of Lessing's books, often at the same time. On the other hand, they would sometimes complain about each other's publishing decisions.

Gottlieb would express anger at Maschler's missing an agreed-upon publishing date. At another time, the situation was reversed, with Maschler accusing Gottlieb of holding up publication, a charge Lessing angrily passed on to the American editor, blaming him for a 'magisterial' publishing pace.

Lessing and Gottlieb enjoyed gossiping about Maschler's social behaviour. After meeting the woman he intended to marry, Lessing wondered whether she was strong enough to put up with Tom. In a letter to Gottlieb she says she could continue for many pages discussing Tom Maschler's behaviour, but in an exercise of self-restraint would refrain from doing so. It's not unlikely, as is often the case in such triads, that Lessing also chatted with Maschler about Gottlieb. Although Juliet O'Hea was talking about the period when Lessing had two English publishers, her comments seemed applicable to Maschler and Gottlieb. In a memo to John Cushman, O'Hea wrote that Lessing 'is extremely hard-headed about her writing and contracts, and has no scruples whatsoever in playing off her English publishers against each other.'

Finding the Way

Writing *The Golden Notebook* was an instrument of change for Doris Lessing. The development of that book opened her to whole new ways of thinking and to experiences that ran counter to the person she thought she was. Rather than push the new aspects of herself away to maintain equilibrium, as some people would do, she embraced them with curiosity and excitement.

She wanted to understand what was creating these new thoughts, many of them incompatible with how she viewed herself at the time, as a 'Marxist and a Rationalist.'[1] As she had done all her life when her interest was piqued, she embarked on a course of reading, this time in mystical, non-rational literature. Several of these books were written by a man named Idries Shah. His work presented her with a philosophical movement of the Islamic religion, called Sufism. Lessing discovered that its teachings reflected many of the thoughts and feelings that were currently concerning her. Not well known at the time, Shah would with Lessing's help, become internationally famous as the world's leading exponent of Sufism

Like other Islamic traditions, Sufism traces its origins back to the Prophet Muhammad and takes inspiration from the divine word of the Koran. However its exact origins are unclear. The term 'Sufi' was not recorded until approximately 100 years after Muhammad's death in 1632. It is adapted from the Arabic word 'suf' which means wool and refers to the simple garb that was worn by holy men. In its earliest incarnations Sufism was a body of thought which could simplistically be described as the mystical side of Islam. Writings which predate the term 'Sufi' might well be considered part of that body of thought, therefore it's hard to define an exact starting point for Sufism. As might be expected over the course of hundreds and hundreds of years, there have been many different ideas contained within the rubric of Sufism, but asceticism and a personal relationship with God are two hallmarks.

With the establishment of Sufi orders in the 12th century – the dervishes whose ecstatic dancing led to the phrase 'whirling dervish' – Sufi teachings became more codified. But the development of Sufism throughout the Islamic world without any central structure had meant its doctrines and practices are in no way uniform. Indeed discussions of

Sufism can lead into a highly subjective realm. In the West this has often taken the form of a debate between a modern wave of Sufi adherents and scholars of Islamic history.

Anyone familiar with Doris Lessing's views of academics would find it easy to anticipate which side of the argument she would land on. Universities have long been a source of irritation for her. She has attacked academic literary analysis for its attention to extraneous detail, and nit-picking. And Lessing has expounded at length about the inane questions she has been subjected to by professors in her many on-campus speaking appearances. About the academic journal which bears her name, *The Doris Lessing Newsletter* she has commented, it is 'acutely embarrassing ... I don't like the cult atmosphere at all.'[2]

Ironically, in a May 1975 article in the magazine *Encounter*, Islamic scholar L.P. Elwell-Sutton attacked Lessing's Sufi mentor Idries Shah on similar grounds, complaining about 'the development of a cult of personality.'[3]

Earlier that year, in the January 8 issue of the *Guardian*, Doris Lessing had written a full page article titled 'If you knew Sufi,' to which Elwell-Sutton's piece was in part a reply. And it contained a brief broadside in his general direction, when she criticised scholars who have 'attacked this figure Shah sometimes viciously.' It was the only sour note in what was otherwise a full page tribute to Idries Shah written in prose so glowing it would make a PR man blush.

After skipping over Idries Shah's birth in Simla, India, in 1924, Lessing explained her version of the amazing facts of Shah's life, beginning with his family. His mother was Scottish, his father's family was of Afghan origin, with ancestors that can be traced back not only to the Prophet Muhammad, but to Abraham of biblical renown. Shah's father helped partition India, and when he wasn't busy lecturing on three continents, he made himself available to Gandhi and Egyptian President, Gamal Abdel Nasser.

Lessing writes that Idries Shah had an education, 'not commonly associated with Princes.' In addition to farm work, and studying at several universities, Shah was sent packing 'without money or support' for a twelve year learning trip where he acquired his extensive knowledge of religion and philosophy.[4] According to Lessing, Shah inherited palaces in India and Afghanistan, controlled hundreds of millions in trust funds, invented electronic devices that were marketed, served on the board of companies in numerous types of business, ranging from 'culture' to 'carpets,' but for some reason, 'supports himself and his family ... entirely by what he earns from writing.'[5] Not content simply to accept his hereditary role as the chief of the Dervishes, Shah had also founded an Institute of Cultural Research to help spread enlightenment to study groups that contain 'nearly as many different professions as there are members.'[6]

In Elwell-Sutton's piece about Shah, a different picture emerges. He disputes the idea that anyone could inherit the role of head of the dervishes because Sufi 'knowledge is not passed on through physical heredity.' Explaining that Shah's inherited title Sayyid 'confers neither sanctity nor authority.' Elwell-Sutton describes, Sayyid as a term applied to 'descendants (real and imagined)' of Muhammad's daughter Fatima.[7] Therefore as a Hashemi Sayyid, Idries Shah could claim descent from the Prophet, but since the number of Sayyids runs into the millions, it is not much of a distinction.

None of the palaces Lessing mentions, appear in Elwell-Sutton's version, there is 'only a modest estate' near Delhi, a present given to the Shah family by the Indian government, after it was expelled from Afghanistan for aiding the British in the First Afghan war in 1841.[8]

Elwell-Sutton's harshest words were reserved not for Shah, himself, but for his teaching. 'This is Sufism (if it deserves that name) without Islam, 'Sufism' without religion, 'Sufism' centred not on God, but on man. Page after page of his writings do not even mention the name of God, the word 'love,' the concept of unity with God through love. He is far more concerned with prescriptions for self-improvement, directions for the achievement of personal happiness, guidelines for a worldly elite.' Shah is, said Sutton, 'a man very much of this world, impressed by big names and revelling in the lionising and the personality cult that centres around him.'[9]

* * *

It wasn't just scholars who were critical of Shah. John Bennett, a seminal figure in what now would be called the New Age movement, wrote an extremely negative account of Shah in his, 1974 autobiography *Witness*. Bennett, devoted much of his life to spiritual pursuits after surviving the trench warfare of the First World War. He had spent time in Asia, and his quest for enlightenment had included time following two famous names in the New Age movement – Gurdjieff and Subud. Bennett also had followers of his own, who were members of his institute at an estate, Coombe Springs, in Kingston, Surrey.

In 1962, Bennett met Shah who was close to half Bennett's age. According to Bennett, Shah had 'come to England to seek out followers of Gurdjieff's ideas with the intention of transmitting to them knowledge and methods that were needed to complete their teaching.'[10] When he and his wife met Shah, they had mixed feelings. Initially, they found the younger man 'restless, he smoked incessantly, talked too much, and seemed too intent on making a good impression. Halfway through the evening, our attitude completely changed. We recognised that he was not only an unusually gifted man, but that he had the indefinable something that marks the man who has worked seriously upon him-self.'[11]

Bennett's description of what follows makes himself seem like a man under a spell. He decided 'to put myself at Shah's disposal and do all that I could to help him.'[12] As the weeks passed, it was clear that what Shah really wanted was Coombe Springs, both the property and those pupils who he felt could help him further his cause. Shah insisted that if Bennett were to turn over the property to him, the gift had to be 'absolute, irrevocable, and completely voluntary.'[13] Bennett agreed, influenced by the fact that Shah was so much younger than himself, and that having him take over Coombe Springs would insure its continu-ation after Bennett's death. Some of Bennett's colleagues urged him instead to sell the property and to give half the money to Shah, while keeping the other half to build himself a retirement home in the country. But Shah was not open to halfway measures about the gift. Pushed to hurry, Bennett moved out of Coombe Springs.

The next few months were extremely difficult. As soon as Shah took over the house, he forbade Bennett's people from visiting, and made Bennett feel so intrusive that he stayed away completely In 1966, Bennett learned that Shah had decided to sell Coombe Springs for one hundred thousand pounds. The sale was made to a developer who would take the – to Bennett – holy land, and build twenty-eight luxury homes for commercial sale. Shah and his family then moved to Langton House in Kent where he was living and working when Doris Lessing met him.

* * *

Lessing's meeting with Shah came about after Doris Lessing read *The Sufis* – or maybe *The Searchers*, Lessing has offered different accounts – and wrote to him. But she had to wait a long time for his response. (Paradoxically, considering how she feels about professors, Doris Less-ing did not feel ready to start her spiritual journey without a teacher.) Lessing wrote to Robert Gottlieb that when she initially found out about Sufism, after more than four years of searching for a discipline to explain and guide her life, she was overcome with joy. Finding Shah seems to have allowed Doris Lessing to surrender many of her defences, built up over the years as one after another, people or disciplines disappointed her.

Gottlieb asked her to tell him about being a Sufi, so that he could understand something that was so important to her, and Lessing somewhat reluctantly began to do so. Part of Lessing's tentative expla-nation to Robert Gottlieb was that Sufis believe there is only a tiny core of the self which can be nurtured and developed. The area that fosters growth is buried deep inside us and will lead us into the light only when it is ready to do so. It was not easy to explain the Sufi way to those not yet ready to grasp it.

This was something Lessing knew from first hand knowledge of watching Sufi teaching in action. One friend remembered her telling about a man in one of Shah's teaching sessions who fell asleep while it was going on. Later, when she asked the man why he had allowed this to happen, he complained that Shah wasn't 'doing anything.'

This was not Doris Lessing's perception. She was perfectly comfortable with the indirect teaching style of Shah's Sufism, a methodology which Shah explained this way: 'The Sufi attitude is undoubtedly that of 'being,' but unlike the familiar type of mystic, he will use 'knowing' as well. He distinguishes between the ordinary knowing of fact and the inner knowing of reality. His activity connects and balances all these factors – understanding, being, knowing.'[14]

If such explanations seem obscure, there is also the suggestion that only those who have reached some higher state of being will be able to comprehend the discipline. As Shah states, 'It is a form of communication among the enlightened ones. It has the advantage of connecting mundane with the greater dimensions; the 'other world' from which the ordinary humanity is cut off.'[15]

Shah felt that Sufism defies conventional definition and he had little patience with people who assumed they understood what Sufism is simply because they have studied or observed it. 'Outward observers are not capable of commenting upon Sufism, only upon its externals. 'Who tastes, knows,' is a Sufi saying. Equally, whoever does not taste, does not know.'[16] In other words – Either you get it, or you don't. The teaching story, the main instrument of Sufi enlightenment demonstrates this dichotomy. To apt students the teaching stories are an important aide to personal growth. Unlike traditional fables or parables, extolling some moral or truth, the tales are open-ended and invite individual interpretation that fosters intellectual and personal development.

Others find the stories oblique or even pointless. Nancy Shields Hardin in her essay 'The Sufi Teaching Story and Doris Lessing' felt that the following story, contained 'zany antics and actions' that 'surprise the listener and encourage him to discover another level of knowledge.'[17]

'Nasrudin finds a king's hawk perched on his window-sill. He has never seen such a strange 'pigeon.' After cutting its aristocratic beak straight and clipping its talons, he sets it free, saying, 'Now you look more like a bird. Someone had neglected you.'[18] It may be safe to say that not every reader will experience the discovery that Shields did. But for students, of Sufism a teaching story can becomes a mirror to see oneself and state of mind. It can foster a holistic way of looking at life, where the right and left brain hemispheres are unified, joining the intuitive and abstract to the rational and logical. Indeed it is one of the purposes of the Sufi teaching story to teach a perceptual change from the linear mode of thought to a more spontaneous, instinctual understanding of life. Lessing's fiction often has aspects of the Sufi teaching story, the dream and real worlds flowing into each other, enabling a reader to look at some life experience in a new way.

* * *

In a *Times* story about Shah's 1994 book, *The Commanding Self,* Doris Lessing wrote that discovering the teaching story taught her how to appraise her own talents. She also used two of the stories in the tribute to Shah. One was about an elephant and a mouse who fall in love and decide to marry. On their wedding night, the elephant keels over and dies. The mouse says: 'Oh Fate! I have unknowingly bartered one moment of pleasure and tons of imagination for a lifetime of digging a grave.'[19]

Lessing adds approvingly, 'There is not a grain of sentimentality in this view of life.'[20] She believes that to understand what it means to think like a Sufi, one must abandon conventional limitations on thought and language. These beliefs have been manifested in her writing. Her characters are often engaged in an evolution of consciousness, as witnessed by, for example, their facility for extrasensory perception.

'Martha could easily hear what Lynda was thinking. Being more sensitive now, by far, than normally, she heard better: normally she could hear an odd phrase, or a key word, or a sentence or two. Summarising what was going on in somebody's head; now it was not far off being inside Lynda's head.'[21]

A Sufi who has reached a certain phase of evolution would be able to see the workings of another person's mind. The influence of this evolutionary aspect of Sufism on Doris Lessing is made clear by her inclusion of this quote from Idries Shah's, *The Sufis* in the epigraph to part four of *The Four Gated City.*

'Sufis believe that, expressed in one way, humanity is evolving towards a certain destiny ... Organs come into being as a result of a need for specific organs ... What ordinary people regard as sporadic and occasional bursts of telepathic and prophetic power are seen by the Sufi as nothing less than the first stirrings of these same organs.'[22]

* * *

It was just these types of sentiments that annoyed many of Lessing's friends when her focus switched from politics to Sufism. They felt that involvement with Sufism had made Lessing become elitist, egotistical and secretive. Others thought Sufism had given her a degree of inner peace that had made her more easy going. Gottlieb, writing with his customary affectionate tone, assured Lessing that he would not reject her beliefs even though they were not his own. Though, in another letter, Gottlieb at first confessed he could not comprehend Lessing's impulse to align herself with a master or teacher, but quickly added that the important issue for both Doris and himself was to keep improving themselves and their lives in whatever ways seemed right for them. It is not likely that Gottlieb would acknowledge any personal criticism of Idries Shah, knowing the extent of Doris Lessing's commitment, one that, in 1979, led her to set up a *Sufi Trust* for one hundred thousand dollars drawn from money that her books would earn from Knopf. The activities of the trust are not generally known.

'I don't understand Shah from nowhere!' said Stuart Hall mockingly. It is a sentiment echoed by many of Doris Lessing's friends and colleagues who knew her in her political days. Clancy Sigal at first assumed they were lovers, a belief shared by many people who saw them together, though Lessing denies this. 'It's the only explanation I can figure for her falling in with that charlatan,' said one sceptic. Elwell-Sutton also puzzled over Shah's hold on intellectuals like Lessing and the poet Robert Graves, whose summation of purpose 'To be in this world, but not of it ... that is the Sufi's ideal' he found totally inaccurate, in terms of historical Sufism.[23]

Referring to Shah's students, Elwell-Sutton commented 'It is significant that the bulk of them come from the intellectual establishment: poets, novelists, journalists, critics, broadcasters.'[24] He wondered if there might also be some kind of pleasure in giving up intellectual control and obeying and following a fixed discipline. And there was the elitist aspect; being *au courant* with a provocative way of thinking, and belonging to some exclusive club that would be out of the reach of less exceptional people.

* * *

All of these possibilities probably hold some clue to Lessing's unequivocal support of Idries Shah. But whatever the mix of reasons for her unquestioning acceptance of his superiority, it is evident from her writing that being a Sufi has both brought her greater peace and intensified her interiorness. Through her interpretation of Sufi thinking, Doris Lessing appears to have been able to put some regrets to rest. As with the Zeitgeist, which is larger than free will, one can believe that some of one's past actions are the result of an as yet unevolved self. One cannot be held responsible for being unenlightened. What's more, one can even regard some of those more turbulent periods as part of one's evolution, where one is finally able to reach a higher level of under-standing.

Like Communism before it, Sufism allowed Lessing a place to belong, while remaining an outsider. On her trips to New York, Lessing would take Shah's books around to religious and New Age bookstores to try to sell them to the storeowners. 'She'd just trot out with a bag full of the books, without making appointments, or saying who she was in ad-vance, just wandering around the city from store to store,' recalled one Knopf editor, still sounding bewildered at the memory. 'I said, if I'd known you were doing that, I would give you a list of certain bookstores. And she said, 'No, rambling about like this is more fun.' She wanted to do it her own way. So I don't know where she went or what she managed to sell. But she was determined to do this for Idries Shah. She wanted to further his work.'

In a London *Telegraph* obituary following Shah's death on November 23, 1996, Lessing wrote, 'It is not easy to sum up 30 odd years of learning under a Sufi teacher, for it has been a journey with surprises all the way, a process of shedding illusions and preconceptions.'[25] Through Sufism, a life that political ideology and artistic achievement could not fully illuminate has become comprehensible. And apparently, Sufism continues to answer Doris Lessing's questions. She quite simply declared in 1990, 'It's the most important thing in my life.'[26]

Will You Love Me in December as You Do in May

In 1973, Robert Gottlieb wrote to Lessing to tell her that 'real excitement' was mounting about her soon to be published tenth novel, *The Summer before the Dark*. Reviewers Richard Locke and John Leonard had both confided how excited they were about it, Leonard saying it was the best novel he had read in a year. Paperback houses were clamouring to buy reprint rights. Gottlieb was allowing himself to do something he rarely did, which was to predict that the book would be an enormous success.

The Summer Before the Dark would indeed be one of Doris Lessing's most popular books, making the best-seller list and generating a great number of admiring reviews. In a virtually unprecedented – and unrepeated – move, John Leonard, then editor of the *New York Times Book Review*, used his 'Last Word,' column to argue against the somewhat negative review appearing in the same issue, written by Elizabeth Hardwick.

'With some diffidence, I would like to dissent from her judgement on the particular novel she is reviewing,' he wrote. 'I think *The Summer Before the Dark* is not only Doris Lessing's best novel, but the best novel to have appeared here since Garcia Marquez's *One Hundred Years of Solitude*.' His essay's final line is, 'Please buy this book.'[1]

* * *

Leonard's rebuttal was seconded by heated letters from readers, insisting that Hardwick had failed to grasp the complexity of Doris Lessing's vision and no letters agreeing with Hardwick's criticism were published.

The story set forth in *The Summer Before the Dark* was a powerful one for women to read in the midst of the feminist revolution of the 1970s. A middle-aged wife and mother, Kate Brown, undertakes – to the point of risking madness – a journey of self-discovery, and of exploring the meaning of life and death. She needs to find what concerns her as a particular individual, rather than mirroring other people's demands and perceptions.

Kate Brown, an upper-middle-class, attractive, healthy woman, has been an attentive, beautiful wife and mother, for twenty–five years. Like many women of her generation, she played the part of wife and mother to the point that the deepest contents of her mind remained hidden from herself. Suddenly, as a summer begins, her services are not needed. Her loving, neurologist husband is going to America for a summer-long visit at a Boston hospital. He does not invite her to accompany him, and once there, she knows, he will engage in the essentially meaningless affairs she has managed to overlook till now.

Three years earlier, her then sixteen-year-old youngest son had accused her of smothering him with her relentless attention and, although she blocked the confrontation from her mind, its message has gnawed at her all this time. This summer, all four of her children are scattering. They want total autonomy, not maternal concern. An emotional gulf opens up as Kate realises she is being forsaken by the people she has built a life around serving. It is a situation that harks back to Doris Lessing's own adolescent confrontations with her mother who, having chosen marriage and family over career, used on her children all the energy she would have applied to the job of matron of a hospital.

Lessing also observed this painful sense of obsolescence in a friend who had reached a certain point in life: 'a woman who has not had a job and whose children grow up and she has to come to terms with the fact that she has no function.'[2]

In *The Summer Before the Dark*, Lessing writes movingly about this confrontation with midlife's diminishments. The middle-aged woman whose children are grown realises one mcrning that she must disengage from their lives. Kate Brown knew this would happen to her one day, but she had not expected it so soon. 'Next summer, or the year after that, yes, but not *now*.'[3]

Although *Ms* magazine ran excerpts of the novel, Margaret Cousins, the fiction and book editor of the *Ladies' Home Journal,* a magazine that spoke to a more traditional reader, declined the opportunity to do so. Regretfully, Cousins explained to Robert Gottlieb that Doris Lessing's commanding prose left no escape. Indeed, she found the impugning of the relationship between mother and child so disturbing she could barely make it home after reading the novel at her office.

As is evident in a 1980 interview with the *New York Times Book Review*, Doris Lessing was not denigrating housewives when she wrote *The Summer Before the Dark*. She commiserated deeply with women like Kate Brown: It was terrible that someone who raises a family is embarrassed to admit that she has no other vocation. She believes that the role of housewife and mother is enormously difficult and exacting, and calls upon a person's noblest instincts.

Kate Brown takes a job as a translator for a conference on coffee when her family flees. She discovers that her nurturing skills serve her well in the world of work. Her employer begs her to stay on to care for another group, because along with her translating she has assumed the role of a conference organiser, a kind of 'tribal mother' to the attendees. She sees the irony in finding public success by continuing the private behaviour that has defined her existence and has resulted in such disappointment. She has spent her life sublimating her needs to others, and now she's doing it again.

Lessing understands that motherhood creates irreconcilable choices for a woman between her biology and her intellectual beliefs, between responsibility to others and personal freedom. Like Lessing, Kate will struggle against having a set identity imposed by her husband and children or even society's vision of an older woman's life. Lessing's own conflicts surrounding motherhood have all been rendered in her fiction, from her hostility toward her mother, to leaving her own children, to trying to combine being a mother with living as a 'free' woman. More often than not, her heroines discover that if they are rewarded in one area of their lives, they will pay a price in another. The unity they seek is ever elusive, but they keep on trying, risking sanity itself in the search.

Kate's attempts to make a new life take her from London to Istanbul to Spain with an ailing young man who becomes her lover. The affair not only does not rescue her but becomes a debacle of sickness and frustration reminiscent of the decline of Lessing's own father. Even so, the relationship is an important leg of her journey to self-understanding. Each new experience, even her brush with madness, brings her nearer to comprehending understanding the complex implications of moving inexorably toward the end of life.

Kate Brown transforms herself physically for her new job. She buys new clothes and dyes her hair the dark red colour of her girlhood instead of the lighter, less dramatic shade her husband found pleasing. Realising that for a good part of her life she had won the approval of her family by creating an appearance that reinforced her role as a wife and mother, she becomes conscious that this has removed her from the arena of sexual attraction.

This realisation hits home when she is ignored by a bunch of workers as she passes their construction site. Out of the men's view, Kate strips of her jacket to reveal a form-fitting dress, rearranges her hair with a scarf, – and hips bouncing strolls back towards the site, to a boisterous chorus of approval. She passes back and forth in front of the construction site, alternating roles. As her normal self she goes unnoticed, but her altered appearance with its seemingly mild sexual provocation continues to elicit a testosterone-laced cacophony. She is filled with rage, initially by being ignored, then by the fact that she has for so long suppressed her own sexuality. The emotions become more complex. She rages at the ludicrous nature of this type of raw male/female interaction and that she has generated so much sexual energy through a facade that is also a denial of self and a trivial one at that.

Real freedom does not mean substituting the flirtatious role-playing of youth for the homemaker identity she has adopted; it means finding a self that is not based on how others react. And find herself she does through a series of dreams about a wounded seal who is really her injured lost self. 'In *The Summer Before the Dark*, I built dreams right into the story, so that the way out for this woman was in fact through her dreams of this magical seal that she found on this hillside.'[4] Through dream after dream Kate tries to protect the seal from all manner of disasters, as she carries it in what she hopes is the direction of the sea. Her burden becomes heavier and heavier, and the creature's pitiful helplessness and dependence on her for direction seem a symbol of her arrested, abandoned selfhood. When she is ultimately able to dream of reaching the coast and placing the seal safely into the water, her emotions, like her arms, are freed of their burden. Before she releases the seal, she realises it is 'full of life, and, like her, of hope.' The light of selfhood shines around her, but '[t]he light that is the desire to please had gone out.'[5]

In an interview with Susan Stamberg, Lessing was asked whether she minded growing older. 'No, I don't mind. When I was young I was quite pretty, I'm sorry that's gone, but I don't care all that much.' She explained that there are many advantages to being older and unnoticed. 'You can sit and watch and listen.'[6] Lessing seems sincerely to enjoy the different stages of her life. Just as she enjoyed the attentions she received from being an attractive young woman, she was fascinated by the new world that was presented when these attentions were stripped away by age. While acknowledging that there's a trade-off, she has found that growing older can be a positive and interesting experience.

Lessing once wrote to Robert Gottlieb about a friend who was bordering on breakdown, helplessly crying with no seeming provocation. There were several reasons for her distress, Lessing said, but one was that she had been an exquisitely beautiful young woman, and now she had turned fifty. It must be more difficult, Lessing mused, to grow old when you are exceptionally beautiful in your youth. On a similar note, in her 1972 interview with Josephine Hendin, she suggested that the process of losing the automatic attention the young women receive is a prime source of female mid-life crisis and depression.

In the last weeks before Kate Brown goes home to her husband, she allows the gray roots to show through her dyed hair. It is a statement of independence. When Josephine Hendin interviewed the fifty-two-year-old Doris Lessing in 1972, she recalls Lessing's own hair was pulled tightly back. Her coat was drab and shapeless. Says Hendin,

'Mrs Lessing sat replete in her eccentricity, an attractive woman in an old woman's guise, scrubbed into a plainness chosen and pervasive as belief.'[7] In the next decade of her life, Lessing would embrace old age even more noticeably. The image of her after sixty is starkly severe, a presentation most people who know her see as exaggerated and deliberate.

Stuart Hall recalls, 'There was a point where she wasn't seen publicly for some while and then she appeared again, and had allowed herself to go gray and her hair was pulled back very austerely. She had, in a very deliberate way, not passed through the transition into being older, but had become – chosen to appear – ten years down the line. It was very striking. I don't think I know anyone else who seemed to have made that decision: 'I will not appear again unless I look manifestly sixty.' It was a very odd thing to do and we all felt she was making some kind of statement.'

Hall's statement may give some clue to Lessing's identity as a woman. Perhaps it was, 'I am taking myself out of the arena of sexual desire.' Perhaps even, 'I will reject before I am rejected.' Well before she made this transformation, Lessing was moving away from the pulls of love. When a younger friend wrote to her of being in love, Lessing replied that she envied her, because love had been absent from her own life for years. It was an absence that at times made her feel sorrowful, but at other times, as if she had finally fled the clutches of a demon.

* * *

In recent years Lessing seems to have changed her mind about celebrating the erosion of erotic and romantic need. Although the face in the photographs on her book jackets is stern and unadorned by makeup, in person she presents a softer, prettier image. She has told friends that she could have fallen in love again, except that the men she was interested in were all at least fifteen years too young, a situation she drew on for her novel *Love, Again* (1996). There, coming full circle, she returns to her most persistent preoccupation, one that affected her feelings about love and sexuality: the withholding mother.

Sarah Durham's rejecting old mother has died at last. Recovering from her own fruitless passion of love for a younger man, Sarah suddenly thinks to herself that she was feeling in her hunger for love what a baby experiences when it needs and desperately desires its mother.

'To fall in love,' sixty-five-year-old Sarah thinks, 'is to remember one is an exile, and that is why the sufferer does not want to be cured, even while crying, "I can't endure this non-life. I can't endure this desert."'[8]

Not long after the publication of *Love, Again*, Lessing revealed to Anthony Clare in the Psychiatrist's Chair, that she had recently been transformed by a love affair with a much younger man. In contrast to Sarah Durham's unendurable desert, Lessing's romantic foray seemed to be something of an oasis.

Lost in Space

Doris Lessing dedicates her series Canopus in Argos to 'my father, who used to sit, hour after hour, night after night, outside our house in Africa, watching the stars. "Well," he would say, "if we did blow ourselves up, plenty more where we came from."'[1] In these five novels, published between 1979 and 1983, Lessing, the exile, doesn't just move to another relationship, another collective, another country, she migrates out of the world itself. Knowing from earliest childhood that things are not always what they seem, she is free to imagine – and create – a whole new cosmos. Originally she had only thought to write one book, *Shikasta*, which would be 'the Bible as science fiction.'[2] But halfway through working on it, she became so happy about the way things were going she knew that more books would follow.

The series revolves around the planet Canopus, an empire of great beneficence. The Canopians watch over the other planets, sending agents to straighten out problems and show the galaxy how to live in peace and purpose. One of the planets they colonise is Shikasta, representing our Earth. Opposing Canopus is the empire of Shammat, evil and treacherous. A third group, the Sirians, are much less reliable and much more bureaucratic than the Canopians. In an obvious echo of her colonial past, Lessing has the Canopians regard themselves as far more advanced than the Sirians. The Sirians in turn are jealous, hostile, and deferential to Canopians.

Shikasta, the first novel of the series, deals with the history of Earth from the paleolithic era up through World War III, a war also depicted in *The Four-Gated City*. Through the reports of Canopian representatives, we learn of Earth's fall from grace. Its inhabitants have become more cruel, more prejudiced, more deceitful, more foolish, causing and experiencing more suffering. Some of the problems they can blame on Shammat, but much of their trouble they have brought on themselves. The biblical connection, as Lessing saw it, was that the Canopian representatives are, in effect, prophets.

The second book in the series, *The Marriages Between Zones Three, Four and Five*, is much less dense, written in the form of an engaging allegory of physical and spiritual love. Lessing is very clear about the inspiration for *Marriages* in her interview with Lesley Hazelton. At a time in her forties when her personal life was deeply unhappy, she fantasised about being part of a very powerful female kingdom that dealt with a similarly powerful and confident kingdom of men. She tried to bolster herself through taking on the persona of this imaginary woman, and found that it helped. She forgot about this technique of giving herself courage until years later, when she was getting ready to write the Canopus series. Hurling a barb at the critics to Lesley Hazleton, she said she trusted they would see that the writing was different in tone from *Shikasta*, and came from a source in herself different from that of the earlier work.

The Sirian Experiments, the third in the series, explores some of the earlier material, and covers the same time period as *Shikasta*, from the first colonisations to the Century of Destruction, but through the report of a single individual, who provides more reader connection than is experienced in *Shikasta*. The Sirian agent is a woman functionary, Ambien II, who exemplifies Lessing's belief that women's better nature is often subsumed by achieving power; in this they are no different from the men whose behaviour they deplore. Ambien II is one of Sirius's five rulers and has been in the Colonial Service for eons. (Sirians do not die; their parts are replaced as they wear out.) Sirians' technical knowledge is superior to that of the Canopians', but their emotions are baser – greed, false pride. Ambien II makes her decisions on the basis of what will most profit the state. She is not concerned with individuals. Before the book ends, she learns to see herself and the world more humanely and honestly.

Lessing told Lesley Hazleton that in 'the third one I go back to a rather shallower level and ... I used Canopus, the 'superior constellation,' for argument's sake, tutoring a more barbaric planet into self-realisation.'[3] This theme seems to come from her history as a student of Sufism. She told Christopher Bigsby that when she began studying under Idries Shah, she went through a long process of removing layers of misconceptions before she could discover truths about herself.

In the fourth volume, *The Making of the Representative for Planet 8*, the story is told not through the coloniser but the colonised. Planet 8 serves as an Eden-like refuge for a group of people who have evolved through genetic breeding. There is neither hardship nor free will on Planet 8. Soon after the colonists, as instructed, build a thick black wall around the planet, snow, which had never fallen before, begins to cascade. Planet 8 moves into an ice age. The people struggle to stay alive, but their energy is sapped by stress, and after a period of deterioration, with criminality and violence, most of them become weakened morally and physically.

The inhabitants of Planet 8 all expire, some by starvation, some by freezing to death or being buried under snow. The novel not only portrays the capacity of human beings to endure but, conversely, it establishes how much greater than the individual is the force of nature.

In *Documents Relating to the Sentimental Agents in the Volyen Empire*, the final book in the series, species grow and decline, territories are conquered, people are enslaved. Language plays a large part in this story, as words are used to create illusion, infect and madden the mind, arouse excess emotion and sentimentality, and incite mob violence.

* * *

'I hate rhetoric of all kinds,' Lessing told the science fiction writer Brian Aldiss in 1988. 'As I went along, I kept coming on these good ideas like the hospital for rhetorical disease ... I've never enjoyed anything so much.'[4] As Lessing transferred the trials of everyday life onto a grand galactic screen, writing the Canopus series – five novels in four years – made her feel more productive than at any previous time in her life.

Lessing has said that she was addressing certain sociological issues in these books, an idea that Robert Gottlieb was not comfortable with. He was wary of his prized author becoming too polemical. He told her that far too often, science fiction simplifies so much that it becomes propaganda, and he did not believe Doris Lessing readers were sympathetic to propaganda. They would have to believe what they were reading in order to accept it.

Marriages was written before *Shikasta* was published, and plans were made to bring the second book out within six to eight months after the first. In a letter, Lessing analysed the time frame for Gottlieb. *Shikasta* would come out in the fall. At least mixed reviews would greet it. Probably while these reviews were still being written, *Marriages* would appear, so different in feel from its predecessor that, sh. said happily, the critics would have to rethink their programmed responses to her work.

Gottlieb's concerns were well founded: many reviewers and readers found the Archives primarily a way for Lessing to lecture. Her 'space fiction' was seen by some as heavy-handed and preachy, not really science fiction at all, with a gap between the form of the genre and the centre of the stories. Critical response to the series was decidedly mixed. John Leonard, her great fan, wrote in his review of *The Sirian Experiments*,

I thought *Shikasta* was a disaster, and found *The Marriages* enchanting and wise. Of course, Mrs Lessing can, and will, do whatever she wants; we are bees stinging her ankles as she lunges toward the ineffable .... She may insist that the cosmology of Canopus in Argos is merely literary; we are obliged to ask how well has she brought if off and then to wonder, as Ambien II wonders about the Sirian empire, 'What for?'[5]

Susan Lardner, writing in the *New Yorker* in 1983, said:

A stranger to the works of Lessing, attracted by the publisher's proclamation of a visionary cycle, and seduced by the author's epiphanic posture, may revel in the pragmatic mysticism of these books, may happily embrace the metaphysics and snuggle in the consoling teleology. A hardened reader may balk, stupefied by the impersonality of the small personal voice, and suspecting ... that the earnest grailchaser has become something of a crackpot. Other readers, who have enjoyed Lessing's other work, may simply find the Canopus series too impenetrable to know what to make of it.[6]

The series, though never popular with Lessing's core readership did win over some enthusiastic new adherents. The composer Philip Glass was so taken with it that he imposed two Canopus-based operas – The Making of the Representative for Planet 8 (1988) and The Marriages between Zones Three, Four and Five (1997).

Nothing angered Doris Lessing more during this period of her life than being told her readers felt abandoned by her flight from the realistic novel. She vehemently insisted to Lesley Hazleton that the Canopus series was being embraced by younger readers all over the world and that many older readers liked it as well. They understood the relevance of her work, that she was addressing the problems of our own world in this fantastic context, she said. Reviewers and critics were too hidebound to see what she was doing.

The young woman who served as Doris Lessing's assistant at this time remembers, 'She was genuinely pissed that people didn't like the space fiction. She was so angry. Every time there would be a review in the London or New York *Times*, or other newspapers, she'd be hysterical if they put down what she was trying to do. 'They're rooted in the past,' she'd rage. 'Can't they see that there are more important things to write about than men and women marrying or having sex? This stuff that I'm writing about now is where it really is.'

Lessing herself has read a great deal of science fiction, and often reviews it. Her critics have probably never read a word of the genre, she asserts. As she indicated to Lesley Hazleton, it is a genre she believes is the ultimate form of social criticism. It infuriates her that so many people don't see this. Of Susan Stamberg she demanded,

Why does a story have to be: 'Mary got up at 6 o'clock and felt terrible and took a sleeping pill and went back to sleep and she knew her heart was going to break because of Dick.' Why is that any more real than: 'Marianne from planet X had a terrible decision in front of her. Was she going to do this or was she going to do that?' ... It seems to me that if people have imaginations so narrow that they can't see themselves as Marianne from planet X, then it's a pity.[7]

Lessing has dismissed the desires of readers who wanted her to return to realism as the complaints of ignoramuses. When Lesley Hazelton told her that women who had seen her as a champion felt abandoned by her sojourn in space, she seemed to find it ludicrous. Her unyielding determination to continue writing the Canopus series, despite the ambivalent reception of her public, brings to mind some lines from *Shikasta*, in the opening paragraphs of what would become the thousand plus page Canopus saga: 'I have known more than once what it is to accept the failure, final and irreversible, of an effort or experiment ... But the ability to cut losses demands a different type of determination from the stubborn patience needed to withstand attrition ...'[8]

New Skin for an Old Ceremony

Lessing's next two novels after the Canopus in Argos series were *The Diary of a Good Neighbour,* published in 1983, and *If the Old Could ...,* published in 1984. For a variety of reasons, she decided to write these two books under a pseudonym, Jane Somers. One reason she later gave for the disguise was to show up the weaknesses of the British and American publishing systems, and those of reviewers in the literary establishment. Despising their publicity-driven marketing methods, she wanted to prove it was more the author's personality and reputation than the literary product that generated publishing and critical interest. The name Doris Lessing was commercially significant. Jane Somers, an unknown novelist – no matter how interesting a writer – was not. Lessing wanted to expose the way that, in the world of publishing, nothing succeeds like success. 'If the books had come out in my name, they would have sold a lot of copies and reviewers would have said, "Oh, Doris Lessing, how wonderful."'[1]

By contrast, the first Jane Somers novel had difficulty finding a publisher. Lessing and her new British agent, Jonathan Clowes, decided to send it first to Lessing's publishers. 'It was fair to start with them,' she said.[2] What she did not say is that it would also make her point particularly sharp if her own publishers rejected a book written by her. Clowes offered the manuscript to Robert Gottlieb during the editor's visit to London in 1982. Gottlieb immediately discerned the truth. 'Who do you think you're kidding,' he impatiently responded.[3]

With some reluctance, Gottlieb agreed to keep silent about the hoax. He also agreed to publish Jane Somers's novel in America, despite believing that sales would be minimal. 'He regards me as a delinquent child, wrong-headed, obstinate and stubborn,' Lessing told an interviewer calmly. But, she added, when the story eventually came out, 'he saw the point of what I've done.'[4]

Actually, Gottlieb is on record as saying the whole exercise seemed pointless. The scanty sales and meagre reviews garnered by Jane Somers admittedly confirmed Lessing's belief that a name often carries more weight than the quality of the writing. But he does not read the same dire messages into the experience as she did. 'My view,' he told the *New York Times,* 'is that what's worthy sooner or later surfaces.'[5]

The manuscript of *Diary of a Good Neighbour* was also delivered by Lessing's young assistant to her British publisher, Jonathan Cape, though not to Tom Maschler himself, who Lessing feared might catch on. 'He would have known it immediately just by the typing,' the assistant who delivered the manuscript says, referring to Lessing's sloppy typing style on an old manual machine. In response the assistant was bemused to hear that in some accounts of the story, the manuscript was supposed to have been retyped to avoid recognition, an apparent embellishment after the fact.

Liz Calder, today a publisher, was then an editor at Jonathan Cape. She was sent the book and passed it on to a 'reader,' a common practice in publishing, particularly for unsolicited manuscripts.[6] Based on the reader's report, Calder turned the novel down.[7] Lessing got the chance to read the reader's report and found it quite condescending.[8]

But Philippa Harrison, the woman in charge of Lessing's first publisher, Michael Joseph, told Jonathan Clowes, 'This reminds me of the early Doris Lessing,' and expressed her willingness to sign the author. 'We got into a panic,' Lessing remembers, 'because we didn't want her going around saying that! So we took her to lunch, and I said, 'This is me, can you go along with it?' She was upset to begin with, but then she really enjoyed it all.'[9]

A French publisher also saw the resemblance and called Lessing to ask whether she had been helping Jane Somers. He too was told the truth and pledged to secrecy. For the next point Lessing wanted to make was about critics. As routinely happens, the book was sent before publication to reviewers, many of whom were familiar with her work. To Lessing's delight, not one of them guessed the truth. Despising as she did the idea of being some scholar's possession, she found this part of the hoax especially rewarding.

When she learned Michael Joseph was going to publish *Diary*, Lessing admitted the truth to Tom Maschler. She knew he would be embarrassed by Cape's rejection of it when the story got out. And there seems little doubt that she always intended to go public at some point in the escapade. For the time being, however, she entreated him to keep her secret. This presented a sizeable dilemma for Maschler – he was not happy about withholding the truth from Liz Calder – 'but whatever sense of betrayal I may have felt was overshadowed by a feeling of loyalty to Doris.'[10]

Because she so enjoyed writing under the pseudonym, Lessing didn't reveal the truth until 1984, after the second Somers book, *If the Old Could* ..., was published to a similarly quiet reception. At that point she decided to confess, and she gave Tom Maschler advance warning, knowing he would be sought out by reporters. 'If it amuses Doris, why shouldn't she do it,' he wrote in the London *Sunday Times*. 'I certainly don't hold it against her, but I'm not sure the exercise proves anything.'[11] He added that when *The Diary of a Good Neighbour* was offered to his publishing house, he would have published it even without knowing the author – if he had thought it was a good book.

Maschler was being somewhat defensive in his appraisal of *Diary*. In fact, the reviews it did get were favourable, even in some literary magazines. Such praise added to Lessing's delight for a particular reason. She admitted a somewhat spiteful pleasure in showing up reviewers who had deplored her Canopus quintet. They had attacked her for abandoning the realistic novel, and intimated that she was dissipating her literary skill by spending so much time on less successful experimentation.

* * *

After the hoax was revealed, Jonathan Yardley wrote a column in the *Washington Post*, wondering whether Lessing's motivation was not so much to prove 'the success syndrome' around a well-known name, as to get back at reviewers who refused to be seduced by her name on Canopus and picked the series to pieces.[12]

Diary of a Good Neighbour was turned down by some British publishing houses for being too melancholy, or too discouraging. Although Lessing is obviously correct when she says that at one time serious publishers did not refuse books because they were too depressing, there is a sense of author retaliation in the novel. It is as if when we read this stark, graphic story of age and deterioration, of a dying woman's incontinence and decay, that Lessing is saying to the critics of the Canopus in Argos books, 'Well, you wanted realism. Here it is. Are you still sure you prefer it to fantasy?'

If the Old Could ... shows Janna, the heroine of *Diary*, continuing to struggle with age. She falls in love and responds like a giddy teenager. In counterpoint to the romantic thrall, she develops a relationship with her niece, an adolescent punker who camps out messily in Janna's pristine flat. The novel exposes the harsh landscape of an ageing woman's unsatisfied desire, and the gap between the generations. It was, even under a pseudonym, a brave book for a sixty-five-year-old woman to write.

The two pseudonymous novels were republished together in 1984 by Michael Joseph (Random House in New York) under the title *The Diaries of Jane Somers*, with an introduction by Lessing, whose name now appeared on the book's cover. 'I wanted to be reviewed on merit, as a new writer, without the benefit of a "name,"' she reiterates in the introduction, ' ... to get free of that cage of associations and labels that every established writer has to learn to live inside.'[13]

But there was perhaps a still deeper reason for the hoax, hinted at in *The Summer Before the Dark*, when Kate Brown experimented with making herself invisible to the ogling workmen by covering her body with a shapeless coat, and letting her hair show its gray roots. Kate was doing nothing less than testing her identity. If the men didn't notice her, did she exist?

It seems that Doris Lessing, the writer, has spent her life in a Sisyphean search for a solid sense of self. The fame that accrues to her name, although she has actively sought it, appears to make her feel less rather than more confident of her identity. She is a woman who is always loath to use her name for special privilege, and perhaps it is not only modesty that restrains her. Too much attention to the public self can erode the inner core. If she is affirmed only because she is Doris Lessing, who is Doris Lessing without the name?

William Phillips remembers an evening when Lessing wanted to take him and Edith Kurzweil, another *Partisan Review* editor, out to dinner. She had a particular restaurant in mind, but when she came by to collect her two friends she told them she'd been unable to secure a reservation. At that moment, Michael Levitas of the *New York Times* phoned to speak to Lessing about a piece she was doing for the newspaper's opinion page. In the course of the conversation she mentioned that they were going out to dinner but weren't able to get into the restaurant of her choice.

Levitas said, 'Hold on,' called the restaurant, and called her back to tell her he had booked her a table. Phillips later asked whether Lessing had given them her name when she made her reservation request. 'Of course not,' she responded curtly. 'When we got there, they were falling all over her,' recalls Kurzweil. But the attention, she recalled, did not please their hostess.

In her introduction to *The Diaries of Jane Somers*, Lessing claims to be 'detached' about her name. One must remember that 'Lessing' is her third surname, she writes, while as for 'Doris,' she reiterates that it was given to her by the doctor who delivered her, 'my mother being convinced to the last possible moment that I was a boy ... I sometimes do wonder what my real name is: surely I must have one?'[14]

The name 'Doris Lessing' immediately bestows identity, but in its recipient's mind, one that is alarmingly superficial. Doris Lessing understands, as Kate Brown came to realise, that identity is too fragile to be determined by other people's recognition. She has fought against such a definition all her life. Over and over again, she has tried to demarcate a personally defined sense of self. Writing under a pseudonym, is like seeing whether there was a deeper self called Doris Lessing, one who was recognised through her writing even if the author was anonymous.

* * *

Janna, the heroine of the Jane Somers novels, is the fiftyish editor of a woman's magazine (the kind Doris Lessing has total contempt for), and the author of popular romantic novels. She is a perfectly groomed woman of impeccable personal habits. Her clothes are beautiful and elegant. Her life is orderly, as are her feelings, to the extent that she is untouched by her husband's and mother's deaths by cancer.

About her mother's worsening illness, she says, 'I hate physical awfulness. I can't stand it ... When it got towards the end ... I couldn't touch her, not really. Not with kindness.'[15]

But after a chance meeting with Maudie, an impoverished ninety-two-year-old Cockney woman who lives in a squalid basement apartment near her own beautiful London flat, Janna will take on the woman's care, and in the process become a more giving person than she is when readers first meet her.

In recalling the genesis of some of the characters, Lessing's assistant during the years she wrote the two novels notes Lessing was 'utterly fascinated with these dotty women who lived very marginal lives. I think they were ladies she met through their passion for stray cats. They would take cats off the streets into their ramshackle rooms, sometimes filling the small, already filthy space with them.'

Among Lessing's models for Janna were one woman who was inordinately concerned with her appearance; another was someone who resolutely clung to the vision of a happy life from childhood through her marriage. But when her husband died, she moved from being a naive middle-aged girl to a whole, impressively autonomous person.

A third model for Janna, says Lessing, was her mother. What would Maude be like if she were a middle-aged woman in the 1980s? Some of the qualities Lessing saw Maude as sharing with Janna as she is when the first novel opens were her efficiency, her energy, her practicality, and her inability to comprehend human frailty.

What Lessing does not explore is what her mother would be like if she lived now as an *old* woman, in London, living near her daughter and needing her care. It is startling that Lessing has never mentioned any connection between her mother and Maudie, the 'fierce ... angry'[16] elderly woman whom she has given her mother's name, though she has discussed the source for characters in multiple interviews and in the introduction to a later paperback edition.

Janna takes total care of Maudie, shops for her, fights with social agencies for services, cleans her rooms, her clothes, her ailing body. When she tends to Maudie, she feels far removed from the Janna who could not meet her mother's or her husband's needs when they were dying. With Maudie, she will sit by her side indefinitely, letting her know that she is emotionally as well as physically taking part in her diminishing life. Indeed, Janna, now that her more selfish self is erased, becomes righteously indignant toward Maudie's family, who had abandoned her years before.

If Lessing has found it difficult to be as emotionally generous as Janna, she has been very generous with money in her life. Not the freewheeling type when it comes to spending, Lessing is nonetheless very, attuned to the financial needs of others, even people she is not particularly close to. One example is Paul Schlueter, the editor of *A Small Personal Voice*, her 1975 collection of non-fiction. In a letter to Robert Gottlieb, where Lessing makes more than one sarcastic reference to being irritated by Schlueter's academic manner, she nonetheless directs that royalties be split fifty-fifty for the book, instead of taking the two-thirds her agent John Cushman said would be appropriate.

When an assistant of Lessing's decided to apply to the London School of Economics, she told her employer she would be able to manage school along with her duties, and Lessing made no negative comments about the plan. Before the young woman heard whether she was accepted at the distinguished institution, she received a call from the States telling her that her father had died.

'The next morning I woke early to make arrangements. Doris was sitting on the stairs drinking coffee. I told her about my father, and she seemed surprised that I was upset. 'I thought you weren't that fond of your father,' she said. I told her he and I had our problems, but it was still a shock to hear of his death. She made no comment except to ask me how soon I would be back. I told her I couldn't say and she didn't seem happy with that answer.' Lessing's assistant was quite used to such minimalist conversations. 'For a person who regularly writes five-hundred-page books, I don't think Doris spoke five hundred words to me in the two years that I lived with her.'

The assistant wrote to Lessing from America telling her when she would return, and received in reply a brief card indicating that some other arrangements might be made at that time. When she arrived back in London, it was to learn that someone else was already living in her room.

'I called a friend who lived down the street and asked if I could stay there. Doris said something about the person who had replaced me needing a place to stay, and then she told me, very casually, that a letter had come to me from the London School of Economics, that she'd opened it and learned I'd been accepted, and sent them a check for my tuition. I was so startled that I didn't say anything, and only afterwards did I begin to think about whether this was a loan or a gift, or whether I was supposed to go on working for her in some capacity as a way of paying her back, since I had no money.'

For about a week, the young woman stopped by the Lessing house to see if there were any errands she could run or duties she could perform, and also to try to speak to Lessing about how she perceived the outlay of money. But Lessing was never available for such a conversation.

'After the end of that week, I got a call from Jenny Diski, who told me to stop going by to see Doris. 'You don't understand,' she said kindly. 'It's over.'

'When I asked about the tuition, Jenny indicated it was a gift. I really had little choice but to accept it, and I did. And although I lived down the street and remained in London for almost another two years, I never spoke to Doris again. She would smile when I passed her on the street, and I delivered presents the first Christmas I was out of the house, but they were never acknowledged.'

'As Jane Somers, I wrote in ways that Doris Lessing could not.' It seems reasonable to conclude that in the Jane Somers novels, Lessing could allow herself to rewrite her life's guilt-producing scenes and, as Janna, *behave* in ways that Doris Lessing could not.

A Literary Rebirth

'A tale of terror ... of accumulating, never-ending fears,' one reviewer wrote about Lessing's 1988 novel – her thirty-fifth book – *The Fifth Child.*[1] 'I hated writing it,' Lessing said. 'It was sweating blood. I was very glad when it was done ....obviously, it goes very deep into me somewhere.'[2] The story of the Lovatt family has the terrifying power of a nightmare in its blend of naturalistic realism and allegorical spectral shapes. Lessing knows that readers are not comfortable with such a mixture. They want realism *or* science fiction, not realism *and* science fiction. She was quite amused by a BBC commentator who kept repeating over and over again that *The Fifth Child* was uncategorisable because of its mix of fantasy and reality.

In her preface to a later edition of *The Golden Notebook*, Lessing chided critics for not noticing that the central theme of the book was breakdown. It is a theme she returns to in *The Fifth Child,* in which a quintessentially happy family disintegrates. The story opens with Harriet and David meeting at an office party. It is the hedonistic sixties, a decade to which these two 'non-dancers' at the raucous gathering do not psychically belong. They recognise themselves in each other, and know 'at once that this was what they had been waiting for. Someone conservative, old-fashioned, not to say obsolescent.'[3]

For a long while, their life has everything they knew they were destined to possess. With the help of David's wealthy father, they buy a huge house, which they proceed to fill with four beautiful children. Harriet and David Lovatt choose steadiness and contentment over intemperance and angst. They take pride in the vast number of relatives and friends who pour through the house every holiday, as if their guests wanted to feed on the purity of the Lovatts' proudly presented life. If the couple seem smug in their conviction that their personal world is enviable, no one could blame them.

In every way the Lovatts seem people immune to catastrophe. Yet, Lessing tells us, they are as vulnerable as we – despite attempts to banish the thought – sense ourselves to be. No one, she insists, no matter how virtuous and stable, escapes the possibility of unforeseeable tragedy. 'I do have a sense, and I've never not had it, of how easily things can vanish. It's a sense of disaster,' she told a reporter during an article about the book.[4]

One day, not having planned to be, but ready to embrace the idea, Harriet discovers she is pregnant with their fifth child. But this pregnancy is terribly different from the preceding four. 'David saw her sitting at the kitchen table, head in her hands, muttering that this new foetus was poisoning her.'[5] At times it does not feel like a baby inside of her at all, but some animal with hooves or claws instead of hands and feet.

When the eleven-pound baby is born – the other children were much smaller – after an excruciating labour – the other children were easily birthed – he seems an alien child. He looks very different from their other children, different from any other child at all. He is large and thick and he hunches over as if ready to spring out at someone. His forehead is angled with a growth of dark yellow hair, and his hands are unusually large.

The parents are repulsed by this Other, whom they name Ben. His siblings are afraid of him. He is fiercely strong and physically precocious, able to lift and climb, although he does not speak at the appropriate age, grunting and shouting instead. When Ben is a year old, the Lovatts' cat and a visiting dog are strangled, and the family is certain Ben is responsible.

People begin to refuse invitations to the house they once flocked to, and the older children lock themselves in their rooms. Harriet tries in vain to get Ben's doctor to agree that the boy is abnormal. The man is reluctant – as other professionals, including Ben's future teachers, will be – only offering that he might be hyperactive, or perhaps a little slower intellectually than other children his age. Yet Harriet feels the professionals, and many of her friends as well, resent having to be disturbed by the presence of Ben, and blame her for creating him.

At the insistence of David, her mother – who has moved into the house to help her in the impossible task of managing Ben – Harriet agrees to send the boy to an institution, to be drugged into oblivion and eventually – although no one will admit this awareness – to death. David's father is more than willing to pay for this service.

'In the days that followed, the family expanded like paper flowers in water.'[6] But while Harriet shares her family's happiness, she keeps thinking of that creature who is her last son – not with loving attachment, but with haunting feelings of guilt at what she has done to him.

One morning after another sleepless night, she gets out of bed knowing she must go to see Ben, to find out what is being done with – to – him. David protests, and she knows as she insists on going that things will change between them because of her decision. A several-hour drive brings her to the dismal-looking building with barred windows that harbours her monster son. After much resistance from the staff since parents do not come to visit their children once they have placed them here, she is taken to Ben's room. The walls and floor are covered with excrement. He lies naked and straitjacketed, on a rubber mattress, dark yellow urine oozing out from under his unconscious body.

She knows she must save him from this place, even though she also knows what bringing him home will mean. The return of this child whom she cannot love will obliterate everything that love previously created.

Ben eventually learns to speak and even goes to school, although he does not learn anything there. Still, he is moved ahead each year. His mother threatens to return him to the institution if he does not control himself, and he manages to restrain his more violent impulses. But his presence hovers over family life until there *is* no family life. David becomes absorbed in the career he never cared about when his personal life was rich. The older children ask to be sent to boarding school to escape the frightening prison their home has become. The child closest to Ben's age grows more and more disturbed.

Ben eventually connects with a bunch of alienated youths. They take over the beautiful house, watching violent programs on television and eating great masses of food Harriet suspects they paid for with stolen money – Ben among the thieves.

As the book ends, Harriet sits alone at her long kitchen table that had once been the centre of family life. She suspects that Ben will drift further into a criminal future.

> The gang would continue to support themselves by theft, and sooner or later would be caught. Ben, too. In police hands he would fight, and roar and stamp about and bellow, out of control with rage, and they would drug him, because they had to, and before very long he would be as he had been when she had found him dying, looking like a giant slug, pallid and limp in his cloth shroud.[7]

Lessing says she wrote *The Fifth Child* twice. The first time she muted the story's horror. She discarded that draft and began again, this time making the story far less pleasant, and far more real.[8]

Reviewers saw *The Fifth Child* as a parable of everything, from AIDS to genetic research to the collapse of the British Empire. Lessing generally and somewhat disingenuously denies any intention of parable. The story is simply an illustration of a human dilemma, she says. When an interviewer commented that there seems no right way to deal with such a child, Lessing agreed and indicated that's what she finds fascinating in the story. If you consider yourself a member of a civilised society, then you have certain values that will make it impossible for you to anticipate or respond to the conflicts created by having a son like Ben.[9] Even when *The Fifth Child* is read at face value as the straightforward horror story Lessing sometimes claims it to be, it makes us understand that we won't always rise above life's assaults. David and Harriet believe that their determined happiness protects them from harm, just as they believe they can perfectly balance personal happiness with responsibility to others. But when the microcosm of society that is the family constantly tries to keep out what is untamed and irrational, it may inevitably create the very thing its inhabitants are trying to escape: something uncivilised, and monstrous in its refusal to be repressed.

With its mix of realism and fantasy the novel is both literal and metaphoric. Lessing is vitally interested in evolution. When, in *The Four-Gated City*, Martha develops extrasensory perception, she thinks to herself that this was what life was about, developing different and higher senses so that you are more aware of yourself and the world than you ever were before. But the clock of evolution can also be turned back. And when it is, mysterious explosions can take place.

One impetus for writing the book was Lessing's fascination with the 'little people' of legend. She had also read a piece by the anthropologist Loren Eiseley, describing a walk along a country road in Maine as night was falling. He was thinking about the Ice Age when he saw a girl ahead of him. When he approached the girl he saw with a shock that she had Neanderthal features.

He briefly spoke with the girl, and as she walked away up to her house, Eiseley thought that the experience he was having could have taken place at any point in the last fifty thousand years. This inspired Lessing to make the leap from ancient anthropology to ancient legend. 'I thought,' says Lessing, 'OK now, a Neanderthal girl. Why not a goblin ...'[10]

She told interviewer Claire Tomlin about yet another spark to light her story – a letter she read in a newspaper from a woman who said that after giving birth to several wonderful children, she had a baby who was the personification of evil, and who caused an entire family to disintegrate. But Lessing asserts that Ben is not evil; he is merely an outsider in this world. Had he lived in an ancient time, in a forest thousands of years before, he would not be singled out as a sinister force. He is probably the result of a gene passed down through centuries.

Lessing has said that it is easier to talk about the ideas that go into a book than to understand the engine that fuels the ideas. It would seem reasonable to assume that the engine for *The Fifth Child*, in part at least, stems from her own anxieties about mothering. The experience of abandoning John and Jean, and her difficulties with Peter and Jenny and other young people that lead her spending much of the 1960s as a kind of housemother to troubled teens', would certainly provide fertile ground for her magnificent depiction of the painful parenting experience of Harriet and David.[11]

'I don't believe that we can hope to explain the figure of Ben ... by an analytic theory or by classical psychiatry,' Lessing says, and to prevent the reader from attempting such an explanation she depicts Harriet and David as supremely perfect parents: loving, attentive, understanding. If *they* could have a child like Ben, any parent could be similarly, blamelessly afflicted.

Some of the descriptions of Ben's life seem to be drawn from Lessing's 1960s 'housemother period'. In 1995, the late Jane Cushman, wife of Lessing's former agent John Cushman, recalled an incident from the late sixties that had an echo of Ben's unruly friends. It happened when the Cushmans were visiting Lessing at a little house she owned in Devon: 'Suddenly there was this great racket, and a car pulled up and three ominous-looking young thugs got out, all dressed in black. They said that Peter had told them Doris would put them up for the night. She just nodded acquiescence. Then they went outside and came back in with this bunch of greasy rags that they swished about. They'd bought a pound of butter to bring 'as a gift,' and it had melted in the car. They thought it was uproarious. My husband and I were terribly uncomfortable.'

Joan Cushman went to visit Lessing in London and Peter joined them for lunch, hunched over his food and not saying a word. Having 'been raised to believe you must jump into a stalled conversation,' she told some mildly amusing anecdote about seeing a rabbit up in a tree outside her hotel window that morning. 'At that Peter became furious. He roared at me for nattering about some stupid rabbit when the world was so full of suffering. He was terribly abusive, and I looked over at Doris and felt she must get this kind of treatment often, and suffer it this way, in stoic silence.' Such episodes seem to have passed. Those interviewed for this book who knew Peter felt that he is extremely bright. One person remembers Lessing saying that Peter was 'caring for me beautifully' when she injured her leg in a fall some years ago.

Lessing's Sufi connection also seems to have helped her cope with her various mothering problems. 'It's as if she feels that destiny dealt her a difficult hand, but by rising to a higher consciousness, she could deal with it,' a colleague remarks. In painting the Lovatts as such paragons of parents, Lessing does seem to stress the idea of fate overpowering individual intention. Nothing Harriet and David did deserved Ben. Fate also gave Doris Tayler two troubled parents, made her marry two men she didn't love, have children she was not ready to have, robbed Peter of a father who might have given him a more stable life. (Peter did reunite with Gottfried in Germany in 1963; in 1979 Gottfried and his third wife were murdered in Uganda, where he was the East German ambassador. Peter took his death hard, his mother told interviewer Fiammetta Rocco in 1992.)

The Fifth Child does not come to a clear conclusion. Harriet's torment and fear have not abated when the last page is turned, just as Ben's future remains uncertain. The reader understands that no parent is ever truly finished with a child's life. At a point when many parents grow apart from their children, she has reached out to all of her offspring. Reuniting with John and Jean in the 1960s, she went on to establish generous trust funds for them and for Peter, who she remains quite close to. So close that she bough him a flat next door to her house. Similarly she purchased Ardroy Estates, a coffee plantation, for her son John (who died in 1990 of a heart attack) to manage. In 1995, she returned to South Africa to visit her daughter and two granddaughters.

'You know, I feel for her,' says a former assistant of Lessing's who lived with her. 'But of course,' she says, wistfully, 'Doris just doesn't deal with human beings very well. She deals with cats very well.'

'People Don't Purr'

'She seemed so lonely to me,' says a former assistant of Lessing's. 'But sometimes, when she lay on her little bed in her space with a beautiful view of the whole city, with lots of pillows and surrounded by her cats, then she seemed happy.' And in a BBC documentary about Lessing, the novelist Margaret Drabble said: 'There's something very nice about the way she always notices the cat population of the world wherever she goes. She's always connected with it, or has an eye open for it …. I think cats, particularly cats, do have her affection.' And British journalist Jane Kelly notes, 'I have never met someone so anthropomorphic about cats. She was constantly saying things during the interview like, "You can't take his picture. He hates being photographed."'

Cats have always been part of Doris Lessing's life. Unlike people, they do not annoy or disappoint her. If *Particularly Cats* is any indication, some of her most vivid and significant memories involve cats, beginning with her earliest childhood in Tehran. During a walk with her Persian nursemaid when she was three years old, she found a starving kitten in the streets, and despite her caretaker's objections, Doris insisted on taking it home. She faced parental resistance to the pet, but with the strong will that was already in evidence she held firm to her demand to keep it. The servants washed the kitten in permanganate to rid it of its filth, and from that first day on, until the family left Persia two years later, the cat slept on Doris's bed.

When the Tayler family set off on their arduous journey across Russia, the cat stayed behind. Doris was told 'soothing lies' when she asked what had happened to it, 'but I did not believe them.'[1] The cat had been her closest companion, a constant loving presence, and then, dead or alive, it was gone from her life. Doris's mother added this story to her repertoire of tales about her difficult daughter, how the little girl was absolutely 'inconsolable' about that mangy, sickly, stray cat.

Lessing's former assistant remembers going with her employer to the vet's to have one of her cats put down. The young woman had to take the animal into the doctor's office, while Lessing stayed in the waiting room, her face etched in grief, too overcome with sorrow to accompany her pet to its death. For years after she had to abandon that Persian cat, Lessing says, a dying feline filled her with pain of an intensity that was far greater than what she experienced when her mother or father or brother died. Many of Lessing's feline memories are attached to Africa, a land which, like a cat – and this independent quality is one of a cat's attractions for Lessing – was always only tentatively tamed.

Wild cats roamed the Tayler farm, and they lured the family's domesticated cats into mating. As it was not practical to spay the female cats, since the nearest vet was seventy miles away in Salisbury, over-population was a serious problem. It was Maude who took charge of ridding the house of unwanted cats, usually by drowning them, just as she was the one to shoot snakes and sickly chickens. Once Doris told Maude she saw a snake in the woodpile, but after Maude shot at the glimpse of grey slithering between two logs, it turned out to be one of Doris's favourite cats. 'It thrashed and yelled among the wood chips, its small bleeding heart showing between fragile broken ribs. It died, while my mother wept and petted it.'[2]

And then, during a year when Doris was at her most combative with her mother, practical, efficient Maude rebelled. She refused to kill any more animals. Her boycott led to the house and surrounding grounds and outbuildings being overrun by them. Clearly, the situation needed remedying. But no matter what Doris or her father said, Maude did not respond. And then, inexplicably, Maude went off on a weekend trip by herself. 'Before she left she said goodbye to her favourite puss, an old tabby who was the mother of them all,' Lessing writes in *Particularly Cats*. 'She stroked her gently, and cried.' The tears startled Doris, for she did not know their source.

After she had gone, Michael placed a call to the vet – no easy task, as twenty other people shared their party line – and asked how to get rid of so many cats. The doctor advised chloroform, and Michael ar-ranged for a pharmacist in Salisbury to put a bottle on the train that came to their village. On the day Maude was due home again, the bottle finally arrived at the train station. Doris and her father took a large cookie tin and placed a tampon soaked in chloroform inside it. Then they lowered an old, sickly cat into the box.

'I do not recommend this method. The vet said it would be instanta-neous; but it was not,' Lessing wrote. Unable to continue the agonising ritual, Michael collected all the cats and placed them in one room. Then he entered the room carrying his revolver from the war. Soon Doris heard the repeated shots, till Michael came back to where his daughter waited. He looked ill, 'very white, with tight angry lips and wet eyes'[3] and he muttered curses before re-entering the other room and finishing his work. When he was done with his ugly task, the servants disposed of the bodies in an unused well.

Maude returned that evening and did not say a word as she went through the house, free now of cats except for her favourite old tabby, which Michael had spared. She sat for a long while, petting the animal and talking softly to it. Then she joined her husband and daughter on the veranda. Michael was still trembling and he solemnly told his wife that this was the last time he would do what he had done that day.

Lessing says she was angry at the 'holocaust of cats,' but she has no memory of grieving herself because she was still armoured against feeling from the loss of the kitten she found in Persia many years before, and from another more recent loss during her very unhappy eleventh year.[4]

She had fallen victim to a recurring, inexplicable illness and was spending a good deal of her time in bed. It was July, and cold, and the blue-grey Persian cat kept her warm as it lay in the bend of her arm. Out at the back of the house was a tub made of wood that was dug into the earth behind the bathroom to catch the bathwater. There were no water pipes on the farm. Servants brought water from a well two miles away, carrying it to the farm on a cart drawn by oxen. In the dry season, the only water for the gardens was the dirty bathwater. One day, during her illness the Persian kitty jumped into the tub when it was filled with hot water. She screamed in pain, and although she was quickly pulled out into the cold air, and placed back in Doris's bed, she began to sneeze and cough and was soon clearly feverish. She had contracted pneumonia, and very soon she was dead. She was dropped down the dry well into piles of garbage and other animal corpses.

It was too much for Doris. She vowed that she would never allow herself such grief again, even though every day as she matured into an adult she compared the cats she passed on the street or saw in friends' homes to that perfect cat of memory. It would be twenty-five years before Doris Lessing allowed herself to have another cat, and the one she sought then was unlike 'that gentle blue-grey purring creature which for me was the cat, the Cat, never to be replaced.'[5]

Nonetheless she is fond of her later cats. Two favourites she has written about are Rufus, a sickly stray she nursed back to health and General Butchkin who stretches out on her typewriter when she is trying to work. In an interview with Alison Nadel, Lessing revealed to the reporter that Rufus is 'a real heartbreaker.'[6]

Lessing has always been reluctant to deprive her female cats of their sexuality. In the way she believes women become invisible when they grow old, she feels a spayed cat loses her looks and has her personality dimmed when she is desexed. Describing one cat she felt compelled to have 'fixed,' she mourns the animal's sudden timidity. She seemed insecure rather than certain of her charm, was petulant rather than seductive. 'In short, she had turned into a spinster cat.'[7]

Lessing once took a visiting journalist up to her bedroom with its balcony looking down on a mass of London gardens. 'I stand here for hours,' she said, resting her back against the railings. 'I love watching all the cats in the gardens, just observing their lives.'[8]

Lessing ends her cat book saying, 'Knowing cats, a lifetime of cats, what is left is a sediment of sorrow quite different from that due to humans: compounded of pain for their helplessness, of guilt on behalf of us all.'[9]

Does that mean, asks the journalist, that she finds it easier to care for cats than human beings?

'Yes,' she laughs. 'People don't purr.'[10]

Epilogue

In 1992, I raised with Doris Lessing the subject of writing her biography. She answered that she was thinking seriously about writing her memoirs. People had been talking to her about it for years, but now, in her seventies, she had reached the time when it seemed 'I had better get on with it.'

Although I believe that memoir and biography complement each other, she disagreed. She would tell her own story, and decided not to cooperate with mine.

Lessing wrote the story of her life across the next few years. The first volume of her memoirs, *Under My Skin*, was published in 1994, the second, *Walking in the Shade*, in 1997. Publication date of the second volume was in October, the month she celebrated her seventy-eighth birthday.

The account Doris Lessing offers, in a voice that is both honest and evasive, ends with 1962. She has said that while she originally planned to write a third volume, she changed her mind because several people in her life were very young and troubled during the 1960s and '70s, and she has misgivings about exposing their history to readers.

For now, however, we have her version of her life only from childhood to her early forties, when she is still exiled from her homeland, Rhodesia. Yet, writing as an elderly woman, her richest meditations are of that young girl and that boundless African land.

Judging by her prickly reaction to interviewers, working on the memoirs has stirred up many emotions. She seems outraged about criticism she received for not going into her feelings about leaving her two children in *Under My Skin*. 'What should I do?' she demanded of journalist Catherine Bennett. 'Write two chapters saying I was unhappy, or what? I should think it was pretty well taken for granted.'[1] Just as feminists clasped *The Golden Notebook* to their breast only to be told they didn't understand what she wrote, the memoirs will probably mean something different to her readers from what they mean to her. *She* is just trying to 'escape the biographers,' to get the *facts* down on paper before someone else distorts them.

The image Lessing presents to the world in her memoirs is assertive, lofty, confident, and courageous. However, there is a shadow on the pages, someone behind them who is insecure, apprehensive, deeply disappointed; an exile, uncertain of her place and her identity, trying to compensate herself for the past's terrible pain.

The Doris Lessing of those pages is often detached from her own behaviour. Yet if her memoir is free of reflection, it is also free of the genre's tendency toward self-aggrandisement and self-pity. We do not know her and she does not want to know us. Clearly, just because she 'changed our lives' doesn't mean she wants us to ring her doorbell and join her for tea. She is a woman who has to write and she can't be distracted by her readers' response to her words. If we misread her, that's not her problem, and in truth, neither is it ours. Our visions of her work and hers don't have to coincide for our needs or hers to be met.

In her late seventies, Lessing still travels a great deal. As much as she professes to dislike book promotion, much of the travel is for that purpose. In the summer of 1997, just before publication of *Walking in the Shade*, she spoke at the Edinburgh Book Festival, and in October flew to New York to begin a three-city tour of interviews and readings.

She remains actively involved in African affairs, organising libraries, speaking to native groups, and continuing to criticise white Zimbabwean society. Ironically, despite this identification with blacks in Zimbabwe, the coffee farm her son managed, Ardroy Estates, on the wooded slopes of the Vumba mountains in the east of the country, is slated for seizure and redistribution to the black population, like a group of 1,500 white-owned properties in November 1997. President Robert Mugabe has acknowledged that not all the farms will go to landless peasants. Half of the properties, which Mugabe claims were originally 'stolen' by nineteenth-century white administrations, will be allotted to black commercial farmers, black businessmen, and guerrilla veterans of the 1980 civil war.

Lessing continues to write, and to experiment with her writing, from a 1994 graphic novel (comic-book) *Playing The Game*, to a 1997 libretto for a Philip Glass opera, *The Marriages Between Zones Three, Four and Five* – her second Canopus-based collaboration with the composer. Lessing's most recent novel is *Mara and Dan*, an apocalyptic adventure story set in the future. Published in 1999, it had the same ambivalent critical reception as many of her other forays into futuristic fiction. But such ambivalence is unlikely to deter Lessing. A sequel to *The Fifth Child* is expected sometime in 2000. And if the past is any gauge, she will continue to explore new paths in literature and life.

There is a compelling aspect to Lessing's search for meaning that makes her a sympathetic figure even when her behaviour is hard to accept. She was not born into an era that encouraged such journeys. As George Orwell, another futurist, wrote in 1947, two years before Doris Lessing arrived in England:

After the age of about thirty, most people almost abandon the sense of being individuals at all – and live chiefly for others, or are simply smothered under drudgery. But there is also the minority of gifted, wilful people who are determined to live their own lives to the end, and writers belong to this class.[2]

Doris Lessing has always lived for herself and most often we are all the better for it. Even when her voice is dismissive, or disapproving – it's original. As her friend, the science fiction writer Brian Aldiss said, 'You don't go to Doris Lessing for tolerance. You go for enlightenment.'[3]

Notes

Because Doris Lessing declined to be interviewed for this book, I have relied on interviews with a great number of people who know her or have known her, the published opinions of people in her circle, reviews of her work, and on her prolific writings, the interviews she granted in the past, and interviews and exchanges of correspondence. From these I have been able to glean insights into the complex person Doris Tayler Wisdom Lessing is, with neither benefit nor hindrance of the subjective lens through which she would have viewed my thoughts. In the process it has become abundantly clear to me how inextricably interwoven Lessing's life and work are. All uses of her fiction and biography are there to offer criticism of her work, ideas and philosophy and have been acknowledged.

In addition to the numbered notes for published sources, unpublished research material (interviews, letters, etc.) is listed by chapter. Information gleaned from Lessing's extensive autobiographical writings has been used as a point of reference throughout the book.

Prologue

My lengthy interviews with Neil Claremon whom Lessing stayed with in Arizona helped shape my own insights about Lessing's ongoing relationship to Africa. Additionally, Laverne Clark, Arizona folklorist, told me of her conversations with, and impressions of, Doris Lessing during Lessing's visit. These sources contributed to the prologue.

1. Lessing, *Going Home*, p. 8.
2. Lessing, *African Stories*, p. 6.

Chapter 1

1. Lessing, 'My Father,' p.83.
2. Ibid.
3. Ibid., p. 86.
4. Lessing, *In Pursuit of the English*, p. 7.
5. Lessing, 'Impertinent Daughters,' p. 56.

Chapter 2

1. Lessing, Notes from interview for 'White Wounded.'
2. Lessing, *Under My Skin*, p. 20.
3. Newquist interview, 'Talking as a Person,' p. 11.
4. Lessing, *Love, Again*, p. 346.

5. Lessing, *Under My Skin*, p. 18.
6. Ibid., p. 19.
7. Ibid., p. 31.
8. Von Schwartzkopf interview, 'Placing Their Fingers in the Wounds of Time,' p. 105.
9. *Martha Quest*, p. 69.

Chapter 3

1. Lessing, 'Impertinent Daughters,' p. 63.
2. Rocco, Notes for interview for Whites Wounded.
3. Lopate interview.
4. Rousseau interview, 'The Habit of Observing,' p. 148.
5. Lessing, *Under My Skin*, p. 50.
6. Ibid., p. 51.

Chapter 4

1. Kaula, *The Land and People of Rhodesia*, p. 1.
2. Thomas, *Rhodes*, p.112-114.
3. Kaula, *Land and People of Rhodesia*, p. 67.
4. Roberts, *Cecil Rhodes*, p. 207.
5. Lessing, *African Laughter*, p. 4.
6. Wachtel interview, *Writers and Company*, p. 245.

Chapter 5

1. Lessing, *Going Home*, p. 31.
2. Ibid., pp. 32-33.
3. Lessing, 'Impertinent Daughters,' p. 66.
4. BBC interviewer, 'Desert Island Discs.'
5. Lessing, *Under My Skin*, p. 64.

Chapter 6

In addition to the list of sources in this chapter, for personal and professional background I drew on my lengthy interview with a publishing colleague who knew Doris Lessing well, personally and professionally. She wishes to remain anonymous.
1. Lessing, 'My Mother's Life,' p. 229.
2. Lessing, *Under My Skin*, pp. 120-121.
3. Lessing, *Love, Again*, p. 346.
4. Lessing, *Under My Skin*, p. 84.
5. Ibid., p. 85.
6. Attallah, 'The *Oldie* Interview,' p. 13.
7. Lessing, *Under My Skin*, p. 87.

Chapter 7

1. Lessing, *Under My Skin*, p. 95.

Chapter 8

1. Lessing, *African Stories*, p. 349, 352.
2. Lessing introduction, *An Ill-Fated People*, p. xiii.
3. Dean interview, 'Writing as Time Runs Out,' p. 87.
4. Connolly, 'A Childhood: Doris Lessing.'
5. Wyndham, 'The Doors of Perception,' p. 41.
6. Bertelsen interview, 'Acknowledging a New Frontier,' p. 134.
7. Ibid.

Chapter 9

1. Lessing, *Under My Skin*, p. 100.
2. Lessing, 'My Mother's Life,' p. 237.

Chapter 10

1. Berkman, *The Healing Imagination of Olive Schreiner*, p. 19.
2. Quoted in ibid., p. 125.
3. Schreiner, *The Story of an African Farm*, p. 171.
4. Lessing, Introduction, *The Story of an African Farm*, pp. vii-viii.
5. Ibid., p. viii.
6. First and Scott, *Olive Schreiner*, p. 47.
7. Schreiner, *The Story of an African Farm*, p. xxvii.
8. Ellis, *My Life*, p. 230.
9. Draznin, ed., *My Other Self*, p. 441.
10. Quoted in Cronwright-Schreiner, *The Life of Olive Schreiner*, p. 210.
11. Lessing, Introduction, *The Story of an African Farm*, p. xxiii.
12. Lessing, *Martha Quest*, p. 1.
13. Schreiner, *From Man to Man*, pp. 224-225.

Chapter 11

In addition to the following sources, I drew on a letter written to me by Philip Paul, who knew Lessing in Rhodesia.
1. Linklater interview, 'Tales of Noddyland,' p. 32.
2. Lessing, *Under My Skin*, p. 183.
3. Ibid., p. 185.
4. Howe, 'A Conversation With Doris Lessing,' p. 11.
5. Walter, 'The Golden Journey.'

Chapter 12

1. BBC, 'Desert Island Discs.'
2. Lessing, *Under My Skin*, p. 207.
3. Lessing, *A Proper Marriage*, pp. 201-203.
4. Ibid., p. 201.

Chapter 13

Additional information in this chapter came from American and English friends of Doris Lessing who wish to remain anonymous.
1. Oates, 'One Keeps Going,' p. 36.
2. Lessing, *Under My Skin*, p. 245.
3. Connolly, 'A Childhood: Doris Lessing.'
4. Newquist interview, 'Talking As A Person,' p. 8.
5. Lessing, *A Man and Two Women*, p. 209.
6. Lessing, *Under My Skin*, p. 256.
7. Lessing, *A Proper Marriage*, p. 201.
8. Seligman, 'The Four Faced Novelist,' p. 8.
9. Lessing, *A Proper Marriage*, p. 340.
10. Bennett, 'Blame Me On The Zeitgeist,' p. 55.
11. Ibid.

Chapter 14

This chapter was supplemented by interviews with anonymous sources who knew Gottfried Lessing, and correspondence between Doris Lessing and Robert Gottlieb.
1. Bertelsen interview, 'Acknowledging a New Frontier,' p. 142.
2. Lessing, *Under My Skin*, p. 261.
3. Lessing, *Ripple From the Storm*, 22.

Chapter 15

This chapter was supplemented by an anonymous observer of Lessing's life, who comments on Doris seeking liberation through sex and communism. Background to Gottfried Lessing's early life was gained through my exchange of letters with Irene Gysi.
1. Torrents interview, 'Testimony to Mysticism,' p. 65.

Chapter 16

1. Lessing, *Under My Skin*, p. 303.
2. Ingersoll interview, 'Describing This Beautiful and Nasty Planet,' p. 230.
3. Lessing, *A Ripple from the Storm*, p. 175.
4. Lessing, 'Language and the Lunatic Fringe,' p. A27.
5. Bertelsen interview, 'Acknowledging a New Frontier,' p. 143.
6. Lessing, *Under My Skin*, p. 326.
7. Lessing, *Stories*, p. 257.

Chapter 17

In addition to the sources listed, I interviewed Paul Hogarth at great length for background on this chapter.
1. Lessing, *Landlocked*, p. 15.
2. Ibid., p. 30.
3. Lessing, *The Four-Gated City*, p. 64.
4. Seligman, 'The Four-Faced Novelist,' p. 10.

5. Ibid., pp. 8-9.

Chapter 18

In addition to her article, and notes for that article about Doris Lessing, I was able to interview Fiametta Rocco about her meeting with Doris Lessing.

1. Lessing, *African Stories*, p. 6.
2. Lessing, *Under My Skin*, p. 304.
3. Quoted in Beck, 'Doris Lessing and the Colonial Experience,' p. 68.
4. Quoted in ibid., p. 69.
5. Schreiner, *Thoughts on South Africa*, p. 361.
6. Rocco interview, 'The White Wounded of Africa.'
7. Quoted in Steele, '"Children of Violence" and Rhodesia: A Study of Doris Lessing as Historical Observer, p. 19.
8. Atallah, 'The *Oldie* Interview,' p. 12.

Chapter 19

My interview with Bernard Kops contributed to this chapter, as did another friend who comments on Doris's behavior but wished to remain anonymous.

1. Vambe, *From Rhodesia to Zimbabwe*, p. 161.
2. Quoted in Veit-Wild, *Teachers, Preachers, Non-Believers*, p. 29.
3. Seligman, 'The Four-Faced Novelist,' p. 10.
4. Lessing, *African Stories*, p. 151.
5. Hartnak, 'Lessing Revisited,' p. 4.
6. Rocco, 'The White Wounded of Africa.'
7. Lessing, *Going Home*, p. 52.

Chapter 20

1. Lessing, *Under My Skin*, p. 353.
2. Ibid., p. 354.
3. Jung, *Psyche and Symbol*, p. 71.

Chapter 21

Supplementing the research for this chapter was an interview with a former assistant who lived for a while in Lessing's home. She spoke to me only on the promise of anonymity. My interview with Stuart Hall provided important insights and background material.

1. Lessing, *Martha Quest*, p. 91.
2. Jung, *Four Archetypes*, pp. 24, 25.
3. Kelly, 'I Hate Sexual Hypocrisy and Feminist Humbug,' p. 31.

Chapter 22

1. Bertelsen interview, 'Acknowledging a New Frontier,' p. 128.
2. Lessing, *The Grass Is Singing*, p. 20.
3. Ibid., p. 192.
4. Lessing, *African Stories*, p. 72.
5. Laing, *The Divided Self*, p. 45-46.

Chapter 23

Some information for this chapter was based on interviews with people who knew Dorothy Schwartz and Gottfried Lessing in England. They wish to remain anonymous. In addition I obtained correspondence of Dorothy Schwartz. My interview with John Mortimer also provided background to the times. The BBC Interview provided the story about the man who told Doris Lessing to stop crying.

1. Lessing, *In Pursuit of the English*, p. 34.
2. Lessing, *Going Home*, p. 7.
3. Quoted in E. Jane Dickson, 'City of the Mind,' Sec. 7, p. 6.
4. Lessing, *In Pursuit of the English*, p. 47.
5. Ibid., p. 210.
6. Ibid., p. 220.
7. Torrents interview, 'Testimony to Mysticism,' p. 69.
8. White, 'New Novels: *The Grass Is Singing*'
9. Gray interview, 'Breaking Down These Forms,' p. 111.

Chapter 24

Material about Gottfried Lessing was supplemented by interviews with anonymous sources who knew him in England and in Germany. Other material came from friends of Doris Lessing during this period who also wish to remain anonymous. The letters from Dorothy Schwartz which I had access to were an additional source for this chapter.

1. Dickson, 'City of the Mind,' *The Sunday Times*, Sec. 7 p. 6.
2. Lessing, *In Pursuit of the English*, p. 220-221.
3. Ibid., p. 238.
4. Foster, 'A Tent-Dweller At Heart.'
5. Langley, 'Scenario for Salvation,' p. 8.
6. Lessing, *Walking in The Shade*, p. 17.
7. Ibid., p. 35.
8. Lessing, *Under My Skin*, p. 414.
9. Lessing, Remarks on receiving Shakespeare Prize.

Chapter 25

I was able to supplement the research for this chapter by interviewing Elaine Dundy, who had been married to Kenneth Tynan, and knew Doris Lessing in London. Interviews with Peter Worsley, Paul Hogarth, Clancy Sigal and an anonymous Communist writer of that period added important background material.

1. Lessing, *African Stories*, p. 59.
2. Ibid., p. 221.
3. Ibid., p. 230.
4. Ibid., p. 244.
5. Ibid., p. 6.
6. Kaufman interview.
7. Tyler, 'Author of Many Characters.'
8. Lessing, *African Stories*, pp. 5-6.
9. Ibid., p. 519.

10. Lessing, *Walking in the Shade*, p. 78.

Chapter 26

1. Lessing, *Walking in the Shade*, p. 43.
2. Ibid., p. 155.
3. Wesker, *As Much as I Dare*, p. 106.
4. Terkel interview, 'Learning to Put the Questions Differently,' p. 21.

Chapter 27

Several interviews with Bernard Kops during the course of writing this book provided significant background information about Doris Lessing, personally, professionally and politically. They served as additional source material for this chapter.

1. Wesker, *As Much as I Dare*, p. 7.
2. Kenneth Tynan, *Curtains*, p. 192.
3. Quoted in Kathleen Tynan, *The Life of Kenneth Tynan*, p. 172.
4. Lessing, *A Small Personal Voice*, p. 6.
5. Maschler, *Declaration*, Introduction.
6. Tynan, 'Theatre and Living,' p. 110.
7. Ibid., p. 116.
8. Osborne, 'They Call it Cricket,' p. 76.
9. Lessing, *A Small Personal Voice*, p. 6-7.
10. Quoted in Cartwright, 'Still Africa's Daughter.'
11. de Bartodano, 'Life Is Stronger Than Fiction,' p. 3.

Chapter 28

My interviews with Bernard Kops are relevant to this chapter. Peter Worsley also agreed to a telephone interview that was most helpful to my research. I conducted several crucial interviews with Paul Hogarth during my London visits. I found Mervyn Jones memoir, *Changes*, extremely helpful, and am grateful to him for allowing me to quote from it extensively. The correspondence between Doris Lessing and Robert Gottlieb was considered for this chapter. An anonymous political colleague told me why Doris Lessing didn't immediately resign from the Communist party after the invasion of Hungary. Raphael Samuel was an important source of information about the politics of this period. A Lesbian friend also contributed her thoughts about Doris Lessing and her sexual attitudes. This woman also wishes to remain anonymous.

1. Quoted in White, 'Pages from Her Own History.'
2. Sigal, *The Secret Defector*, p. 33.
3. Jones, *Chances*, p. 124.
4. Ibid.
5. Ibid., p. 140.
6. Ibid., p. 119.
7. Lessing, *Retreat to Innocence*, back cover.
8. Ibid., p. 333.

Chapter 29

Paul Hogarth's interviews were vitally important to this chapter.

1. 'Rhodesian Status Jarred by Racism,' *The New York Times*, 25 October, 1953, p. 27.
2. Ibid.
3. Creighton, *The Anatomy of Partnership*, p. 104.
4. Lessing, *Going Home*, p. 250.
5. Lessing, *Walking in the Shade*, p. 198.
6. 'Federation Stand Irks South Africa,' *The New York Times*, 31 October, 1953, p. 5.
7. Lessing, *Going Home*, p. 7.
8. Ibid., p. 31.
9. Lessing, *Walking in the Shade*, p. 196.
10. Lessing, *Going Home*, p. 78.

Chapter 30

Interviews with people who did not wish to be named supplied information about Doris Lessing's political sentiments at this time. Ralph Miliband, John Seville, and Raphael Samuel also provided background material. Stuart Hall was a thoughtful source of information on a number of cultural and political issues that were part of Doris Lessing's life, as well as reflections on her writing. Clancy Signal provided an intimate perspective on the climate of this time. In addition to his memoir, William Phillips permitted me to interview him about a number of issues relevant to this chapter.

1. Lessing, *The Golden Notebook*, p. 360.
2. Rousseau interview, 'The Habit of Observing,' p. 152.
3. Chun, *The British New Left*, p. 11.
4. Ibid.
5. Lessing, 'The Cult of the Individual.'
6. Thompson, 'On the Trail of the New Left,' p. 94.
7. Lessing, *Stories*, p. 86.
8. Phillips, *A Partisan View*, p. 206.
9. Ibid.
10. Newquist, 'Talking as a Person,' p. 9.
11. Phillips, *A Partisan View*, p. 206.
12. Ibid., pp. 206, 207.

Chapter 31

Additional information for this chapter was provided by Clancy Sigal who was interviewed extensively at his Los Angeles home, by telephone, and through correspondence. Ralph Miliband and Raphael Samuel addressed him, and his relationship with Doris Lessing during our interviews. Other sources only spoke on promise of anonymity. Ann Edwards also granted me an interview.

1. Lessing, *The Golden Notebook*, p. 543.
2. Sigal, *The Secret Defector*, prologue; p. 7.
3. Sigal, 'The Boys of Watergate.'
4. Lessing, *The Golden Notebook*, p. 553.
5. Sigal, *Going Away*, p. 503.
6. Sigal, '"You Can't Do It," I Shouted.'
7. Lessing, *Walking in the Shade*, p. 224.

Chapter 32

I called on my interview with Stuart Hall for this chapter. Someone who knew Lord Russell well also provided background, and wished no attribution. My interview with Lesley Hazleton was very helpful. Ralph Miliband, in our interview was equally important to my research. Clancy Sigal continued to be a valuable source of opinion and information. In addition to her newspaper interview with Doris Lessing, Jane Kelly allowed me a telephone interview. Others who knew Clancy Sigal and Doris Lessing were interviewed without attribution.

1. Jones, *Chances*, p. 143.
2. Sigal, *The Secret Defector*, p. 49.
3. Kathleen Tynan, *The Life of Kenneth Tynan*, p. 194.
4. Jones, Chances, p. 149.
5. Whaley, 'Move Along, Miss Cummings,' *Daily Mail*, 14 September, 1959.
6. 'Lord Russell Resigns CND Presidency,' *Manchester Guardian*, 25 October, 1961.
7. 'Prison for 32 Anti-Nuclear supporters,' *The Times*, 13 September, 1961, p. 5.
8. Wesker, *As Much As I Dare*, pp. 508-510.
9. Jones, Chances, p. 181.
10. Lessing, 'Our Minds Have Become Set in the Apocalyptic Mode,' *The Guardian*, 14 June, 1982.
11. Kelly interview, 'I Hate Sexual Hypocrisy and Sexual Humbug,' p. 31.
12. Sigal, 'Goodbye Little England.'

Chapter 33

In preparation for this chapter that deals with the publication of The Golden Notebook my interviews with Clancy Sigal, Stuart Hall, John Leonard were extremely helpful. Lesley Hazleton also provided important recollections of Doris Lessing's response to the novel's impact on readers. The letter from the 'happiest day' fan who was told 'don't exaggerate was written to me in response to my author's query in *The New York Times*.

1. Lessing, *The Golden Notebook*, pp. 576-577.
2. Hurren, review of *Play with a Tiger*.
3. Tynan, 'Lillith in Earth's Court.'
4. Gomery, 'The Women Whose Play Hits London Tonight.'
5. Ean interview, 'The Older I Get, the Less I Believe,' p. 201.
6. Sigal, '"You Can't Do It!" I shouted,' p. 14.
7. Lessing, *The Golden Notebook*, p. 531.
8. Ibid., p. 603.
9. Ibid., p. 639.
10. Ibid., p. xiv.
11. Gornick, 'Opening the *Golden Notebook*: Remembering the Source,' p. 4.
12. Howe, 'Neither Compromise nor Happiness,' p. 18.
13. Leonard, 'The African Queen,' p. 528.
14. Lessing, Golden Notebook, p. ix.
15. Brownmiller, 'Doris Lessing in N.Y.C.'
16. Hazleton, Notes for 'Doris Lessing on Feminism, Communism and "Space Fiction,"' p. 2.
17. Linklater, 'Tales of Noddyland,' p. 32.

Chapter 34

Interviews with Robin Blackburn, Clancy Sigal, Dr Bob Mullan and R.D. Laing's widow, Jutta Laing contributed greatly to this chapter.

1. Sigal, *The Secret Defector*, p. 31.
2. Storr, 'The Divided Legacy of R.D. Laing.'
3. Both quoted in Mullan, ed., *Mad to Be Normal*, p. 303.
4. Perott, 'The Man Who Says We're All Mad.'
5. Laing, *The Politics of Experience*, p. 58.
6. Laing, *The Divided Self*, p. 17.
7. Laing, *The Politics of Experience*, pp. 133, 129.
8. Ligal, '"You Can't Do It," I Shouted,' p. 13.
9. Mullan, ed., *R.D. Laing, Creative Destroyer*, p. 215.
10. Laing, Wisdom, Madness and Folly, pp. 132, 133.
11. A. Laing, *R.D. Laing: A Biography*, p 71.
12. Laing, 'What Is Schizophrenia?' p. 68.
13. Quoted in Palling, 'Insanity Is Not Illegal,' p. 52D.
14. A. Storr, 'Divided Legacy of R.D. Laing.'
15. A. Laing, *R.D. Laing*, p. 110.
16. Sigal, *Zone of the Interior*, p. 68.
17. Mullan, ed., *Mad to Be Normal*, p. 180.
18. Ibid., pp. 188, 172.
19. Ibid., p. 188.
20. Mullan, ed., R.D. Laing: Creative Destroyer, p. 215.
21. A. Laing, *R.D. Laing*, p. 123.
22. Ibid., p. 124.
23. Mullan, ed., *R.D. Laing: Creative Destroyer*, pp. 215, 216.

Chapter 35

For background on this chapter I used my interview with a former assistant of Doris Lessing who lived in Lessing's home for more than two years. She requested anonymity as a requirement for our discussion. Similarly, a publishing colleague spoke to me under the same conditions.

1. MacKenzie, 'True Stories.'
2. Stevenson, *Bitter Fame*, p. 286.
3. MacKenzie, 'True Stories.'
4. Lessing, *The Four-Gated City*, p. 529.
5. Leonard, 'The Children of Violence Are Mutants.'
6. Lessing, *The Four-Gated City*, p. 531.
7. Oates interview 'One Keeps Going,' p. 35.
8. Hendin interview, 'The Capacity to Look at a Situation Coolly,' p. 49.
9. Ibid.
10. Laing, *The Politics of Experience*, p. 157.

Chapter 36

The collected letters of John Cushman provided some of the information for this chapter. I also reviewed Robert Gottlieb's extensive correspondence while he was head of Alfred W. Knopf. Lesley Hazleton was a rich source of material in her recollections of her own interview with Doris Lessing. An anonymous publishing colleague was also a source of information. I observed the incident at Rutgers University.

1. MacFarquhar, 'Robert Gottlieb: The Art of Editing,' p. 183.
2. Knopf PR Department, Press Material.
3. MacFarquhar, 'Robert Gottlieb,' p. 187.
4. Ibid., p. 184.
5. BBC documentary, p. 1.
6. Ibid., p. 15-16.
7. MacFarquhar, 'Robert Gottlieb,' p. 216.
8. de Bertodano, 'Life Is Stronger Than Fiction,' p. 3.
9. Lessing, 'In Fact, Only a Minority of Journalists Are Any Good,' p. 50.

Chapter 37

The correspondence between Robert Gottlieb and Doris Lessing provided background for this chapter. My interview with Stuart Hall provided context. raised important questions for my understanding of Sufism. Clancy Sigal also spoke to me about Doris Lessing and Idries Shah as did another friend who wished to remain anonymous. Numerous anonymous sources who knew Lessing in the fifties and sixties served as background. Another anonymous source was a publishing colleague.

1. Torrents interview, 'Testimony to Mysticism,' p. 66.
2. Bertelsen interview, 'Acknowledging a New Frontier,' p. 121.
3. Elwell-Sutton, 'Sufism and Pseudo-Sufism,' p. 12.
4. Lessing, 'If You Knew Sufi,' *The Guardian*, Jan. 8, 1975, p. 12.
5. Ibid.
6. Ibid.
7. Elwell-Sutton, 'Sufism and Pseudo-Sufism,' p. 14.
8. Ibid.
9. Ibid., p. 15.
10. Bennett, *Witness*, p. 355.
11. Ibid.
12. Ibid., p. 358.
13. Ibid., p. 360.
14. Shah, *The Commanding Self*, p. 2.
15. Shah, *The Sufis*, p. 74.
16. Ibid., p. 338.
17. Hardin, 'The Sufi Teaching and Doris Lessing,' p. 122.
18. Ibid.
19. Shah, *The Commanding Self*, p. 43.
20. Review of *The Commanding Self*, London Times, 5 May, 1994, p. 40.
21. Lessing, *The Four Gated City*, p. 519.
22. Ibid., p. 466-67.
23. Elwell-Sutton, 'Sufism and Pseudo-Sufism,' p. 16.
24. Ibid., p. 15.
25. Lessing, 'Idries Shah' (obituary), 1996.
26. de Bertadano, 'Life is Stronger Than Fiction.'

Chapter 38

I reviewed the correspondence between Doris Lessing and Robert Gottlieb for this chapter. Stuart Hall also offered some crucial observations about Lessing and aging. A younger friend who wishes to remain anonymous spoke of her correspondence with Lessing.

1. Leonard, 'The Last Word.'
2. Thomson interview, 'Drawn to a Type of Landscape,' p. 186.
3. Lessing, *The Summer Before the Dark*, p. 23.
4. Hendin interview, 'The Capacity to Look at a Situation Coolly,' p. 54.
5. Lessing, *The Summer Before the Dark*, pp. 266, 269.
6. Stamberg interview, 'All Things Considered,' 1984, p. 5.
7. Hendin, 'Doris Lessing: The Phoenix 'Midst Her Fires,' p. 83-84.
8. Lessing, *Love, Again*, p. 350.

Chapter 39

My interview with Lesley Hazleton informs this chapter, as did Lessing's correspondence with Robert Gottlieb. Lessing's former assistant shared her recollections of this period in Lessing's life.

1. Lessing, Canopus in Argos: *Archives*, p. vii.
2. Gray interview, 'Breaking Down These Forms,' p. 116.
3. Hazleton interview notes, p. 5.
4. Aldiss interview, 'Living in Catastrophe,' p. 170.
5. Leonard review of *The Sirian Experiments*.
6. Lardner, 'Angle on the Ordinary.'
7. Stamberg, 'An Interview with Doris Lessing,' p. 3.
8. Lessing, Canopus in Argos: *Archives*, p. 5.

Chapter 40

My interview with William Phillips provided material for this chapter, as did my interviews with Lessing's assistant. Lessing's assistant also gave me, on the promise of anonymity, shared recollections of this period in Doris Lessing's life.

1. McDowell, 'Doris Lessing Said She Used Pen Name.'
2. 'Doris Lessing Talks About Jane Somers,' *Doris Lessing Newsletter*, Spring 1986, p. 3.
3. Tomalin, 'Mischief.'
4. Ibid.
5. McDowell, 'Doris Lessing Said She Used Pen Name.'
6. Tomalin, 'Mischief.'
7. Maschler, 'The Lesson of Lessing.'
8. Frick interview, 'Doris Lessing.'
9. Ibid.
10. Maschler, 'The Lesson of Lessing.'
11. Ibid.
12. Yardley, 'Lessing Is More.'
13. Lessing, *The Diaries of Jane Somers*, p. vii.
14. Ibid., p. viii.
15. Ibid., p. 7.
16. Ibid., p. 28.

Chapter 41

I interviewed the late Jane Cushman, the wife of Doris's former agent John Cushman, for this chapter. My interview with Lessing's former assistant was also used in the chapter's development. Other friends who knew Peter and Doris commented on their relationship on the condition of anonymity.

1. Jones, 'Alien,' p. 31.
2. Quoted in Rothstein, 'The Painful Nurturing of Doris Lessing's "Fifth Child."'
3. Lessing, *The Fifth Child*, p. 3.
4. Rothstein, 'Painful Nurturing.'
5. Lessing, The Fifth Child, p. 32.
6. Ibid., p. 76.
7. Ibid., p. 132.
8. Rothstein, 'Painful Nurturing.'
9. Tomalin interview 'Watching the Angry and Destructive Hordes Go Past,' p. 177.
10. Ibid., p. 176.
11. deMontremy interview 'A Writer is Not a Professor,' p. 198.

Chapter 42

Journalist Jane Kelly was interviewed by telephone for this chapter. My interview with Lessing's former assistant also informs the writing.

1. Lessing, *Under My Skin*, p. 38.
2. Lessing, *Particularly Cats ...and Rufus*, p. 8.
3. Ibid., p. 12.
4. Ibid.
5. Ibid., p. 17.
6. Nadel, 'Animal Passions.'
7. Lessing, *Particularly Cats ...and Rufus*, p. 49.
8. Nadel, 'Animal Passions.'
9. Lessing, *Particularly Cats ...and Rufus*.
10. Nadel, 'Animal Passions.'

Epilogue

1. Bennett, 'Coolhead.'
2. Orwell, 'Why I Write,' p. 183.
3. BBC documentary.

Bibliography

Novels (chronological)

The Grass Is Singing. London: Michael Joseph; New York: Crowell, 1950.

Martha Quest (Children of Violence, vol. 1). London: Michael Joseph, 1952. Reprint. New York: Plume, 1970.

Five: Short Novels. London: Michael Joseph, 1953.

A Proper Marriage (*Children of Violence*, vol. 2). London: Michael Joseph, 1954. Reprint. New York: Plume, 1970.

Retreat to Innocence. London: Michael Joseph, 1956. Reprint. New York: Prometheus, 1959.

A Ripple from the Storm (Children of Violence, vol. 3). London: Michael Joseph, 1958. Reprint. New York: Plume, 1970.

The Golden Notebook. London: Michael Joseph; 1962. Reprint. New York: Bantam, 1981.

Landlocked (Children of Violence, vol. 4). London: MacGibbon and Kee; New York: Simon & Schuster, 1965. Reprint. New York: Plume,1970.

The Four-Gated City (Children of Violence, vol. 5). London: MacGibbon and Kee; New York: Knopf, 1969. Reprint. New York: HarperPerennial, 1995.

Briefing for a Descent into Hell. London: Jonathan Cape; New York: Knopf, 1971.

The Summer Before the Dark. London: Jonathan Cape; New York: Knopf, 1973.

The Memoirs of a Survivor. London: Octagon, 1974. Reprint. London: Picador, 1976.

Colonised Planet 5, Shikasta: (Canopus in Argos: Archives, vol. 1). London: Jonathan Cape; New York: Knopf, 1979.

The Marriages Between Zones Three, Four, and Five (Canopus in Argos: Archives, vol. 2). London: Jonathan Cape; New York: Knopf, 1979.

The Sirian Experiments (Canopus in Argos: Archives, vol. 3). London: Jonathan Cape; New York: Knopf, 1981.

The Making of the Representative for Planet 8 (Canopus in Argos: Archives, vol. 4). London: Jonathan Cape; New York: Knopf, 1982.

Documents Relating to the Sentimental Agents in the Volyen Empire (Canopus in Argos: Archives, vol. 5). London: Jonathan Cape; New York: Knopf, 1983.

The Diaries of Jane Somers. New York: Random House, 1984. Two novels originally published under the pseudonym Jane Somers. *The Diary of a Good Neighbour* and *If the Old Could.* Michael Joseph; New York: Knopf, 1983-84;.

The Good Terrorist. London: Jonathan Cape; New York: Knopf, 1985.

The Fifth Child. London: Jonathan Cape; New York: Knopf, 1988. Reprint. New York: Vintage, 1989.

Canopus in Argos: Archives (all five Canopus novels in one volume). New York: Vintage, 1992.

Playing the Game: (graphic novel); Charlie Adlard, artist. London: HarperCollins, 1995.

Love, Again. New York: HarperCollins, 1996.

Mara and Dan. London: HarperFlamingo, 1999.

Non-fiction (chronological)

Going Home. London: Michael Joseph, 1957. Reprint. New York: Popular Library, 1968.

In Pursuit of the English. London: MacGibbon and Kee; New York: Simon & Schuster, 1960. Reprint. New York: HarperPerennial, 1996.

Particularly Cats. London: Michael Joseph; New York: Simon & Schuster, 1967.

A Small Personal Voice: Essays, Reviews, Interviews. Edited and introduced by Paul Schlueter. New York: Knopf, 1974. Reprint. New York: Vintage, 1975.

Prisons We Chose to Live Inside. A series of 5 lectures broadcast in 1985 by CBC Radio. London: Jonathan Cape, 1987.

The Wind Blows Away Our Words. London: Picador, 1987.

Particularly Cats and More Cats. Illustrated by Anne Robinson. London: Michael Joseph, 1989.

Particularly Cats ... and Rufus. Illustrated by James McMullan. New York: Knopf, 1991.

African Laughter: Four Visits to Zimbabwe. New York: HarperCollins, 1992.

Under My Skin: Volume One of My Autobiography, to 1949. London, New York: HarperCollins, 1994.

Walking in the Shade: Volume Two of My Autobiography, 1949-1962. New York: HarperCollins, 1997.

Short Story Collections (chronological)

This Was the Old Chief's Country. London: Michael Joseph, 1951.

The Habit of Loving. London: MacGibbon and Kee, 1957.

A Man and Two Women. London: MacGibbon and Kee; New York: Simon & Schuster, 1963. Reprint. New York: Touchstone, 1984.

African Stories. London: Michael Joseph, 1964. Reprint. New York: Touchstone, 1981.

The Black Madonna. London: Panther, 1966. Winter in July, London: Panther, 1966.

The Temptation of Jack Orkney. New York: Knopf, 1972. Published in U.K. as *The Story of a Non-Marrying Man and Other Stories*. London: Jonathan Cape, 1972.

This Was the Old Chief's Country. Vol. 1 of *Doris Lessing's Collected African Stories*. London: Michael Joseph, 1973.

The Sun Beneath Their Feet, Vol. 2 of *Doris Lessing's Collected African Stories*. London: Michael Joseph, 1973.

Stories. New York: Knopf, 1978.

London Observed. London: HarperCollins, 1992. Published in U.S. as *The Real Thing: Stories and Sketches*.

Drama (chronological)

Mr. Dolinger. Unpublished play. Produced 7 July 1958 at the Oxford Playhouse.

Each His Own Wilderness. In New English Dramatists: Three Plays, edited by
  E. Martin Browne. Harmondsworth, England: Penguin, 1959.
The Truth About Billy Newton. Unpublished play. Produced 18 January 1960
  at Salisbury Arts Theater, Salisbury, Wiltshire, England.
Play With a Tiger: A Play in Three Acts. London: Michael Joseph, 1962. Reprint.
  London: Flamingo, 1996.

Poetry

Fourteen Poems. Northwood, Middlesex, England: Scorpion Press, 1959.

Opera (chronological)

Libretto for *Making of the Representative for Planet 8* by Philip Glass, Dun-
  vagen Music Publishers, 1988. Premiere by Houston Grand Opera, 1988.
Libretto for *The Marriages Between Zones Three, Four and Five* by Philip Glass.
  Premiere in Heidelberg, Germany, 1997.

Miscellaneous (chronological)

'Myself as Sportsman.' *New Yorker,* 21 January 1956 pp. 92-96.
'The Cult of the Individual.' Letter to the Editor. *Reasoner,* 3 November 1956,
  pp. 11-13.
'London Diary.' *New Statesman,* 15 March 1958, pp. 326-327.
'Crisis in Central Africa: The Fruits of Humbug.' *Twentieth Century,* April 1959,
  pp. 368-376.
'Smart-Set Socialists.' *New Statesman,* 1 December 1961, p. 822.
'The New Man.' *New Statesman,* 64 7 September 1962, pp. 282-283.
'What Really Matters.' *Twentieth Century,* Autumn 1963, pp. 97-98.
'All Seething Underneath. ' *Vogue,* 15 February 1964.
'Elephant in the Dark. ' *Spectator,* 18 September 1964, p. 373.
'Zambia's Joyful Week.' *New Statesman,* 6 November 1964, p. 692.
'Allah Be Praised.' Review. *The Autobiography of Malcolm X* with Alex Haley.
  New Statesman, 27 May 1966.
'The Gray Princess.' *McCall's,* March 1967, pp. 110-111.
'An Ancient Way to New Freedom.' *Vogue,* 15 September 1971, p. 98.
'Spies I Have Known.' *Partisan Review,* Winter 1971, pp. 50-66.
'In the World, Not of It.' *Encounter,* August 1972, pp. 61-64.
'Vonnegut's Responsibility.' *New York Times Book Review,* 4 February 1973,
  p.35.
'Afterword to *The Story of an African Farm* by Olive Schreiner.' *In A Small
  Personal Voice.* New York: Knopf, 1974.
'If You Knew Sufi.' *The Guardian,* January 8, 1975, p. 12.
'My Father.' *In A Small Personal Voice.* New York: Knopf, 1974. Reprint. New
  York: Vintage, 1975.
'Being Prohibited.' *In A Small Personal Voice.* New York: Knopf, 1974. Reprint.
  New York: Vintage Books, 1975.
'A Revolution' *New York Times,* 22 August 1975, p. 31.
Remarks on receiving Shakespeare Prize of the F.V.S. Foundation for 1982.
  Anglo-German jury, under chairmanship of Dr. Rudolf Haas, Hamburg
  University, Hamburg, Germany. Hamburg: F.V.S. Foundation, 1982.

'Our Minds Have Become Set In The Apocalyptic Mode.' The Guardian, 14 June, 1982.

'Impertinent Daughters.' *Granta*, Winter 1984.

'My Mother's Life' *Granta*, Autumn 1985.

Lecture Transcript 'Doris Lessing Talks About Janet Somers.' *Doris Lessing Newsletter*, no. 1, Spring 1986.

Introduction to *The Story of an African Farm* by Olive Schreiner. New York: Crown, 1987.

'The Day the Cats Finally Had to Die.' *Daily Mail*, 21 October 1989.

The Doris Lessing Reader, Excerpts from novels, short stories and non-fiction. London: Jonathan Cape; New York: Knopf, 1989.

'In Fact, Only a Minority of Journalists Are Any Good.' Opinion. *London Sunday Correspondent*, 28 January 1990.

'Language and the Lunatic Fringe. Op ed. *New York Times*, 26 June 1992, p. A27.

Review of *The Commanding Self. London Times*, 5 May 1994, p. 40.

Obituary, Idries Shah. *Electronic Telegraph* #563, 7 December 1996.

Works about Doris Lessing

Interviews (alphabetical)

Aldiss, Brian. 'Living in Catastrophe. In *Doris Lessing: Conversations*. Earl G. Ingersoll, ed. Princeton, NJ: Ontario Review Press, 1994.

Attallah, Naim. 'The Oldie Interview: Doris Lessing.' Portrait by Jane Brown. *The Oldie*, March 1996, pp. 12-14.

BBC 'Desert Island Discs' program, 21 November 1993.

Bennett, Catherine. 'Cool head, cool heart.' *Guardian*, 17 October, 1994, p. 8.

———. 'Blame Me on the Zeitgeist,' Supplement to the weekly *Mail & Guardian*, 25 November to 1 December 1994, p. 55.

Bertelsen, Eve. 'Acknowledging a New Frontier. In *'Doris Lessing: Conversations*. Edited by Earl G. Ingersoll. Princeton, NJ: Ontario Review Press, 1994.

Bigsby, Christopher. 'The Need to Tell Stories. In *'Doris Lessing: Conversations*. Edited by Earl G. Ingersoll. Princeton, NJ: Ontario Review Press, 1994.

Dean, Michael. 'Writing As Time Runs Out.' In *Doris Lessing: Conversations*. Edited by Earl G. Ingersoll. Princeton, NJ: Ontario Review Press, 1994.

de Bertodano, Helena. 'Life Is Stronger Than Fiction.' *London Daily Telegraph*, 7 April 1996, Sunday review section.

de Montremy, Jean-Maurice. 'A Writer Is Not a Professor.' In *Doris Lessing: Conversations*, edited by Earl G. Ingersoll. Princeton, NJ; Ontario Review Press, 1994.

Ean, Tan Gim and Others. 'The Older I Get the Less I Believe.' In *Doris Lessing: Conversations*, edited by Earl G. Ingersoll. Princeton, NJ: Ontario Review Press, 1994.

Frick, Thomas. 'Caged by the Experts.' In *Doris Lessing: Conversations*, edited by Earl G. Ingersoll. Princeton, NJ: Ontario Review Press, 1994.

———. 'Doris Lessing.' *Writers at Work: The Paris Review Interviews*, edited by George Plimpton. Ninth series. New York: Viking Penguin, 1992.

Gomery, Donald. 'The Woman Whose Play Hits London Tonight.' *London Daily Express*, 3 March 1962.

Gray, Stephen. 'Breaking Down These Forms.' In *Doris Lessing: Conversations*, edited by Earl G. Ingersoll. Princeton, NJ: Ontario Review Press, 1994.

Hazleton, Lesley. 'Doris Lessing on Feminism, Communism and 'Space Fiction.' *The New York Times Magazine*, 25 July 1982, section 6, p. 21.

———. Notes from interview conducted with Doris Lessing for 'Doris Lessing on Feminism, Communism and 'Space Fiction.' '

Hendin, Josephine. 'The Capacity to Look at a Situation Coolly.' In *Doris Lessing: Conversations*, edited by Earl G. Ingersoll. Princeton, NJ: Ontario Review Press, 1994.

Howe, Florence. 'A Conversation with Doris Lessing.' *Contemporary Literature*, Autumn 1973.

Kaufman, Richard. Pacifica Radio Archive BB3368, 1963.

Kelly, Jane. 'I Hate Sexual Hypocrisy And Feminist Humbug.' *Daily Mail*, 7 November 1992, p. 31.

Langley, Lee. 'Scenario for Salvation.' *Guardian*, 14 April 1971.

Linklater, Andro. 'Tales of Noddyland.' *London Telegraph Magazine*, 24 January 1992, p.31-32.

Lopate, Lenny. 'New York & Company.' WNYC radio, 25 October 1994.

McDowell, Edwin. 'Doris Lessing Says She Used Pen Name to Show New Writers' Difficulties.' *New York Times*, 23 September 1984, p. 45.

Nadel, Alison. 'Animal Passions.' *London Telegraph Weekend*, 7 October 1989.

Newquist, Roy. 'Talking as a Person.' In *Doris Lessing: Conversations*, edited by Earl G. Ingersoll. Princeton, NJ: Ontario Review Press, 1994.

Oates, Joyce Carol. 'One Keeps Going.' In *Doris Lessing: Conversations*, edited by Earl G. Ingersoll. Princeton, NJ: Ontario Review Press, 1994.

Raskin, Jonah. 'The Inadequacy of the Imagination.' In *Doris Lessing: Conversations*, edited by Earl G. Ingersoll. Princeton, NJ: Ontario Review Press, 1994.

Rocco, Fiammetta. 'The White Wounded of Africa.' *Independent on Sunday*, 25 October 1992.

———. Notes from interview conducted with Doris Lessing for 'White Wounded of Africa.'

Rousseau, Francis-Olivier. 'The Habit of Observing.' In *Doris Lessing: Conversations*, edited by Earl G. Ingersoll. Princeton, NJ: Ontario Review Press, 1994.

Stamberg, Susan. 'All Things Considered.' Washington, DC: National Public Radio, 24, 25 April 1984.

———. 'An Interview with Doris Lessing.' *Doris Lessing Newsletter*, 8., no. 2 (Fall 1984).

Terkel, Studs. 'Learning to Put the Questions Differently.' In *Doris Lessing: Conversations*, edited by Earl G. Ingersoll. Princeton, NJ: Ontario Review Press, 1994.

Thomson, Sedge. 'Drawn to a Type of Landscape.' In *Doris Lessing: Conversations*, edited by Earl G. Ingersoll. Princeton, NJ: Ontario Review Press, 1994.

Tomalin, Claire. 'Watching the Angry and Destructive Hordes Go Past.' In *Doris Lessing: Conversations*, edited by Earl G. Ingersoll. Princeton, NJ: Ontario Review Press, 1994.

Torrents, Nissa. 'Testimony to Mysticism.' Translated by Paul Schlaeter. In *Doris Lessing: Conversations*, edited by Earl G. Ingersoll. Princeton, NJ: Ontario Review Press, 1994.

Von Schwarzkopf. 'Placing Their Fingers on the Wounds of Our Times.' In *Doris*

Lessing: Conversations, edited by Earl G. Ingersoll. Princeton, NJ: Ontario Review Press, 1994.

Wachtel, Eleanor. *Writers and Company*. In *Doris Lessing: Conversations*. San Diego: Harcourt Brace, 1993.

White, Lesley. 'Pages from Her own History,' *London Sunday Times*, 9 October, 1994.

Books, Articles, Essays, and Reviews (alphabetical)

Angier, Carole. 'Despising the Sham.' Review of *Love, Again*. *Spectator*, 20 April 1996.

Appelbaum, Brooks. 'She Can't Help It.' Review of *Love, Again*. *New Yorker*, 10 June 1996, pp. 88-89.

Beck, Antony. 'Doris Lessing and the Colonial Experience.' *Journal of Commonwealth Literature*. 19, no. 1 (1984) University of Liverpool.

Brownmiller, Susan. 'Doris Lessing in New York City: Best Battles Are Fought by Men and Women Together.' *Village Voice*, 22 May 1969.

Cartwright, Justin. 'Still Africa's Daughter.' *London Daily Telegraph*, 11 October 1997.

Clemons, Walter. 'What's in a Literary Name?' *Newsweek*, October 1 1984, p. 89.

Connolly, Ray. 'A Childhood: Doris Lessing.' *London Times*, 17 November 1990, Saturday review section, p. 62.

Dickson, E. Jane. 'City of the Mind.' *London Sunday Times*, 10 May 1992, sec. 7, pp. 6-7.

Foster, William. 'A Tent-Dweller At Heart.' *Scotsman*, 4 October 1971.

Gail, Godwin, David Crownfield, John Lindberg, Richard Brook. 'The Personal Matter of Doris Lessing.' *North American Review*, Summer 1971.

Gornick, Vivian. 'Opening the Golden Notebook: Remembering the Source.' *Pen Newsletter* #79 (October 1992), from a symposium 25 November 1991.

Hardwick, Elizabeth. 'What is a Woman of 45 to Do?' Review of *The Summer Before the Dark*. *The New York Times Book Review*, 13 May 1973, p. 1.

Hardin, Nancy Shields. 'The Sufi Teaching Story and Doris Lessing.' In Doris Lessing, edited by Harold Bloom. New York Chelsea House, Modern Critical Views series, 1986.

Hartnack, Michael. 'Lessing Revisited.' *Daily Dispatch* (Zimbabwe), 27 May 1995.

Hendin, Josephine. 'Doris Lessing: The Phoenix 'Midst Her Fires.' *Harper's*, June 1973, pp. 83-86.

Howe, Irving. 'Neither Compromise nor Happiness.' Review of *The Golden Notebook*. *New Republic*, 15 December 1962.

Hurren, Kenneth. Review of 'Play with a Tiger.' *London Observer*, 30 March 1962.

Jones, D. A. N. 'Alien.' Review of *The Fifth Child*. *New York Review of Books*, 30 June 1988, pp. 30-31.

Kakutoni, Michiko. 'Family Relations, Society and a Monstrous Baby.' Review of *The Fifth Child*. *The New York Times*, 30 March 1988, p. C24.

———. 'Who Exactly Is This Sexagenarian Sex Kitten?' Review of *Love, Again*. *New York Times*, 15 March 1996, p. C30.

Knapp, Mona. *Doris Lessing*. New York: Ungar, 1984.

Lardner, Susan. 'Angle on the Ordinary.' *New Yorker*, 19 September 1983 P. 140.

Leonard, John. 'The African Queen.' *Nation*, 7 November 1994, pp. 528-529.

──. Review of 'Under My Skin' *CBS Sunday Morning*, 23 October 1994.

──. ' The Last Word: More on Lessing..' Review of *The Summer Before the Dark*. *New York Times Book Review*, 13 May 1973.

──. 'The Children of Violence Are Mutants.' Review of *The Four-Gated City*. *New York Times*, 15 May 1969, p. 45.

──. Review of *Re: Colonised Planet V Shikasta*. *New York Times* (23 October 1979).

──. Review of *The Making of the Representative for Planet 8*. *New York Times*, 7 February 1982, p. 1.

──. Review of *The Marriages Between Zones Three, Four and Five*. *New York Times*, 27 March 1980.

──. Review of *The Sirian Experiments*. *New York Times*, 13 January 1981, p.C14

Maschler, Tom. 'The Lesson of Lessing.' *London Sunday Times* 27 January 1985.

Morrison, Blake. 'Reds in the Bed.' *Independent on Sunday*, 12 October 1997, p. 31.

Rothstein, Mervyn. 'The Painful Nurturing of Doris Lessing's "Fifth Child."' *New York Times*, 14 June 1988.

Sage, Lorna. *Contemporary Writers: Doris Lessing*. London: Methuen, 1983.

Seligman, Dee. 'The Four-Faced Novelist.' *Modern Fiction Studies* 26 (Spring 1980), pp.3-16.

Showalter, Elaine. *The Female Malady: Women, Madness, and English Culture, 1830-1980*. New York: Pantheon, 1985.

Sigal, Clancy. '"You Can't Do It!" I Shouted, "Oh, Can't I?" She Shouted Back.' *The New York Times Book Review*, 12 April 1992, pp. 13-14.

Sprague, Claire. 'The Politics of Sibling Incest in Doris Lessing's 'Each Other.' ' *San Jose Studies*11 (1985), pp.42-49.

Sprague, Claire, and Virginia Tiger. *Critical Essays on Doris Lessing*. Boston: G. K. Hall, 1986.

Steele, M.C. "Children of Violence' and Rhodesia: A Study of Doris Lessing as Historical Observer.' Salisbury, Rhodesia: Central Africa Historical Association, 1974.

Taylor, Jenny. *Notebooks, Memoirs, Archives: Reading and Rereading Doris Lessing*. Boston: Routledge & Kegan Paul, 1982.

Thorpe, Michael. *Doris Lessing's Africa*. London: Evans Brothers, 1978.

Tomalin, Claire. 'Mischief.' *London Sunday Times*, 23 September 1984, p. 15.

Tyler, Christian. 'Author of Many Characters.' *London Observer*, 15 September 1994.

Tynan, Kenneth. 'Lillith in Earl's Court.' Review of *Play with a Tiger*. *London Observer*, 25 March 1962.

Walter, Natasha. 'The Golden Journey.' *Independent*, 15 October 1994.

White, Antonia. 'New Novels: Grass Is Singing.' *New Statesman and Nation*, 1 April, 1950.

Wyndham, Francis. 'The Doors of Perception.' *London Sunday Times*, 18 November 1979, p. 41.

Yardley, Jonathan. 'Lessing Is More: An Unknown Author and the Success Syndrome.' *Washington Post*, 1 October 1984, p. B1.

Select General Bibliography

Bart, Pauline B. 'Depression in Middle-Aged Women.' In *Woman in Sexist Society: Studies in Power and Powerlessness*, edited by Vivian Gornick and Barbara K. Moran. New York: Basic Books, 1971.

Benson, Mary. *South Africa: The Struggle for a Birthright*. New York: Funk & Wagnalls, 1969. First published as *The African Patriots*. New York: Funk & Wagnalls, 1963.

Berkman, Joyce Avrech. *The Healing Imagination of Olive Schreiner: Beyond South African Colonialism*. Amherst: The University of Massachusetts Press, 1989.

Bowlby, John. *Attachment and Loss,* Vol. 1, *Attachment*. London: The Hogarth Press, 1969.

———. *Attachment and Loss,* Vol. 2, *Separation*. London: The Hogarth Press 1973.

———. *Attachment and Loss,* Vol. 3, *Loss*. London: The Hogarth Press 1980.

Chun, Lin. *The British New Left*. Edinburgh: Edinburgh University Press, 1993.

Creighton, T. R. M. *The Anatomy of Partnership: Southern Rhodesia and the Central African Federation*. London: Faber and Faber, 1960.

Cronwright-Schreiner, S. C. *The Life of Olive Schreiner*. London: Unwin, 1924.

Diski, Jenny. *Skating to Antarctica: A Journey to the End of the World*. London: Granta Books, 1997.

Draznin, Yaffa Claire, ed. *'My Other Self': The Letters of Olive Schreiner and Havelock Ellis, 1884-1920*. New York: Peter Lang 1992.

Eliot, T.S. 'The Waste Land' *The Top 500 Poems*. William Harmon, ed. New York Columbia University Press (1992)

Ellis, Havelock. *My Life*. Cambridge, MA: Riverside Press, 1939.

Elwell-Sutton, L.P. 'Sufism and Pseudo-Sufism.' *Encounter*, May 1975, pp. 9-17.

First, Ruth, and Ann Scott. *Olive Schreiner: A Biography*. New York: Schecken, 1980. Reprint New Brunswick, NJ: Rutgers University Press, 1990.

Gurdjieff, G. I. *Meetings with Remarkable Men*. New York: Dutton, 1963.

Hall, Stuart. *Stuart Hall: Critical Dialogues in Cultural Studies*, edited by David Morley and Kuan-Hsing Chen. London: Routledge, 1996.

Hogart, Paul. 'Some Impressions from a Recent Visit to Rhodesia and South Africa.' Journal Fifty-Two of the Society of Industrial Artists August 1956.

Jones, Mervyn. *Chances: An Autobiography*. London: Verso, 1987.

Jung, C.G. *Four Archetypes: Mother, Rebirth, Spirit, Trickster*. Translated by R.F.C. Hull. Bollingen Foundation, 1958. Reprint. Princeton, NJ: Princeton University Press, 1959.

———. *Psyche and Symbol: A selection from the Writings of C. G. Jung*, edited by Violet S. de Lazlo, translated by Cary Baynes and R. F. C. Hull. Garden City, NY: Doubleday, 1958.

Kaula, Edna Mason. *The Land and People of Rhodesia* Philadelphia: Lippincott, 1967.

Kops, Bernard. *The Dissent of Dominick Shapiro*. New York: Coward-McCann, 1966.

Kotre, John. *White Gloves: How We Create Ourselves Through Memory*. New York: Free Press, 1995.

Laing, Adrian Charles. *R. D. Laing. A Biography*. London: P. Owen, 1994.

Laing, R. D. *The Divided Self: A Study of Sanity and Madness*. London: Tavistock, 1960. Reprint. Hammondsworth, England: Penguin, 1990.

————. *Knots*. New York: Pantheon, 1970.

————. *The Politics of Experience*. New York: Pantheon, 1967.

————. *The Politics of the Family and Other Essays*. London: Tavistock, 1971. Reprint. New York: Vintage, 1971.

————. *Wisdom, Madness, and Folly: The Making of a Psychiatrist*. New York: McGraw-Hill, 1985.

————. 'What Is Schizophrenia.' *New Left Review* no. 28, p. 68

MacEoin, Denis and Ahmed Al-Shahi, editors. Islam in the Modern World. London: Croom Helm, 1983.

MacFarquhar, Larissa. 'Robert Gottlieb: The Art of Editing.' *Paris Review*, Fall 1994, pp. 182-223.

MacKenzie, Suzie. 'True Stories.' Interview with Jenny Diski. *Guardian*, 9 October 1991.

Maschler, Tom, ed. *Declaration*. London: MacGibbon and Kee, 1958.

Miliband, Ralph. *Marxism and Politics*. Oxford: Oxford University Press, 1977.

Moers, Ellen. *Literary Women*. Garden City, NY: Doubleday, 1976.

Mortimer, John. *Clinging to the Wreckage. A Part of Life*. New Haven, CT: Ticknor & Fields, 1982.

————. 'Don't Blame the Sixties – or the Young.' *London Evening Standard*, 5 June 1995.

Mullan, Bob, ed. *Mad to Be Normal: Conversations with R. D. Laing*. London: Free Association Books, 1975.

————. *R. D. Laing: Creative Destroyer*. London: Cassell Wellington House, 1997.

Orwell, George. 'Why I Write.' In *Decline of the English Murder and Other Essays*. Reprint. Harmondsworth, England: Penguin, 1965.

Osborne, John. 'They call it cricket,' In *Declarations*, edited by Tom Maschler. London: MacGibbon and Kee, 1958.

Palling, Bruce. 'Insanity Is Not Illegal.' *Newsweek*, 24 October 1977, p. 52.

Perrott, Roy. 'The Man Who Says We're All Mad.' Introduction to R. D. Laing. *London Observer*, 20 September 1970.

Phillips, William. *A Partisan View: Five Decades of the Literary Life*. New York: Stein & Day, 1983.

Roberts, Brian. *Cecil Rhodes: Flawed Colossus*. New York: Norton, 1988.

Rowbotham, Sheila. *Woman's Consciousness, Man's World*. Harmondsworth, England: Penguin, 1973.

Russell, Bertrand. *Common Sense and Nuclear Warfare*. New York: Simon & Schuster, 1959.

Schreiner, Olive. *From Man to Man: or Perhaps Only*. London: Unwin. 1926

————. *The Story of an African Farm*. 1883. Reprint. Introduction by Doris Lessing. New York: Crown, 1987.

————. *Woman and Labor*. New York: Frederick A. Stokes, 1911.

————. *Thoughts on South Africa*. London: Unwin, 1923.

Shah, Idries. *The Commanding Self*. London: Octagon Press, 1994.

————. *The Sufis*. London: Octagon Press, 1964.

————. *The Way of the Sufi*. London: Jonathan Cape, 1971.

Sigal, Clancy. 'The Boys of Watergate.' Eulogy for H. R. Haldeman. *New York Times*, 27 November 1993, p. 19.

————. *Going Away*. Boston: Houghton Mifflin, 1962. Reprint. New York: Dell, 1962.

———. 'Goodbye Little England.' *Weekend Guardian*, 17-18 June 1989.

———. 'The Karma Ran Over My Dogma.' *Nation*, 18 May 1992, p. 649.

———. *The Secret Defector*. New York: HarperCollins, 1992.

———. *Weekend in Dinlock*. London: Secker & Warburg, 1960.

———. 'Working with Laing' Letter to the Editors. *New York Review of Books*, 19 December 1996, p. 84.

———. *Zone of the Interior*. New York: Crowell, 1976. Reprint. New York: Popular Library, 1978.

Stevenson, Anne. *Bitter Fame: A Life of Sylvia Plath*. Boston: Houghton Mifflin, 1989.

Storr, Anthony. 'The Divided Legacy of R. D. Laing' *Observer*, 27 August 1989.

Thomas, Antony. *Rhodes: The Race for Africa*. New York: St. Martin's Press, 1997.

Thompson, Dorothy. 'On the Trail of the New Left.' *New Left Review*, January/February 1996, pp. 93-100

Tynan, Kathleen. *The Life of Kenneth Tynan*. New York: W. Morrow, 1987.

Tynan, Kenneth. 'Theatre and Living.' In Declarations, edited by Tom Maschler. London: MacGibbon & Kee, 1958.

———. *Curtains*. New York: Athenaeum, 1961.

Vambe, Laurence. *An Ill-Fated People: Zimbabwe Before and After Rhodes*. London: Heinemann, 1972.

———. *From Rhodesia to Zimbabwe*. Pittsburgh: University of Pittsburgh Press, 1976.

Veit-Wild, Flora. *Teachers, Preachers, Non-Believers: A Social History of Zimbabwean Literature* (*New Perspectives on African Literature*, 6). London: Hans Zell, 1992.

Wesker, Arnold. *As Much as I Dare: An Autobiography*. London: Century, 1994.

Whaley, Peter. 'Move along Miss Cummings,' London *Daily Mail*, 14 September 1959.

Index